EXTRAORDINARY *Latinas*

VOLUME V
RECLAIMING COURAGE, HEALING & THE POWER WITHIN

PRESENTED BY
ILHIANA ROJAS SALDANA &
SANDRA NOEMI TORRES

EXTRAORDINARY LATINAS VOL V
RECLAIMING COURAGE, HEALING & THE POWER WITHIN

Published by:
Ilhiana Rojas Saldana
& Sandra Noemi Torres
www.unitedlatinas.com

Editing by Lora Denton
Masters in Clarity | www.mastersinclarity.com

ISBN: 979-8-9925568-3-4

Published in the United States of America

To the Latinas who came before me, whose courage made space.
To those who walk with me now, whose encouragement fuels the journey.
And to those who will follow, who will rise with even greater freedom.

This book is rooted in healing, strengthened by courage, and guided by truth.
It honors the pride we carry, the accomplishments we often minimize,
and the legacy we build—one choice, one voice, one act of bravery at a time.
May you see yourself reflected here, and remember how powerful you already are.

Ilhiana

Before stories ever reach pages, they were lived through moments of adversity, strength, courage and healing.

Scars often remain but resilience lives in our ancestry. It echoes in the women who came before us; all those who sacrificed, nurtured, used their voices to stand up for others and believed in just futures.

This is an invitation to remember your power.
To reclaim the courage that may have been quieted.
To honor healing as strength, not weakness.
To recognize that the power within you has always been there, waiting to be fully embraced.

May you reconnect to your voice, your truth, and your purpose.

You are not starting from nothing.
You are continuing a legacy.

With deep love and sisterhood,

Sandra Noemi Torres
CEO & Founder, UNITED LATINAS

TABLE OF CONTENTS

ACKNOWLEDGEMENTS

This volume was born from courage—quiet courage, bold courage, and the kind of courage that emerges after deep reflection and healing. We extend our heartfelt gratitude to every woman who trusted this space enough to share her story. To our extraordinary authors: your vulnerability, wisdom, and truth are the heartbeat of this book. Each chapter is a testament to resilience, reclamation, and the power that unfolds when we choose to rise fully as ourselves. Thank you for your bravery and for allowing your voices to guide others forward.

We are deeply grateful to our editor, Lora Denton, and the Masters in Clarity team for their steady partnership and thoughtful guidance throughout this journey. Your care for the process, attention to detail, and belief in the message carried this book from vision to reality with integrity and intention.

To the UNITED LATINAS community—this work exists because of you. Your presence, your leadership, and your unwavering commitment to lifting one another continue to remind us that healing is not a solitary act, and power is amplified in community. Thank you for creating spaces where stories are honored, voices are expanded, and transformation is possible.

Finally, we extend our gratitude to every reader who picks up this book with an open heart. By engaging with these stories, you become part of a collective movement—one rooted in courage, restoration, and possibility. May these pages meet you where you are and inspire you to reclaim what has always been yours.

With deep appreciation,

Ilhiana & Sandra

MightyHUB

Power Up Your Network and Become a part of the UL Online Community

unitedlatinas.mn.co

THERE IS NO ONE PATH.
THERE IS YOUR PATH

FOREWORD BY:

LUCY PÉREZ

When I look back at my life, I do not see a straight line.

I see a series of pivots. Of moments where I questioned whether I belonged. Of choices that made little sense to others but felt deeply aligned to me.

Looking back matters.

It is easy, especially for high-achieving individuals, to live in forward motion — measuring ourselves by the next milestone, the next promotion, the next goal. But reflection offers something different. It offers perspective. It reveals the throughlines. It reminds us that what felt uncertain in the moment was often shaping us for something we could not yet see.

I was born in Puerto Rico to parents who emigrated from Spain. That immigrant mindset, rooted in relentless work ethic, resilience, and gratitude, was the air I breathed growing up. My parents believed deeply in two things: family and opportunity. They believed that if you worked hard, doors would open. And if they did not, you created another path.

That mindset has been both a gift and a responsibility.

It instilled in me a deep appreciation for education, for effort, and for excellence. It also instilled in me a quiet awareness that we do not all start from the same place, and that if I was given opportunities, I had an obligation to widen the door for others.

The second defining thread in my life began with my great-grandmother. Recovering from a stroke, I would walk beside her, helping her move through the house. I was young, but I understood something fundamental: without health, nothing else is possible.

For a long time, I thought that meant becoming a physician. A memorable high school anatomy class made it clear that I was better suited to advancing health in ways that didn't involve a scalpel. That moment taught me something important: purpose is constant, but the form it takes can change. My path took me into chemistry labs, cancer research centers, and then into consulting, where I increasingly focused on advancing health more equitably and effectively. The "how" evolved. The "why" did not.

And there was also the pivot to life in Boston.

Leaving Puerto Rico for college was the first time I felt the weight of being different. In Puerto Rico, I was one of many. In Boston, I became "the minority." I often describe that period as becoming a "double only" — typically the only woman and the only Latina in the room.

It changes you.

You learn quickly how to read a room. You learn how to prepare twice as hard. You learn how to translate between cultures. You carry not just your own aspirations, but the expectations of your family and community.

But you also learn something else: you deserve to be there.

Over time, I realized that belonging is not something granted to you. It is something you claim. And leadership is not about conforming to a template; it is about expanding the template.

That is one of the central truths I hope you feel in this book:

There is no one path. There is your path.

This Volume is a testament to that truth.

The women whose stories you are about to read did not follow identical scripts. What connects them is not sameness. It is agency.

Some paused when the world expected them to push forward. Some rebuilt after trauma. Some trusted their own timing when external clocks grew loud. Some transformed survival into boldness. Some rooted themselves in purpose. Some turned pain into progress. Some redefined the equation entirely. Some honored their roots while extending their reach.

There is something transformative about reading the lived experience of another Latina — uncurated, unpolished, unapologetic. These stories are rooted in Latina identity, but their lessons travel far beyond it. When our stories are not told, narratives get written about us. When our stories are told by us, they shape what others believe is possible.

We are navigating complexity — in business, in health, in identity, and in community. The world needs leaders who are resilient and relational. Ambitious and empathetic. Strategic and grounded in purpose.

Latinas have long cultivated these capabilities — not as leadership theories, but as lived experience. In doing so, they offer lessons in navigating multiple worlds, translating across cultures, building networks of support, and pushing forward when systems were not built with you in mind.

This Volume does not ignore systemic barriers. It acknowledges them. But it does something equally powerful: it showcases what leadership looks like anyway.

Too often, we think leadership is the title. These women remind us it is the practice.

Looking back at my own journey, I can see that the moments that shaped me most were not the predictable milestones. They were the decisions that felt risky — the ones that required trust, courage, and clarity about who I wanted to become.

Perfection is a myth that silences too many of us.

We must retire the phrase *"calladita te ves más bonita."* Silence has never been our superpower. Voice is.

This Volume amplifies that voice.

It also reminds us that success is not singular.

There is no one path. There is your path.

Whether you see yourself directly reflected in these pages or are here to listen and learn, I hope these stories inspire you with what leadership can look like.

May these stories remind you that leadership can look like you.
May they challenge you to speak when it matters.
May they encourage you to trust your timing.
May they inspire you to build with purpose.
May they affirm that your roots are a source of strength, not limitation.

Most of all, may they leave you hungry to turn the page and ready to claim your own path forward.

With admiration for the extraordinary Latinas who shared their stories, and with belief in the many more whose stories are still unfolding.

Lucy Pérez

~ ~ ~

Lucy Pérez is a Senior Partner at McKinsey & Company based in Boston, global co-leader of the McKinsey Health Institute, and a leader within the McKinsey Institute for Economic Mobility. A senior leader in the firm's Life Sciences practice, she advises CEOs and executive teams globally on growth strategy, innovation, and organizational transformation. With a Ph.D. in Chemistry from Harvard University and early experience as a cancer researcher at Memorial Sloan-Kettering Cancer Center, Lucy brings scientific rigor and strategic clarity to complex challenges in life sciences, public health, and healthcare systems. She is passionate about leveraging advances in science and technology to improve patient outcomes and reshape health systems worldwide.

A champion for health equity and Latino economic mobility, Lucy has led groundbreaking research with the World Economic Forum highlighting the $1 trillion opportunity to close the women's health gap—work recognized with a Presidential Award from the American Medical Women's Association. She co-leads McKinsey's Hispanic and Latino Network and sponsors research on Latino economic advancement, while serving on the Advisory Board of the Aspen Institute's Conexion Program. A resident of Boston, Lucy is proud to serve on the boards of MassBio and the Massachusetts Business Roundtable. Recognized as one of Amplify LatinX's inaugural LatinX 100 Leaders, one of ALPFA's 50 Most Powerful Latinas, and a Greater Boston Chamber of Commerce's Pinnacle honoree, Lucy's leadership reflects both excellence at the highest levels of business and a deep commitment to inclusive impact.

~ ~ ~

Connect with Lucy:
https://www.linkedin.com/in/lucy-perez/

INTRODUCTION BY:

ILHIANA ROJAS SALDANA

Stories have always been how we find one another.

They are how we make sense of what we've lived, how we name what we've overcome, and how we remember that our experiences, no matter how personal, are rarely ours alone. When stories are shared, they create connection. When they are honored, they create belonging. And when they are told with courage, they become a source of strength for others who are still finding their way.

For many years, I didn't fully understand the power of that.

I moved quickly through life — achieving, producing, succeeding. I built a 20-year career in Fortune 500 companies. I climbed. I delivered. I led. From the outside, everything looked strong. Yet inside, there was a season when I felt disconnected from myself. I had learned to adapt, to assimilate, to perform. I had learned to be strong — but not always to be seen. I rarely paused long enough to name what I had survived, what I had built, or what it had cost.

It wasn't until I began listening deeply to the stories of other women, of other Latinas — stories of courage, doubt, reinvention, resilience — that something shifted in me. Their words felt like mirrors. I saw my own fears reflected back. I saw my own strength reflected back. And I realized something profound:

When we share our stories, we don't just inspire others.
We recognize ourselves.

And that recognition matters.

It validates the quiet battles. It honors the invisible labor. It reminds us that every chapter — especially the complicated ones — deserves to be acknowledged.

I learned this lesson even more deeply after my mother passed.

As I began going through her belongings, I discovered pieces of her life I had never known. Letters. Notes. Evidence of dreams fulfilled and sacrifices made quietly. I found myself wishing I had asked more questions. Wishing I had documented more of her journey in her own words.

Her story — a bold young woman in 1960s Mexico who declared at fifteen that she would see the world and then made it happen — shaped everything about how I see courage. But what moved me most was not only what she accomplished. It was how much of her strength went unnamed while she was living it.

That realization changed me and reshaped how I live my life.
I no longer wait for someday to honor the story. I honor it now.

Our stories deserve to be documented while we are still living them. Not decades later. Not rewritten by someone else. But now — in our own words.

Because legacy is not only what others say about us when we are gone. It is what we choose to preserve about ourselves while we are here.

The stories in this book are exactly that.

They are stories of grit, resilience, and determination. Stories of women who have navigated uncertainty, carried responsibility, faced barriers — many of them unseen — and continued forward anyway. Stories shaped by lived experience, by cultural pride, by sacrifice, and by an unwavering commitment to creating something meaningful in the world.

Again and again, we hear that Latinas are underrepresented in leadership, influence, and spaces of power. Yet these pages tell a fuller, more honest truth. Latinas are building, leading, creating, and transforming every day. They are shaping industries, organizations, families, and communities — often without recognition, but never without impact. What has been missing is not achievement. It is visibility.

Each author in this series brings her own journey, her own voice, and her own definition of success. Together, they reveal the extraordinary breadth of Latina leadership — across fields, backgrounds, and life paths. There is no single way to be powerful. No single story that defines us. What unites these women is not sameness, but courage: the courage to show up fully, to persist through doubt, and to claim space in a world that does not always make room.

As Latinas, we come from a lineage of women who carried immense responsibility with quiet determination. Our mothers, grandmothers, aunts, and ancestors often moved mountains without being named for it. Their courage lives on through us — not as pressure to be perfect, but as a reminder that resilience is part of who we are. We are not starting from nothing. We are continuing a legacy.

In a world filled with noise — where narratives are simplified, distorted, or spoken for us — owning our voice matters more than ever. Telling our stories in our own words is an act of agency. It is how we preserve truth, reclaim authorship, and ensure that the fullness of our experiences is seen and valued. When Latinas speak, we don't just share stories — we expand what leadership looks like.

This book is also a testament to the power of community. None of us were meant to navigate life alone. When we come together, when we listen deeply, when we recognize ourselves in one another's journeys, the path becomes lighter. Stories become bridges. And possibility expands.

To the women who chose to share their stories here — thank you. Your willingness to be seen is an act of leadership. Your courage creates space for others.

And to you, the reader:

As you turn these pages, I invite you to consider your own story.
What moments shaped you?
What did you survive that no one saw?
What have you built quietly?

Your journey matters. Your voice carries weight. And your story — in all its evolving chapters — deserves acknowledgment.

Document it. Honor it. Share it when you are ready.

Because legacy is not built in grand gestures alone. It is built in the brave decision to say: *This is who I am. This is what I lived. And it mattered.*

With gratitude,

Ilhiana Rojas is a seasoned Business Strategist, Executive and Leadership Transformational Coach, a Diversity & Inclusion Consultant, an Award-winning Advocate for women and Hispanics, a multiple Bestselling Author, and an International Motivational Speaker. She is a possibility thinker and a firm believer that nothing is impossible. Ilhiana uses her 20-plus years of corporate experience and certified coaching expertise to help build resilient, collaborative, and high-performing leaders and cultures. Ilhiana also serves on multiple Boards supporting initiatives that center on empowering women and Hispanic populations.

~ ~ ~

Connect with Ilhiana
https://www.linkedin.com/in/ilhiana-rojas7
www.ilhianarojas.com
www.belivecoach.com
Email: ilhiana@unitedlatinas.com

Schedule time with Ilhiana:

https://calendly.com/ilhiana-rojas/20-min-meeting

DR. ALEXANDRA COLÓN-RODRÍGUEZ

"Discomfort was never a sign that I did not belong; it was a signal that I was becoming."

- Alexandra Colón-Rodríguez

~ ~ ~

Alexandra Colón-Rodríguez, PhD is a scientist, educator, and community builder whose work bridges scientific excellence with purpose-driven impact. Trained as a neurotoxicologist and shaped by her roots in Santurce, Puerto Rico, she now serves as Principal Program Manager of the Postdoctoral Program at Genentech, where she leads initiatives centered on mentorship, professional development, and inclusive workforce growth within a global scientific community. Beyond industry, Dr. Colón-Rodríguez is the founder and president of STEAM100X35, a nonprofit dedicated to amplifying Puerto Rican women in STEM and inspiring the next generation through culturally relevant education, mentorship, and access to opportunity. Across academia, industry, and community spaces, her leadership reflects a deep commitment to representation, service, and the belief that expanding access to science strengthens both innovation and society.

~ ~ ~

For my daughters, with all my love; may you always know that your DNA is filled with strength, purpose, and legacy, and that you are unstoppable.

FROM ROOTS TO REACH:
A NONLINEAR JOURNEY OF PURPOSE AND IMPACT

THE JOURNEY

I was born and raised in Santurce, Puerto Rico, and educated entirely within the island's public school system. My upbringing was grounded in community, resilience, faith, and the belief that education was both a privilege and a responsibility. While I did not grow up surrounded by scientists or professionals in science, technology, engineering, and math (STEM) fields, I was surrounded by people who worked hard, cared deeply for one another, and believed in doing right by others. From an early age, I learned that perseverance was not optional; it was a way of life shaped by necessity, dignity, hope, and faith that things could be better.

As a student, I was curious and driven, but I did not always see myself reflected in the careers presented to me. Science was something I enjoyed and excelled at, yet it often felt distant and abstract, disconnected from people who looked like me or shared my lived experiences. During my undergraduate years, I worked continuously to pay for my education, sustain myself, and help my mother as much as I could. She was a single mother for most of my upbringing, and I was intentional about not adding financial stress to her life. Independence was not just a goal; it was a responsibility I carried with pride.

My longest job as an undergraduate student was at the largest mall in my area, working at a small booth selling ties, pens, and jewelry. I vividly remember one day when someone I had met in college, who had already graduated, saw me there and said, "You are still here? I thought you were going to get a bachelor's degree in science and become a professional." I never hid the fact that I came from a low-income family and worked to sustain myself. Still, that comment crystallized something I already knew: for someone like me, a Latina woman interested in science, raised by a single mother and navigating economic limitations, the path forward carried not only ambition, but pressure, judgment, and invisible expectations.

I did not have a direct or traditional path into science. While completing my bachelor's degree, my life was profoundly altered with the loss of my father, who had recently been diagnosed with a brain disorder. As I processed my grief, I became deeply curious about the brain, how it works, and how disease alters it. During this time, I learned about the field of neuroscience and, for the first time, I clearly understood what a scientist is and what scientists do. Science no longer felt abstract; it felt purposeful. I saw in it a career with noble intent and the potential for both impact and personal fulfillment.

By the time I decided to pursue a PhD, I was a junior in college. I quickly realized that I was behind by traditional standards. I had no formal background in neuroscience and had never participated in research, both of which are critical requirements for doctoral training. The gap between where I was and where I hoped to go felt overwhelming. Still, I chose not to interpret "late" as "impossible."

I applied to a summer research internship and was accepted at Michigan State University (MSU), an experience that would prove life-changing. I still remember the phone call from Dr. Nettavia Curry. It was the first time in my life I was offered an opportunity that I knew, deep in my core, would alter the trajectory of my future. In that moment, something clicked: it was okay to dream big.

That summer empowered me in ways I could not have imagined. Ten weeks were enough to reveal the breadth of what science could be and, just as importantly, to show me that people from backgrounds like mine were also pursuing, and thriving in, scientific careers. After that transformative experience, I returned to Puerto Rico and completed my bachelor's degree in microbiology with renewed confidence, clarity, and purpose.

After completing my bachelor's degree, I pursued a postbaccalaureate program to become competitive for a PhD in a field I had never encountered: neurotoxicology. That year became a bridge between aspiration and preparation. I conducted research, took advanced coursework, and immersed myself in an academic environment at a Big Ten university (MSU). It was transformative, but also deeply challenging.

I moved to a state where I knew very few people. The culture, pace, and climate were vastly different from Puerto Rico, and Spanish, my first language, was no longer the norm. Beyond the academic rigor, I struggled with technical English, especially in fast-paced lectures filled with unfamiliar terminology. Determined not to fall behind, I asked professors if I could record lectures so I could review them at night until I fully understood the material. When one professor refused, I learned that persistence sometimes requires advocacy.

I sought support from my mentor, Dr. William D. Atchison, who has been my strongest professional supporter since the very beginning. His advocacy was pivotal, not only in addressing the immediate challenge but in reinforcing that I belonged in those spaces and deserved access to the tools I needed to succeed. That experience shaped how I understand mentorship and leadership.

Leaving Puerto Rico to pursue advanced training was one of the most difficult and transformative decisions I have made. My doctoral focus area was not available on the island, and stepping away from my home, culture, and support system forced me to grow in ways I had not anticipated. As a neurotoxicologist in training, I entered spaces where I was often one of the few, if not the only, Latina present. These experiences were both empowering and challenging, teaching me how to advocate for myself while remaining grounded in my identity.

Throughout my academic journey, I faced moments of self-doubt, imposter syndrome, and uncertainty. Rather than retreating, I sought feedback, mentorship, and opportunities to learn. I came to understand that growth does not happen in isolation; it happens through reflection, community, and a willingness to ask for help. Discomfort was never a sign that I did not belong; it was a signal that I was becoming.

A defining aspect of my journey has been realizing that success is not measured solely by individual achievement but by impact. For the past decade and a half, as I became increasingly aware of the privilege of occupying spaces, often the first, the only, or one of very few, I committed myself to widening access to others. While advancing my scientific training, I became deeply involved in mentoring, program development, and science education initiatives focused on increasing access and visibility for underrepresented communities. This understanding eventually led me beyond the bench to my current role as Principal Program Manager of the Postdoctoral Program at Genentech, and to founding an education nonprofit dedicated to amplifying the work of Puerto Rican women in STEM and inspiring the next generation.

Today, my life is grounded in purpose, impact, and presence. I serve as the Principal Program Manager of the Postdoctoral Program at Genentech, where I am proud to support early-career scientists during one of the most formative stages of their professional journeys. Beyond my role in biotech, I lead an education nonprofit dedicated to amplifying the work of Puerto Rican women in STEM and expanding access through mentorship, hands-on learning, and scholarships. What I am most proud of is that my job now reflects both who I am and what I value, using my scientific training beyond the bench to build programs, shape systems, and invest in people, while living a life rooted in faith, family, community, and purpose.

Every positive and negative experience along my journey has shaped who I am today: a leader, guided by service and committed to creating pathways for others. I did not always know where my journey would lead, but I have always known why I walk it: to open doors, build bridges, and ensure that those who come after me see possibility where I once saw uncertainty.

THE LEARNINGS

My journey has been shaped not only by milestones but by struggle, loss, and moments when the path forward was unclear. Many of my most important learnings emerged during periods when I felt out of place, underprepared, or emotionally stretched. These challenges did not break me; instead, they clarified my purpose and shaped how I lead, mentor, and serve.

One of the most pivotal realizations was that my path would not be linear. Coming from a low-income background, navigating higher education while working, grieving the loss of my father, and later entering a field in which I had no prior exposure required constant recalibration. I often felt behind, academically, professionally, and emotionally, especially when comparing myself to peers who had access to research opportunities, mentorship, and familiarity with academic systems from an early stage. Learning to release comparison became essential. I learned to focus instead on progress, effort, and growth.

> *Feeling out of place did not mean I did not belong; it often meant I was expanding into spaces not originally designed with people like me in mind.*

Another significant challenge was navigating environments where I was often one of the few, or the only, Latina, first-generation, or multilingual individual in the room. This manifested as imposter syndrome, self-doubt, and at times, the pressure to overperform to prove that I belonged. Overcoming this required reframing how I interpreted discomfort. I learned that feeling out of place did not mean I did not belong; it often meant I was expanding into spaces not originally designed for people like me in mind.

Inner strength came from purpose. Losing my father and discovering neuroscience gave meaning to my academic pursuits, anchoring my persistence in something more profound than achievement alone. When things felt overwhelming, I reminded myself why I was doing the work. I developed practical strategies that sustained me: seeking feedback early, breaking significant goals into manageable steps, and allowing myself to be a learner without shame. Asking for accommodations, seeking mentors, and advocating for my needs, especially as a non-native English speaker, became acts of courage and essential tools for survival and growth.

While there were moments I navigated challenges independently, I was never truly alone. My family, friends, and mentors played a critical role, particularly those who saw my potential before I did. Advocacy from mentors such as Dr. William D. Atchison's reinforced that support systems matter, not just for access, but for belonging. At the same time, I learned the importance of becoming my own advocate, building confidence in my voice and trusting my lived experience as valid and valuable.

As I moved into leadership roles, I also began to challenge established norms. Traditional academic and scientific systems often reward productivity over people and hierarchy over humanity. I chose to disrupt that model by centering mentorship, transparency, and empathy, especially when addressing power dynamics, accessibility, and representation. I learned that disruption does not always look like confrontation; sometimes it seems like redesigning systems, asking better questions, and consistently advocating for those who are often unheard.

Perhaps the most important learning has been this: resilience is not about enduring in silence. It is about adapting with intention, asking for help, and using your experiences to make the path more accessible for others. The challenges I once viewed as obstacles are now the foundation of my leadership. They allow me to lead with empathy, build inclusive environments, and create pathways where none previously existed.

These learnings continue to guide my work and my purpose. They remind me that growth is ongoing, leadership is relational, and impact is measured not only by what we achieve, but by who we uplift along the way.

THE INSPIRATION

My inspiration has always been deeply rooted in the women who raised me and shaped my understanding of strength, resilience, and purpose. I am inspired, first and foremost, by my mother and my grandmothers, women who navigated life with courage, dignity, and determination, often under circumstances that demanded more of them than they ever asked of themselves. They taught me that strength does not always announce itself loudly; sometimes it shows up quietly, in perseverance, sacrifice, and unconditional love. Watching them face challenges head-on instilled in me a deep sense of responsibility to honor their legacy through how I live, lead, and serve others.

As my journey evolved, so did my sources of inspiration. As a leader, I am deeply inspired by Jacinda Ardern and her ability to lead with empathy, authenticity, and moral clarity. Her leadership challenged traditional notions of power and showed that compassion and decisiveness are complementary strengths rather than opposing forces. Seeing a woman lead unapologetically, with humanity, reinforced my belief that leadership rooted in care, listening, and integrity is not only possible but also transformative.

My inspiration continues to evolve as I meet people and learn about individuals who lead with purpose, courage, and intention. I am inspired by everyday acts of kindness, by mentors who lift others as they climb, and by communities that choose collaboration over competition. These encounters remind me that inspiration is not static; it grows as we remain open to learning from others.

On a deeply personal level, my husband's discipline and faith inspire me daily. His steadiness, commitment, and values ground me, especially during moments of uncertainty or fatigue. He reminds me of the importance of consistency, reflection, and trust in something greater than oneself.

> *Inspiration is not static; it grows as we remain open to learning from others.*

Above all, my greatest inspiration today is my children. Becoming a mother reshaped my understanding of purpose and legacy. They have given me a renewed sense of urgency and passion to build something lasting, not just professionally, but ethically and emotionally. I am inspired to create a legacy they can be proud of, one rooted in service, courage, and love. Whether they choose to carry that legacy forward in their own ways or simply draw strength from it, my hope is that they always know that they come from a long line of strong women, and that their story, too, matters.

THE ADVICE

If I could speak to my younger self, or to anyone navigating a similar journey, I would offer a few lessons I learned gradually, often through challenge, but now carry with clarity and intention.

1. Your path does not need to be linear to be legitimate.

For a long time, I believed that success required following a clearly defined, traditional trajectory. When my path diverged, when I discovered new fields later than expected, needed additional training, or began considering roles beyond the bench, I questioned whether I truly belonged. I now understand that nonlinear paths often build the most adaptable and fulfilled leaders. Exposure changes perspective. It is hard to aspire to what you have never seen, and it is okay to pivot when new information reveals a better-aligned path. Choose paths that move you closer to where you want to be in five years, or even one year, knowing that you are allowed to change your mind as you grow.

2. Ask for help, and build a community, not just a single mentor.

I was raised to work hard, endure quietly, and not burden others. While resilience matters, I learned that progress accelerates when you allow yourself to be supported. No single person can meet all your needs. Build a community of mentors, some who guide you professionally, others who support you personally, and some who help you navigate life decisions. Learning to ask for feedback, advocate for myself, and lean into community fundamentally changed my trajectory.

3. Do not confuse discomfort with inadequacy.

Many of the moments when I felt the most uncertain, being one of the few Latinas or women in a room, entering a field I had never been exposed to, leading in unfamiliar spaces, were moments of expansion, not evidence that I did not belong. I wish I had learned earlier to reframe discomfort as a signal of growth. You will often feel uncomfortable when you are stretching beyond what is familiar. That feeling does not mean you are failing; it usually means you are becoming.

4. Invest early in financial literacy; it is a tool for freedom.

Coming from a low-income background, I did not grow up with conversations about financial planning, investing, or wealth-building. I now understand that financial literacy is about more than money; it is about choice, security, and breaking generational cycles. Learning how to manage resources and build generational wealth allows you to make decisions based on values rather than fear. Financial knowledge creates options, and options create freedom.

5. Reflect often, and let your values, not fear, guide your decisions.

Self-reflection has been one of the most important habits in my personal growth. It helped me make peace with one of my hardest decisions: stepping away from the bench as a scientist. For a long time, I struggled with the idea of leaving a path I had worked so hard to enter. Through reflection, I realized that continuing on that path would not align with the life I wanted, particularly being a present mother to my children. I know myself, and I know that in that environment, I would always be working.

Leaving the bench did not take away my preparation, my training, or my degree. I will always be a scientist. My scientific thinking, rigor, curiosity, and problem-solving skills did not disappear; they evolved. Choosing a different path was not a loss of identity; it was an expansion of how I use my training to create impact. Science is not confined to the bench, and neither is purpose.

6. Measure success by impact, not just achievement.

Early on, I equated success with titles, milestones, and external validation. Over time, my perspective shifted. True fulfillment came from impact, mentoring others, creating access, building inclusive spaces, and contributing to something larger than myself. Habits that supported this shift included regular reflection, seeking honest feedback, and staying grounded in purpose rather than comparison. I learned to ask not only *What am I achieving?* but *Who am I helping along the way?*

To anyone walking a similar path, my advice is this: give yourself permission to reflect, to pivot, and to redefine success. Honor your story, trust your voice, and remember that the experiences you once saw as obstacles may become the very foundation of your leadership and legacy.

THE PATH FORWARD

As I look ahead, I carry with me the lessons that have shaped my journey: that paths can be nonlinear, that asking for help is a strength, that discomfort signals growth, and that success is measured not only by what we achieve but by the lives we impact along the way. My hope is that these lessons do not end with my story, but continue through the choices others feel empowered to make because of it.

To anyone navigating spaces where you feel, or are, underrepresented, overlooked, or unseen: you do not need to wait for permission to become who you are meant to be. You belong in rooms you have not yet entered, in careers you may not yet know exist, and in leadership spaces that are still learning how to make room for voices like yours. Your background, culture, and lived experiences are not obstacles to overcome; they are sources of insight, resilience, and strength. Bring them with you.

My call to action is simple but intentional: reflect often, choose boldly, and move forward with purpose. Seek exposure to new paths, build communities of support, invest in your growth, financially, professionally, and personally, and give yourself permission to pivot when your values or season of life change. You are allowed to redefine success. You are allowed to pursue a life that honors both your ambition and your humanity.

I also invite you to lead with impact. As you advance, look back and ask who you can bring with you. Mentor someone. Share information that was once inaccessible or withheld. Create access where it did not exist before. Legacy is not built through titles alone; it is built through generosity, intention, and service.

What lies ahead for me is a continued commitment to building pathways and systems that expand access and opportunity. Through my work in biotech leadership, education, and nonprofit spaces, I will continue advocating for inclusive cultures, mentorship-driven environments, and greater visibility for individuals and communities historically excluded from science, leadership, and decision-making spaces. I remain committed to using my scientific training because I will always be a scientist, in ways that influence policy, programs, and people, even beyond the bench.

At the heart of everything I do is legacy. I want to leave behind a legacy rooted in courage, compassion, and possibility. One where Latinas see themselves not only surviving in spaces where they are underrepresented, but thriving and leading with authenticity. And on a deeply personal level, I want my children to grow up knowing that their roots are powerful, their dreams are valid, and that they come from a lineage of people who chose to rise and to lift others as they climbed.

If there is one final message I leave you with, it is this: your story matters. Your timing is your own. And your presence can change what is possible. Walk forward with intention. Lead with heart. And trust that the path you are creating, however unconventional, is worthy, impactful, and yours.

ABOUT DR. ALEXANDRA

Alexandra Colón-Rodríguez, PhD, is a neurotoxicologist by training, educator by calling, and community builder at heart. She currently serves as Principal Program Manager of the Postdoctoral Program at Genentech, one of the world's first and leading biotechnology companies, where she oversees a large, interdisciplinary postdoctoral community and leads strategic initiatives focused on scientific excellence, mentorship, professional development, and inclusive workforce development.

Born and raised in Santurce, Puerto Rico, Dr. Colón-Rodríguez completed her undergraduate training in microbiology before pursuing doctoral studies in comparative medicine, integrative biology, and environmental toxicology. Her scientific work has been grounded in understanding how environmental exposures affect the nervous system, while her career has evolved to center on creating systems that support scientists, trainees, and communities, particularly those historically underrepresented in STEM.

Dr. Colón-Rodríguez is the founder and president of STEAM100X35, Inc., an education-focused nonprofit with a mission to amplify the work of Puerto Rican women in STEM and to inspire the next generation of scientists through culturally relevant, hands-on workshops, global webinars, mentorship, and research scholarships. Through STEAM100X35, she has built programs and partnerships that remove financial barriers, increase visibility, and empower girls and young women to see themselves as scientists and leaders.

Across academia, industry, and the nonprofit sector, Dr. Colón-Rodríguez is recognized for her commitment to service, mentorship, and science education. Her work reflects a deep belief that access, representation, and opportunity are essential to advancing both scientific innovation and social impact.

To learn more about her efforts, visit alexandracr.com or STEAM100X35.com and follow her work in science education, mentorship, and community leadership.

Learn more about Alexandra and connect with her:

https://www.linkedin.com/in/alexandracr/
https://www.alexandracr.com/
https://www.steam100x35.com/

ANA SAGAON

"One day your younger self will visit you in a memory. Meet her there with gentleness— and remind her to trust the process, embrace the lessons, and turn fear into fuel."

\-   Ana Sagaon

~ ~ ~

Visionary leader, coach, and mentor passionate about unlocking human potential and turning purpose into impact. With 25+ years leading Talent, Culture and Human Resources across diverse global environments. I help individuals and organizations rise above limits, embrace change with confidence, and create futures that matter.

My leadership style blends empathy with strategic clarity and disciplined execution—building cultures where people thrive, teams perform, and business results accelerate.

A senior People executive leader with an MBA in Strategy & Leadership, I hold SHRM-SCP, Hogan, and Lean Six Sigma Green Belt certifications, Trained in neuroscience and subconscious-mind reprogramming practices.

I believe fear can be a teacher and courage a daily practice. My purpose: create environments where potential becomes power, and power serves purpose.

~ ~ ~

To Abril, my sister, whose soul is always with me wherever I go.
To my husband, Víctor, for being my unwavering support; to my children, Ana Lucía, Andrea, and Víctor Santiago, for filling my life with joy and purpose; and to my mom, Coco, whose love and wisdom shaped the person I am today. This is for all of you—my heart, my strength, my inspiration.

WHAT KIND OF PERSON DOES THE WORLD NEED FROM YOU?

THE JOURNEY

Golden autumn leaves drifted effortlessly alongside I-64 as I drove through Virginia's long, winding highways, the sunlight draping the landscape in warm amber hues. The world outside my window felt almost cinematic—trees glowing gold, the crisp air brushing my skin, the hum of my Porsche vibrating with quiet confidence beneath me. But the beauty of that moment wasn't in the car, or the road, or even the peaceful freedom of the drive.

The beauty was in the gratitude rising within me—steady, grounded, overwhelming.

Not the kind of gratitude people list casually at Thanksgiving.
Not the polite kind that quickly fades.
But the deep, full-body gratitude of a woman who remembers her origins.

The gratitude of someone who has walked through difficult moments,
those that most people never see.
Who has rebuilt herself more than once.
Who has learned that strength isn't born from comfort—strength is carved by fire.

That afternoon on I-64, I whispered a quiet thank you—to God, to life, to the little girl I once was, and to the woman I chose to become.

Because nothing in my life was handed to me.
Everything was earned.
Every inch.
Every step.
Every opportunity.
Every second chance.

I did not wake up one day into a better life.
I built it—with discipline, sacrifice, heartbreak, courage, resilience, and the willingness to keep believing even when the world felt heavy.

Through every chapter—poverty, early responsibility, education, career growth, motherhood, devastating loss, immigration—one question guided me like a compass:

"What kind of person does the world need from you?"

This question shaped my childhood.

It has shaped my career and the decisions we have made at every step as a family.
It shaped the advocacy work that came after the tragedy.
And it shapes who I am today.

My story is not a story of perfection. It is a story of becoming.

And I share it for every Latina who has ever wondered if she is strong enough.

For every woman who has ever rebuilt her life quietly.
For every girl who dares to imagine something more.

ROOTS: Growing Up in Monterrey, Mexico

I was born in Monterrey, Mexico—the youngest of four children in a home bursting with movement, noise, love, and hardship. We didn't have luxuries, but we had each other. And in our small, crowded home, there was always life—laughter, arguments, the smell of food, the sound of my mother's footsteps, the energy of survival, resilience, a mindset of perseverance, effort, and courage mixed with the deep loyalty of family.

My mother was the heart of our home—strong in her softness, powerful in her persistence. She was the kind of woman who turned scarcity into sustenance and exhaustion into fuel. She taught us resilience not through speeches, but through example.

My father brought another kind of strength— thoughtful, wise, bookish. Though money was tight, he insisted that books were non-negotiable. Education, he believed, was our ticket to more than survival mode—it was our path to possibility.

He once told me: "Hija, el mundo allá afuera es grande y puedes aprenderlo a través de los libros; quien domina el conocimiento domina el mundo."

"The world out there is big, and you can learn about it through books; whoever masters knowledge masters the world."

Those words became part of me before I even understood them.

A Memory That Became My Compass

One afternoon when I was eight years old, my mother and I boarded a crowded public bus. We ended up standing on the very last step—dangerously close to the open door, wind blowing hard against us, the floor shaking beneath our feet.

At a red light, I looked outside and saw a man in a small sedan—air-conditioned, clean, comfortable. He looked to me like he belonged to a different world.

My mother followed my gaze, then asked me gently:

"¿Quieres estar un día en un carro así…
o quieres seguir aquí en el último escalón?"

Do you want to be in a car like that one day,
or do you want to stay here on the last step?

Before I could respond, she added:

"Si quieres una vida diferente, la puedes tener.

Pero tienes que estudiar. Tienes que enfocarte. Tienes que decidir bien. Todos los días. De lo contrario, puedo asegurarte que seguirás viajando en el último escalón del autobús."

"If you want a different life, you can have it. But you have to study. You have to focus. You have to make good decisions. Every day. Otherwise, I can assure you that you will continue to travel on the last step of the bus."

That moment didn't shame me—it woke me.
It handed me a map.

I learned that day that life offers choices, not guarantees.
And I silently promised myself: I would choose boldly.

THE WORK YEARS: Learning Hustle and Grit

Responsibility came early: I had to bring money home and help my parents. While other kids played after school, I worked.

At twelve, and for ten years, I performed in children's shows— dancing, singing, entertaining other kids. Later, I waited tables, cleaned at restaurants, worked cash registers, and assisted at events. I worked not because it was expected, but because it was necessary.

Those jobs became my foundation in leadership, although I wasn't aware at that time:

- How to learn and adapt quickly
- How to stay calm under pressure
- How to communicate clearly
- How to treat everyone with respect
- How to navigate conflict
- How to solve problems immediately with little information
- How to keep going, even when I was exhausted

But more than anything, I learned that leadership is not about authority. Leadership is about humanity and how much you can serve and help others.

BECOMING: Discovering My Professional Purpose

When it came time to choose a university major, I did the practical thing: I followed what my sister studied, I was good at Math, and went to study Industrial Engineering. It promised stability and opportunity, but I didn't have a clear understanding of whether I liked it or not. The only thing I knew was that you could always find a job easily and quickly after graduating.

But it wasn't until I was in my internships that something felt off.
My mind understood the work, but my heart wasn't in it.

I found myself drawn instead to people—their stories, their motivations, their frustrations, their potential.

Slowly, I realized, I was meant to develop and help people.

That's when I pursued Talent Management and Human Resources—a field that combined strategy, psychology, empathy, leadership, communication, and development.

At 27, I became a Human Resources manager.
I remember that I was proud but terrified at the same time.
I questioned myself constantly.

But I showed up anyway.
Fear became my teacher , and Courage became my habit.

And for the first time, I felt aligned with my purpose.

THE TURNING POINT: When Life Changes Without Warning

There are moments in life that arrive without warning—moments that crack your world open and force you to see life differently.

A few years ago, 6 to be exact, my family lived one of those moments.

It was a normal day—ordinary, uneventful—until a phone call shattered everything. My sister Abril, a woman known for her generosity, loyalty, and quiet strength, had been killed in a femicide in Mexico City.

The news hit like ice.
My mind couldn't comprehend it.
My heart couldn't accept it.
I remember the sudden heaviness in my chest.
The world spinning.
The sound of my brother's trembling voice when he was telling me what happened.
My own breath disappearing.

The life of our entire family changed forever the night we received that call telling us that my sister, Abril, had been shot. The news was devastating—two bullets, one in her neck and another in her head, fired by a hired assassin while she was in her car with her children in Mexico City. In that moment, Abril became another statistic in Mexico's epidemic of femicide, but to me, she was so much more: my companion, my confidant, and someone who always stood by my side.

What makes Abril's story even more painful is that she tried to protect herself. Months before her murder, she had bravely pleaded with the authorities for protection, expressing her fear and desperation in court because she had already suffered violence and feared for her life. Unfortunately, her pleas were ignored.

There is a particular grief that comes when someone you love is taken violently—a grief that is sharp, disorienting, and completely unprepared. It's not just emotional; it's physical. It lives inside your bones.

For days, our family existed in a fog of disbelief.
How could someone so loved, so vibrant, so needed, be gone?
She was not just our sister; she was a mom of 3 beautiful kids, who now needed to face the cruel reality of never seeing her again. She was full of

energy, motivation, and a love for life; suddenly, without warning, she was gone.

Losing Abril could have broken us. It was just the love of my husband, my 3 children, our entire family, and seeing my mom suffering with resilience that we were able to stay on our feet.

Abril's story is not unique. It's a reflection of the countless women who suffer violence and are failed by the system. Her death ignited a determination in me to speak out, not just for Abril, but for all the women whose voices have been silenced. My daughter started raising awareness through social media, first, to heal her pain for the loss of her aunt, Abril, but later as a way to educate others, support those in need, and fight for real change—so that no one else has to endure what my sister did. I joined her effort and started raising our voice and demanding action for those suffering violence. Abril's legacy lives on in the fight for justice and in every effort to make our society safer and more compassionate.

Slowly—through tears, prayers, and conversations that lasted deep into several days and nights—we made a decision where her story would not end in darkness, her name would not fade , and her life would not be reduced to the manner of her death. We chose to turn pain into action. We created the ONG La Voz de Abril to speak out about everything that Abril wanted to say and provide awareness to other women.

Of course, nothing can bring her back, but her story now can help and protect others.
Her light continues through the lives she helps save.

THE DECISION: Why We Left Mexico

After losing Abril, my family and I found ourselves at a crossroads. The pain was overwhelming—memories, unanswered questions, and the pain surrounded us. Yet, even in the midst of grief, I remember one of many values that my family has always had. It is in the worst moments that character is revealed. Now, more than ever, we needed and we must kept moving forward, solving each immediate challenge as it came, with resilience, no matter what. Day by day, I poured myself into my Family and my work, supported by the incredible love and patience from my husband and children, determined to transform pain into purpose and progress.

Despite the uncertainty, I remained committed to my career and personal growth. My dedication did not go unnoticed. After years of perseverance, I was recognized as a talent and was offered the opportunity to migrate to the United States—a chance to rebuild in a new environment. My husband, who is the smartest person I know, was also transferred from his job to the US. We embraced this opportunity, but the journey was not easy. Migrating to a new country with a different language is not easy at all, but we were committed to shaping it with resilience, hard work, and the belief that even in the darkest times, new possibilities can emerge.

Immigrating to the United States was not glamorous.
It was humbling, terrifying, lonely at times, and exhausting many days.

Suddenly, everything was new—school systems, cultural norms, workplace expectations, social rules, even the way people communicated.

But every challenge reminded us why we came:
Because we wanted to demonstrate that we, as Mexicans, can thrive wherever we are, we wanted our children to live new experiences, open their minds, and above everything, understand and prove that we can achieve all that is in our minds, all dreams are possible, if we really want them. We can live the life we want, the life we deserve.

REINVENTING: A New Life in a New Land

Little by little, we built our life in Virginia.
I rebuilt my career from the ground up—this time as a Latina leader navigating two cultures with pride. I learned new systems, adapted to new environments, and expanded my skills.

At home, we raised three extraordinary children—
Ana Lucía, powerful, brave, wise, and kind;
Andrea, smart, courageous, tender, and intuitive;
Victor Santiago, astute, curious, and full of unlimited potential.

We wanted them to know their heritage is a gift.
That their identity is power.
That they are the bridge between two worlds.
That resilience flows in their blood.

In this new land, I found not just a career—but a purpose.
Not just a home—but a healing space.
Not just safety—but the freedom to dream again.

THE LEARNINGS

What Life Has Taught Me So Far

Life doesn't deliver wisdom with a bow—it reveals it through moments that shape who you are. Every challenge, every crossroad, every quiet reflection became an invitation to rise stronger, wiser, and braver. These lessons were not setbacks—they were stepping stones. They taught me that resilience grows from hope, that education unlocks limitless possibilities, and that fear can be transformed into fuel for bold action. They remind us that leadership is a privilege to serve, that pain can ignite purpose, and that family is the foundation that keeps us grounded while we reach for the sky. These are not just words—they are truths I've lived, and they can inspire you to lead, love, and rise beyond what you ever imagined.

Here are my lessons learned:

1. Resilience is built, not inherited.

You get stronger by surviving and learning, not by avoiding the storm.

I learned this after losing my sister. Grief taught me that resilience isn't a gift—it's built through pain and persistence. I love this quote that my brother Victor Hugo once shared with me:

"Once the storm is over, you won't remember how you made it through, how you managed to survive. You won't even be sure whether the storm is really over. But one thing is certain. When you come out of the storm, you won't be the same person who walked in. That's what this storm's all about." -Haruki Murakami

2. Education changes destinies.

Knowledge creates choices—and choices create freedom.

Education was my escape route when I had nothing. Every book opened doors and gave me options I never imagined. Make sure you learn something new and exciting every day, after a year, you will have 365 new wonderful knowledge in your backpack.

3. Once you overcome your fears, you have an exponential positive change.

Leaving your comfort zone could be scary, but thinking about how many opportunities you have let slip by because the thought of grasping them made you hesitate and doubt yourself?

Every time you step outside your comfort zone, you experience growth—growth you would never find by staying the same.

Each time I said "yes" despite fear, my world expanded. Fear became fuel—and that changed everything. Try to do that single thing that is always in your mind, but you don't feel brave enough to do it, just do it, don't overthink about it, we all know life is short, but for some reason we behave as if we had all the time and strength to become that person we really want to be.

4. Leadership is service, and pain can become purpose.

It is always about lifting others. Sometimes it is at the worst times that you can find how strong you really are. When you transform grief, you may be transforming generations.

By serving others, I learned that leadership means turning grief into action that protects them. Even though you are not fully aware of how this will unfold or who might be transformed by a single word you spoke to them.

5. Family is a root system where integrity is a legacy.

It grounds you, nourishes you, teaches you, and strengthens you.

The big moments—new roles, wins, finished projects—are exciting, but for me, ordinary courage is built in the invisible. It was built in those days when you made little decisions. Ordinary courage looks like admitting to your kids when you get something wrong and letting them watch you try again. It looks like saying "I don't know" and then learning about it. It looks like building a family story where strength and softness are not enemies. It is built when you allow your kids to make mistakes and learn from them.

There are days when my sister's absence is a sharp ache that surprises me in the middle of something mundane—a person in the street, a laugh from a stranger that sounds like hers, or when people ask how we are doing. But what keeps me steady is knowing that our family chose to answer with action. That our voices, joined with others, helped strengthen protections through our ONG, **La Voz de Abril**. That now, my daughter has the passion and fire inside to continue Abril's purpose. That somewhere, a woman gets a faster response, a safer option, a different outcome—and our choice to act is part of that. Love is not only a feeling. It is a series of decisions that become actions.

THE INSPIRATION

My first inspiration was my mother.

A woman who carried entire worlds in her hands without ever calling it extraordinary. She taught me that strength is not always loud—it is often the quiet decision to keep going. She showed me that love can be both discipline and tenderness, that scarcity can be transformed into possibility, and that a mother's belief can become a daughter's compass. Her resilience was the rhythm of my childhood, and her footsteps became the blueprint for my own.

My father inspired me in a different way.

He gave me the gift of knowledge, the belief that books were doors, and that education could rewrite destinies. He taught me to think boldly, to question deeply, and to trust that my mind could take me further than my circumstances.

My siblings shaped me too.

Growing up in a home full of movement and noise, they were my first community, my first teachers in loyalty, conflict, forgiveness, and love. And then there is Abril—my sister, my friend, my mirror. Her life inspired me long before her death did. She inspired me with her generosity, her courage, her devotion to her children, and her ability to love fiercely. And after she was taken from us, her story became a fire inside me. She inspires me still— every day—to speak, to protect, to advocate, to transform pain into purpose. She reminds me that legacy is not what we leave behind; it is what we ignite in others.

My husband has been one of my greatest inspirations. His intelligence, patience, and unwavering belief in me have carried me through seasons when I doubted myself. He has been my partner in every sense—steady when life shook, brave when the path was uncertain, loving when grief felt unbearable. His support taught me that strength is multiplied when shared.

And then—my children. Ana Lucía, Andrea, and Victor Santiago.

They inspire me in ways I never expected. They are my daily reminder that the world can be rebuilt through love, that courage can be inherited, and that our stories matter because they shape the next generation. Watching them grow into thoughtful, brave, curious human beings pushes me to be better, to rise higher, to lead with integrity. They are the reason I choose courage over comfort, purpose over fear, and truth over silence.

But inspiration has also come from places beyond my family.
From every woman who has rebuilt her life quietly.
From every immigrant who started over with an accent and a dream.
From every Latina who dared to imagine more than what the world expected of her.
From every survivor who turned her pain into a voice.

And today, what inspires me most is possibility. The possibility of a world where women are safe. Where daughters inherit confidence instead of fear. Where purpose is louder than pain.

Where our stories—especially the ones born from struggle—become bridges for others.

I am inspired by the idea that we can honor our past while building a future that would make our younger selves proud.

That every step forward becomes an invitation for someone else to rise.

THE ADVICE

THE IMMIGRANT CHAPTER: Two Languages, One Life

When we first arrived in the U.S., I used to rehearse sentences in my head before I spoke them aloud, smoothing the edges of my accent in professional rooms. I don't do that anymore. I still work on clarity—that's respect—but I no longer apologize for the soundtrack of my story. Spanish taught me tenderness and cadence; English taught me reach and precision. I don't pick between them. I let them braid.

My children are fluent in both and fluent, too, in the idea that they do not have to choose. They can love pan dulce and apple pie, with roots in Mexico and the US. They expanded their horizons and know they can shine in any new environment; the sky is the limit. They can be many without being divided, because wholeness can be mixed. They now know they have the potential to do whatever they want and become a better version of themselves every day.

When I mentor my children, I don't give them a script; I try to give them a mirror. I tell them what I wish someone had told me sooner:

- You don't need to be twice as good; you need to be yourself as fully as possible.

- Learn to name your value in words that the room understands. Don't be shy and hide your strengths.

- Document your wins. Have a grateful notebook. Your future self will thank you.

- When in doubt, don't decide; ask better questions.

- Be kind, not small. There's a difference.

- And remember: boundaries protect your calling.

GRATITUDE and SELF LOVE

I used to write gratitude lists like they were homework. Now I try to practice gratitude more like breathing. Small, steady, honest. I thank the day for letting me learn. I thank my body for carrying me, especially when I ignored it. I thank the people who tell me the truth before the world does. I thank my husband and children for making this family our safe space. I thank my mother for the map she gave me, and my father for the books that felt like doors.

And I thank the part of me that didn't quit—the part that believed there was more even when evidence was scarce.

Driving down I-64 that afternoon, the sun melting into the horizon and the golden leaves dancing like they'd been waiting for me, I felt a truth rising— not loud, but undeniable. My life has not been easy. But it has been meaningful. It has been mine.

I thought of the little girl on the last step of a crowded bus in Mexico. She could not have imagined this version of us: a woman leading with steadiness, loving with intention, raising children who believe in both roots and wings, honoring a sister she will always miss, building safety where she can, choosing courage when it counts.

Here I am—not because doors opened politely, but because I learned how to push, how to knock again, how to build a new door when the hallway ended. Here I am—not untouched by

Here I am—not because doors opened politely, but because I learned how to push, how to knock again, how to build a new door when the hallway ended

pain, but transformed by it. Not without fear, but moving anyway. Not perfect, but whole.

And in that quiet stretch of highway, I heard the question that has followed me since childhood—the one that steadies my hands and sets my direction:

What kind of person does the world need from you?

The world does not need the smaller version of you.
It does not need the one who apologizes for taking up space, who folds herself to fit, who calls herself "lucky" when what she really is is powerful.

The world needs the version of you that dares.
The version that speaks truth, even when her voice shakes.
The version that dreams without asking for permission.
The version that says yes to purpose and builds after loss, loves after risk, and leads without losing herself.

If my journey proves anything, it is this:

You do not need a perfect beginning to create an extraordinary life. You need courage. You need clarity. You need the discipline to keep going and the humility to begin again. You need people—a few good ones—who will remind you who you are when you forget. And you need to keep listening to that quiet voice inside, the one that has been speaking since you were a child, the one that already knows the answer.

So pause. Breathe. Ask yourself with honesty and tenderness:

What kind of person does the world need from YOU?

Because inside every Latina lives a revolution,
a voice strong enough to bend the future,
a tenderness deep enough to heal a room,
a resilience that remembers how our grandmothers survived and insists that our daughters will thrive.

And if I could rise, then so can you.

Step forward. Step boldly. Step without apology.
Become the woman your younger self needed.
Become the woman your children will remember with pride.
Become the woman the world has been quietly waiting for.
Because the truth is simple and it is yours to claim: **You are exactly the kind of person the world needs—and it's time to live like it.**

A Note to the Next Extraordinary Latina

Especially those navigating unfamiliar rooms, languages, or expectations never designed with you in mind, see these lessons not as rules but as tools. Let your story inform your confidence, not diminish it. Use your languages, your culture, your questions, and your perspective as assets, not adjustments. Pay attention to where you feel pressure to shrink, and choose instead to clarify, contribute, and stay rooted in who you are. You do not have to erase parts of yourself to succeed. You are allowed to take up space with integrity, lead with kindness, and grow without apology. Your voice, exactly as it is, belongs.

If you are reading this and wondering whether it's your turn, let me offer you this: there is no committee that will tap your shoulder and declare you ready. Readiness is often a decision, not a feeling. I waited years for the surge of certainty that never arrived. In the end, I moved because the cost of staying small became more painful than the risk of stepping forward.

You don't have to fix everything to begin. You don't need a perfect plan, only an honest one. Start where you are, with what you have, and who you already are. The rest you can grow into. Courage expands with use. Confidence compounds. Clarity arrives in motion.

> *If you carry a loss, bring it tenderly with you. Let it teach you to cherish the ordinary and to answer harm with action*

If you carry a loss, bring it with you tenderly. Let it teach you to cherish the ordinary and to answer harm with action. Speak about your people's stories. Protect their legacies by living yours fully. Love can be both soft and steel.

If you are an immigrant, or the daughter of one, know this: bilingual hearts beat in wider rooms. Your accent is geography. Your mixed metaphors are bridges. You belong in every space your work and integrity can sustain. Don't try to sand away your imperfections; learn to manage them.

Celebrate your wins out loud. Archive them. Teach others to do the same.

And if doubt is still in your head, try to answer these questions and review your answers again in 6 months. Growth makes old answers obsolete.

- What moment from childhood still shapes what you reach for?

- Whose voice lives in your head—and which sentence do you need to retire?
- What kind of person does the world need from you this year, not just someday?
- What is One single action you would take if you weren't afraid?

One day your younger self will visit you in a memory. Meet her there with gentleness. Tell her she did enough. Tell her that their effort was not invisible. Tell her you took the map she made and carried it farther than either of you imagined.

When the world asks, "What kind of person does it need from you?"—answer with courage, from the heart. There has always been the answer.

Remember: you don't have to be fearless to be faithful to your calling. You only have to be willing. Willing to begin. Willing to continue. Willing to believe that your voice matters here.

It does. You do. You just need to Start now.

THE PATH FORWARD

Today, I stand in a place I once only dreamed of—not because life was easy, but because I chose to keep moving when it wasn't. I've learned that resilience is not a destination; it's a daily decision. Education opened doors, courage turned fear into fuel, and pain became purpose. My story is proof that storms don't define you—your response does.

The road ahead isn't a straight line—it's a living journey of courage and choice. Every challenge became a stepping stone, every loss a lesson, every doubt an invitation to grow stronger. If you're reading this, know this: your story is still unfolding, and the next chapter begins now. Not tomorrow. Not "someday." Today.

Trust the process. Embrace the lessons. Push past the limits you've placed on yourself. When fear whispers, answer with courage. When doubt knocks, open the door with action.

Rise boldly. Build courageously. Love deeply. Become unstoppable. The world is waiting for your light—go claim it.

ABOUT ANA

I am Ana Sagaon—a visionary leader, coach, and mentor committed to unlocking human potential and turning purpose into impact. My mission is to help individuals and organizations rise above limits, embrace change, and create futures that matter. Leadership, to me, is not a title but a responsibility: to inspire courage, ignite curiosity, and build systems where people thrive and results follow.

My journey began in Mexico, shaped by Japanese roots and an international life across **two countries**. Those experiences taught me resilience, adaptability, and the conviction that fear can be a teacher and courage a daily practice. With a foundation and an MBA in Strategy & Leadership, I've spent over two decades **leading Talent and Human Resources areas in global environments**, driving transformation, reimagining structures, elevating performance, and cultivating cultures that prioritize dignity and growth.

I am passionate about mentoring and coaching leaders to discover what lights them up and align it with meaningful impact. My work spans leadership development, organizational design, and cultural reinvention, always anchored in the belief that purpose is the ultimate competitive advantage. When people connect to their "why," they don't just perform—they innovate, collaborate, and lead with humanity.

As a loving mom and lifelong learner, I bring empathy and clarity to every conversation. My vision is bold: to create environments where potential becomes power, and power serves purpose.

Learn more and connect with Ana at:

https://www.linkedin.com/in/ana-sagaon-shrm-scp-9892415/

ANDREA VELÁZQUEZ

"When we are young we are taught to color inside the lines, to strive for perfection, to conform to other's standards. As an Afro Latina, I've learned to color outside the lines and create my own masterpiece!"

- Andrea Velázquez

~ ~ ~

Andrea "Drea" Velázquez is an unapologetic Afro-Latina leader, mentor, and bridge-builder whose life's work embodies purpose, pride, and impact. With over 25 years of experience in Diversity, Equity, and Inclusion—and more than two decades as a Spanish Medical Interpreter and Trainer—Drea has dedicated her career to breaking linguistic and cultural barriers in healthcare. A powerful advocate and coach, she founded What's Your Legacy Coaching to empower others to live with intention and create lasting change for future generations. Guided by her deep love for her family and community, Drea leads with authenticity, joy, and a fierce commitment to helping others find their voice, embrace their heritage, and build their legacy.

~ ~ ~

I dedicate this chapter to the women in my family and my son who have played a role in shaping me into the woman I am today. A Mis Abuelas, Andrea (who I was named after) and Francisca, God rest their souls. They taught me how to be strong, courageous and wise in the midst of chaos. To stay true to my Puerto Rican roots no matter the trials or tribulations. A mi Madre Julia, for her resilience, boldness and fierceness, traits that I am proud to claim. To my querubin GRANDdaughter who God sent to save my life. And last but definitely not least to my son, Benjamin, thank you for giving me the gift of being your mother and learning so much in the process.

FROM THE BRICKS TO BOLDNESS: A JOURNEY OF FAITH AND EMPOWERMENT

THE JOURNEY

Being raised in the South End of Boston was one of the best experiences of my childhood. I grew up in a housing project that was truly a melting pot. I was surrounded by families unlike my own, yet our differences never mattered; we got along and cared for one another as family. We were different in race, ethnicity, culture, color, religion, and even language—but it never seemed to matter. All of us kids went to the same elementary school, and we all became great friends.

As I got older, I realized that this experience was both a blessing and a curse. Growing up as an Afro-Latina in "the bricks" (aka public housing project) was wonderful, but it was a culture shock when I started at Michelangelo Middle School in Charlestown. It was my first time on a school bus, my first time traveling outside my comfort zone, and my first time being completely alone in a new environment. I was excited to see what was beyond the bricks, but I was also nervous. I thought everyone would be just as kind and accepting as the people from my neighborhood. That did not happen.

Discovering I Was "Different"

In middle school, I learned that I was "different." The white Latinas said I had *pelo malo*—coarse hair—and told me I was too dark to be Puerto Rican, even though I spoke fluent Spanish. The Black girls weren't too welcoming either, because although I looked like them, I spoke with a Spanish accent. I was bullied simply because I was different.

That was the first time I questioned my very existence. *Who am I? Why am I here? What did I do wrong?* Those questions stayed with me for a long time. But through that pain, I learned empathy. I vowed never to bully anyone because I knew what it felt like to be on the receiving end—the isolation, the shame, and the ugly thoughts that creep into your mind when you're treated as less than.

Family and Early Life Lessons

I was raised in a two-parent home with three of my seventeen siblings. I come from a blended and complicated family dynamic—one that I chose to love despite the hate imposed on me by some my older siblings, not raised with me. Being the youngest came with the benefits of being spoiled, but it also meant inheriting generations of trauma.

My father was abusive toward my mother, and my mother was the backbone of our family. She stayed because she didn't want us to grow up without a father. Living in that environment taught me early on that a two-parent home isn't always the healthiest one. Although my Papi sobered up and became a changed man/father, the trauma taught me what resilience looks like and what it costs.

Pivotal Moments That Changed My Life

Those early lessons followed me into adulthood, but I still found myself following in my mother's footsteps. After separating from my son's father, I found myself in an abusive relationship. For ten years, I thought I could love my way through the abuse. Unfortunately, it was not until I almost lost my life at the hands of my abuser that I realized it was time to set myself free. Even though I thought about staying, God sent me a sign that enough was enough. I walked away and vowed to love myself enough to stand tall, to be bold, courageous, and fierce. I thought about the scripture 1 Corinthians 13:4-8 on love and decided to wait for that kind of love. LOVE DOES NOT HURT!

There was also a time in my life when I allowed others to name me, blame me, and shame me—for my mistakes and even for theirs. My upbringing taught me to be tough and to wear that toughness on my face. Being tough carried with it an image of being a mean person. As an AftoLatina, I faced the additional challenge of being told that speaking up or standing up for myself was interpreted as having an "attitude" or as not being a good person or team player.

As long as I allowed people to use me and abuse me in my personal or professional life, I was considered a nice person. However, as soon as I spoke up for myself, people automatically labeled me as having an attitude or being mean. The truth is, I was a nice person; however, that image stuck with me, and people used it against me. I allowed it for many years because I wanted to be seen in a different light. I wanted to fit in. I wanted to be seen as a nice person, but it did not seem to make a difference. People still treated me as if I were the "mean, Black woman with an attitude." Eventually, I reclaimed control of my life and my narrative. I no longer allow anyone to define who I am or use my past against me.

Embracing My Identity and Roots

My background and upbringing have reminded me that I should never be ashamed of my Puerto Rican roots—my language, my heritage, and the texture of my hair. My ancestors endured so much to survive, and I am *extremely* thankful for their sacrifices. I often say that I'm the proudest Puerto Rican alive because I feel I must keep proving to those who only see the color of my skin or the texture of my hair that I am 100% Puerto Rican. I am deeply thankful to God for the culture I was born into.

Turning Pain Into Purpose

I've accepted that I cannot change the past, nor do I want to. There may be things I would do differently, but both the positive and negative experiences have taught me to be resilient, courageous, and faithful. They've helped me step out on faith and live in my purpose.

The past has shaped me into a better person—one who lives unapologetically and allows others to do the same. I've learned to transform pain into power, shame into self-love, and fear into faith.

Today, I live boldly, courageously, and unapologetically. I honor my past, my heritage, and my journey. I am the woman I am because of everything I've lived through—and I use that strength to empower others to reclaim their stories, embrace who they are, and live fully in their truth.

THE LEARNINGS

The most pivotal challenges I faced were the ones that came from trying to be what someone else wanted or liked. For a long time, I allowed people to treat me in unhealthy ways, to hold my mistakes over my head, and to make me feel less than.

About twelve years ago, I decided that I was done living that way. I chose to take my life back and embrace my uniqueness. I stopped relaxing my hair and started wearing it in its natural state, "con rizos." My rizos (curls) weren't tamed at that time, but oh, how I felt so free. I embraced them with so much love. Family and friends questioned the change and even thought it wasn't a good idea. Some people looked at me like I was crazy, but I didn't care what others thought. I was over what people thought about me and what I looked like. Sometimes stepping outside of the 'norm' can look crazy to some, but I consider myself 'not the norm.' I love being different. That's what being unique is all about.

I turned my challenges into stepping stones instead of stumbling blocks. I hired a life coach (shout-out to Clara Angelina Diaz), attended workshops, and did deep self-assessments. I made a commitment to myself that I would no longer allow anyone to name me, blame me, or shame me for my past mistakes. I thought about my younger self and realized that if I had learned this earlier in life, it would have been a game-changer. And that's where my idea of becoming a Youth Life Coach began. My goal now is to help youth embrace themselves and create a purposeful life that leaves a lasting legacy.

The Challenge of Being Seen and Heard

As an Afro-Latina woman, speaking up often came with consequences. When I used my voice, I was seen as aggressive, mean, uncooperative, troublesome, too loud, or too extra. I can admit I was sometimes defensive—but that came from being constantly taken for granted and overlooked. Whether it was in my personal life or in the workplace, I had to work twice as hard to prove myself, only to be passed over for opportunities I had earned.

That constant pressure to prove my worth became exhausting. The turning point came when I realized that trying to fit into other people's expectations was slowly destroying my spirit. I was tired of being tired. Change is good; however, changing to fit into someone else's box or standards can diminish who you are and what you stand for. Love me or hate me, I know that I am fearfully and wonderfully made, and I show up as an unapologetic AfroLatina with all the boldness God has created me with.

Finding Inner Strength

My strength came from family, prayer, coaching, mentoring, and honest self-reflection. I had to do the inner work. Growth doesn't happen without change, and I was ready for change. A changed mindset, a changed environment, changing habits, and even the people I associated with.

I wanted to be an example for my family and my community. I couldn't change who God made me to be — but I could change how I showed up. That realization became my power. I began living my truth, boldly and unapologetically. I also find strength in supporting others in their growth, and I love celebrating others' victories.

Strategies That Helped Me Heal

One of the most powerful strategies that kept me grounded was reminding myself that I am "fearfully and wonderfully made" (Psalm 139:14). I am here for a reason, with a purpose. I am enough. My life and story matters.

I began showing up for myself — and for those who didn't yet have a voice. Having a life coach was truly a blessing. Through that journey, I gave myself permission to forgive myself for my past mistakes and to keep moving forward. Forgiveness became my freedom.

I gave myself permission to forgive myself for my past mistakes and to keep moving forward. Forgiveness became my freedom.

Building a Support System

For most of my life, I tried to fix everything on my own. But I eventually learned that we aren't meant to do life by ourselves. I began leaning on my family, and on a small group of women I trust dearly (too many to name).

My Mom, sister Ileana, and nieces Kaisha, Monique, and Keomi have played a pivotal role in my journey. They've kept me grounded and sane while cheering me on to the next level.

There's a saying: *It takes a village to raise a child.* I believe it also takes a village — a support system — to be successful in every area of life. My village has been my strength on the days when I felt weak and my encouragement when I started to doubt myself.

Challenging the Status Quo

After graduating from high school, I went straight into the workforce. At the time, I thought taking a year off before college would help me figure out what I wanted to do. But that "year off" turned into an unexpected blessing. My son was born. And although it was the best time of my life, I knew that I had to work harder to make sure he had everything he needed. Entering the workforce as a young Afro-Latina mom showed me how hard it can be to be seen, respected, and taken seriously, especially without a degree.

Still, those experiences taught me resilience, confidence, and faith. They showed me that I could challenge the systems that tried to hold me back simply by refusing to give up — by showing up, speaking up, and standing tall in who I am.

Living Unapologetically Authentic

The journey hasn't been easy, but it's been worth it. Every challenge has helped shape me into the woman I am today — bold, grounded, and unafraid to live authentically. I've learned that empowerment begins the moment you decide that your life belongs to you.

Today, I stand proudly in my truth, not as who others wanted me to be, but as who God created me to be: *fearfully, wonderfully, and unapologetically authentic.*

THE INSPIRATION

Throughout my life, I've been blessed with incredible sources of inspiration — people, faith, and experiences that have carried me through even the hardest seasons. Each one has played a special role in shaping who I am and the legacy I want to leave behind.

My greatest inspiration has always been my mother. She could make a dollar out of fifteen cents, literally. My mother raised and provided for four children here in the States while also supporting her three eldest children in Puerto Rico — and still managed to save for a rainy day. She helped me raise my son while I worked and somehow made it all look so easy, even while carrying the weight of her own trauma. Watching her do the impossible with grace, strength, and faith taught me what resilience truly looks like. She showed me that love and determination can move mountains.

When times got tough, my son became my reason to keep pushing forward. We went through some very difficult moments together, but we always stuck by each other and cheered one another on. Our life felt a little like the movie *The Pursuit of Happyness* — full of challenges, uncertainty, and moments that tested our strength — but we kept believing that better days would come. He was, and still is, my motivation to rise each day, to keep going, and to become the best version of myself.

Through every chapter of my life, my faith has been my compass. The Bible and prayer have guided me through some of the most challenging times, reminding me that I am never alone, even when life feels overwhelming. These days, I continue to draw strength and spiritual inspiration from powerful words and teachings. I often listen to *Hello Tomorrow and Goodbye Yesterday* by Cindy Trimm. Her wisdom and faith-filled messages help me stay grounded in purpose and in the promise of what lies ahead.

Someone who had a profound impact on my journey was my dear friend, Marion Sargeant — God rest her soul. Marion was one of the hardest-working women I've ever known. She was the first to tell me that I didn't have to settle for less. Her encouragement and belief in me helped me raise my standards and recognize my worth. My sister, Ileana Velasquez, has also been one of my biggest inspirations. Her marriage, her work ethic, and her unwavering support continue to inspire me. She is my sounding board, my unofficial counselor, and one of my greatest blessings.

Today, my inspiration comes from my grandchildren. They remind me every day to be better, to do better, and to create something meaningful that will outlast me. They inspire me to leave a legacy of courage, faith, and empowerment — not just for them, but for the generations that will follow. Starting my business, *What's Your Legacy Coaching*, came from that desire. I wanted to help guide the next generation to embrace their identity, their purpose, and their power — just as I've learned to embrace mine.

THE ADVICE

The advice I would offer my younger self is simple: it's okay to learn from other people's mistakes. You might reach your destination or goal faster if you take the time to observe what others have done — what worked for them and what didn't. Your path may not look exactly the same, but at least you'll have a model to guide you.

Be curious. Ask questions about the things that intrigue you. Read more. Explore the world like a child seeing it for the first time. Travel, experience, and witness God's creation — it will awaken your imagination and keep your creative spirit alive.

Show up for yourself the same way you show up for others. Give yourself those pep talks you're so quick to offer a friend when they're feeling down. Take your own advice! Step out on faith, because fear is a horrible place to stay.

Be unapologetic about starting over, again and again. You can begin anew whenever you choose.

Write your vision and make it plain (Habakkuk 2:2). Know what you want, and map out where you want to go. Life is a journey — sometimes you'll need a map to stay on course, and sometimes you'll wander without one, simply exploring where the road takes you. Either way, start early. Give yourself the time to learn if the road you're on is truly your path.

And remember — it's *your* journey. Be unapologetic about starting over, again and again. You can begin anew whenever you choose.

Take time to sit and talk with your elders — your abuelos and abuelas, your parents, your tíos and tías. There's wisdom and history in their stories, waiting to be heard. Learn from your bloodline's past so you can create a better present and future for yourself, your loved ones, and even for the world.

And don't forget to care for yourself along the way. Whether it's through prayer, meditation, gardening, or giving back to your community, find what nourishes your soul. Think about what was missing when you were a young girl — and share that light with the next generation.

THE PATH FORWARD

Life is a journey, and your journey may not look like anyone else's. Own it, and make it what *you* want it to be. Embrace the gems that life throws your way — and don't be afraid to let go of the ones that no longer serve you.

You will make mistakes along the way; we all do. Don't let those mistakes keep you stuck. Give yourself grace, brush yourself off, and keep moving forward. The hills and valleys you face, and the people you meet along the way, will either make you or break you — but both have something to teach you.

Strive to live a life that feels true to you. Your footprint is your legacy and what makes you unique. Leave a lasting imprint on the next generation—one that inspires them to do the same. Color outside the lines and create your own masterpiece. Somewhere out there, someone may be waiting for you to be *boldacious* — to write your story, build your business, step out on faith, and share your light with the world.

My call to action is simple: reach back and lift others as you rise. Our next generation of Latina leaders is watching, waiting for a helping hand, a word of encouragement, or a seat at the table. Hold that space for those who are still finding their voices.

And if you're ready to take the next step toward leaving a legacy that endures, reach out and schedule a *cafecito* with me. Let's map out your plan to create the life, the impact, and the legacy that only *you* can build.

ABOUT ANDREA

Andrea 'Drea' Velázquez is an unapologetic, Afro-Latina born and raised in Boston, Massachusetts, with Puerto Rican roots. Andrea's superpower is bringing the best of both worlds of her AfroLatinidad to the table. She has the power to bridge linguistic and cultural gaps in the medical and community arenas.

Andrea is a Spanish Medical Interpreter and Trainer at Brigham and Women's Hospital. She serves on the hospital's Ethics Committee and the Schwartz Rounds Advisory Committee. She has more than 25 years of Diversity, Equity and Inclusion experience and has been a Medical Interpreter for over 20 years. As a Medical Interpreter Language Coach for over 15 years, she has trained and mentored more than 200 professional Interpreters throughout her career.

Andrea continues to inspire and mentor young professionals in this field. Andrea is the proud mother of an amazing, AfroLatino young man and grandmother to 5 beautiful grandchildren. She is always looking to create opportunities to make the world a better place for her son, grandchildren and her community. Drea is happiest when she is coaching and mentoring others to achieve their goals and live in their purpose. Through coaching and mentoring, she has found her sense of purpose in life, which led her to start her life coaching business. 'What's Your Legacy Coaching' is dedicated to supporting youth and adults in creating a long-lasting legacy.

Andrea currently serves on the United Latinas Board, Beth Israel Lahey Plymouth Advisory Board, and The Pathway Initiatives, Inc. Board. Andrea prefers to color outside the lines and create her own masterpiece.

You learn more and connect with Andrea at:

CANDY PAHUA

'When you multiply trust by opportunity, you get transformation!

-    Candy Pahua

~ ~ ~

Candelaria "Candy" Pahua Oros is a bilingual healthcare leader, educator, and equity advocate whose work is transforming access to life-saving care across rural and underserved communities in Northern California. As a champion within the Every Woman Counts program, she leads breast and cervical cancer prevention initiatives across 16 counties—bringing culturally responsive education, compassion, and hope to the women who need it most. With an MBA in Healthcare Administration, Lean Six Sigma expertise, and a proven record in operations and policy innovation, Candy designs data-driven solutions that reduce preventable hospitalizations and strengthen community health systems. Recognized by the Korn Ferry Foundation and the National Association of Latino Healthcare Executives, she is a rising voice in healthcare equity, committed to mentoring the next generation and building a future where every community has access to dignified, high-quality, and culturally centered care.

~ ~ ~

For my parents, whose sacrifices built the foundation for my dreams and for every Latina leader turning community strength into systemic change.

THE LATINA EQUATION WHERE TRUST MEETS OPPORTUNITY, TRANSFORMATION BEGINS

THE JOURNEY

I was raised in the heart of rural Northern California, where community wasn't a word; it was a way of life – neighbors dropping off fruits after a harvest and music spilling from backyard gatherings. My family, like many Latino families, built our lives on faith, resilience, and service to others – the kind of faith that shows up in veladoras on the kitchen table and Spanish music floating in the background like a soundtrack to my life. They immigrated to the United States decades ago, carrying little more than courage, a few photographs, and the dream of a better future for their children.

My mother worked in the fields, and my father worked in the almond orchards. We didn't have much, but we had each other. I watched my parents work hard and grow through adversity. They made sure we had a roof over our heads and food on our plates. Our house always had warmth, filled with laughter and fun banter, and it became a haven for my extended family. It taught me that skills are learned and that leadership takes many shapes. It often begins at the kitchen table, where Latino families pass down wisdom, values, and responsibility to our people. My parents didn't speak English and always made sure we took advantage of opportunities, reminding us that educación is not just schooling, it's dignity, mobility, and the legacy they came here to build. I grew up being the interpreter at medical appointments, school open houses, and everyday errands – a role many first-generation daughters know well. That early responsibility shaped my calling long before I ever knew what public health was.

Growing up, I didn't see many Latinas in positions of power, especially in healthcare. What I did see were outreach folks speaking Spanish and informing people about important health issues. They weren't called executives or fancy titles, but they were leaders in every sense of the word. I didn't know it then, but that grassroots leadership model would later define my entire career.

My path into healthcare began with education, as a first-generation college student at CSU, Chico. I majored in Health Science with a health education option. It wasn't an easy journey. I struggled with navigating a system that I was unfamiliar with, and my mental health declined. There were moments of extreme doubt—times I thought I couldn't survive this. I began thinking that the opportunity wasn't meant for me. But every time I volunteered for an event, helped a friend out, or participated in a community initiative, I felt a sense of purpose that kept me moving forward.

After earning my degree, I worked as a contract employee at California Health Collaborative, where I conducted community outreach for *Every Woman Counts*. Suddenly, I wasn't just doing health education; I was empowering entire communities to access and improve healthcare related to cancer prevention. In small towns across Northern California counties, I met women who reminded me of my mother, my tías, and my neighbors. Many were hesitant about cancer screenings like mammograms. Through classes – including bilingual classes – outreach events, and trust-based relationships, I saw transformation firsthand.

But the deeper I got into community work, the more I saw the gaps. How often were decisions made about communities without including their voices? I realized that while education is vital, systems change saves generations. That realization became a turning point. I decided to pursue my MBA in Healthcare Administration from Northern Arizona University, determined to bridge the gap between community experience and executive decision-making.

Balancing graduate school, full-time work, and advocacy wasn't easy, but it taught me discipline, resilience, and strategy. I learned to see healthcare not only through the lens of compassion but also through the lenses of data, design, and efficiency. During my MBA consulting practicum, I learned how data and statistics help shape programs and policies. It proved that heart and strategy could coexist.

> *Each opportunity reinforced a lesson my community had taught me early on: leadership isn't about authority; it's about access.*

Parallel to my professional growth, I also grew as an advocate. I joined advisory committees, mentorship programs, and leadership initiatives. Each opportunity reinforced a lesson my community had taught me early on: leadership isn't about authority; it's about access. The more rooms I entered, the more I saw how critical it was for Latinas to take up space, speak up, and lead with authenticity.

Of course, the journey wasn't linear. There were seasons of burnout, moments of imposter syndrome, and tears running down my face as I questioned whether my efforts were enough. But every setback became a seed of growth. Losing fellowship opportunities taught me patience and persistence. Working through a pandemic taught me empathy and adaptability. Every time I saw a promotora in outreach, it reignited my purpose.

Today, as a CHES®—a Certified Health Education Specialist, Lean Six Sigma Green Belt, and MBA graduate—I see myself as both a product and a promise of what's possible when community and leadership intersect. My background taught me humility; my education taught me strategy; and my lived experiences taught me courage.

Becoming an empowering changemaker wasn't a single moment. It was a series of ordinary acts done with extraordinary effort and intention. It was saying yes to selective opportunities that scared me, speaking up in rooms where my voice shook, and building pathways for others who might never have believed they belonged there.

I often think back to those early days watching the *promotoras*. They didn't wait for permission to lead. They led because their communities needed them to. That's what drives me today—to create a visible, sustainable pipeline where Latinas like *promotoras de salud* can evolve into public health professionals, program directors, and healthcare executives.

Because when Latinas rise, communities thrive.

The Latina Equation in action: Trust × Opportunity = Transformation.

THE LEARNINGS

My journey wasn't a straight line. I wish it had gone according to plan. Instead, it was a mosaic of detours, rejections, and redirections. Each challenge pushed me to grow in ways I never anticipated.

One of the first significant challenges I faced was learning how to lead without a roadmap. As a first-generation college student and professional, there was no inherited playbook for navigating higher education or healthcare systems. I often found myself translating not just for patients, but for my own future. I had to learn to interpret policies and jargon that no one had ever explained to me. The imposter syndrome was real. For years, I felt like I had to overperform just to belong. But over time, I realized that belonging isn't granted—it's claimed. I stopped trying to blend in and began leading with the authenticity that had once made me feel "different."

Another pivotal moment came when I decided to pursue my MBA. Balancing graduate studies, full-time work, and community advocacy was demanding. There were nights I cried from exhaustion, questioning if my efforts and sacrifices were worth it. But I kept reminding myself that I wasn't doing this for me alone; I was doing it for every Latina who thought leadership was out of reach. That mindset turned perseverance into purpose. My coping mechanism became reframing stress as a form of growth. Each deadline wasn't an obstacle—it was preparation for the executive roles I hoped to hold one day.

At work, I also encountered systemic barriers, where community insight was often undervalued relative to academic credentials. I learned to challenge that norm by bringing data and lived experience to every conversation. When I presented cancer-screening outcomes or outreach metrics, I paired numbers with narratives. It shifted perceptions—suddenly, the community's voice carried weight because it came wrapped in evidence.

My greatest strength emerged from collaboration. Over time, I built a support system of mentors, colleagues, and fellow Latina professionals who reminded me that leadership doesn't have to be lonely. I found spaces where purpose met professionalism. I met mentors who helped me see that advocacy isn't just about speaking up—it's about staying in the room long enough to change the conversation.

When opportunities didn't pan out—like fellowship rejections—I used reflection as a tool instead of resentment. I'd ask myself: *What did this experience teach me that success couldn't?* Usually, the answer was resilience, adaptability, and grace. Those lessons became part of my leadership toolkit.

Perhaps my most transformative learning was understanding that disruption is a form of love. In healthcare, advocating for equity often means questioning outdated systems. I learned to disrupt respectfully—by asking hard questions, designing process improvements, and pushing for cultural competence in decision-making. My Lean Six Sigma training taught me to challenge processes with data; my community taught me to do so with empathy.

The main line of every challenge has been this: strength doesn't come from never falling—it comes from rising with wisdom. Each setback redefined my capacity for compassion, patience, and persistence. I now see leadership as the art of turning lessons into leverage—not just for yourself, but for others who follow.

If "the journey" was about building credibility, "the learnings" are about building character. I learned that courage isn't the absence of fear; it's the decision to act despite it. I learned that leadership isn't about titles; it's about trust. I learned that when we stand firm in our values, even the systems that once excluded us begin to evolve.

Those lessons are the foundation of who I am today: a Latina leader who turns obstacles into opportunities—and who believes that every challenge is an invitation to grow and to lift others as we rise.

THE INSPIRATION

When I think about what keeps me moving forward, I think of my parents. My mom taught me that it is okay to be bold and loud, and my father taught me that there is strength in being steady and quiet. They are my first and most enduring teachers of resilience, faith, and hard work.

My father taught me that perseverance is non-negotiable—that every challenge is an opportunity to build strength. My mother taught me that using my voice is powerful and is best when I yield it strategically. Together, they modeled a form of leadership built on humility, service, and passion.

Growing up, I watched them navigate life with limited resources but unlimited determination. They showed me that dignity isn't defined by status but by how you treat people. Their sacrifices, late nights, long workdays, and unwavering belief in the value of education are the foundation for everything I do. When times were tough, I remembered their example. When I questioned my path, I heard their voices reminding me that purpose is greater than fear.

Beyond my parents, my inspiration came from the *promotoras* in my community—the women who carried public health on their backs long before it was recognized as a profession. They reminded me that leadership doesn't start with a title; it begins with trust. Every time I see a woman gain the confidence to schedule her first screening or advocate for her own health, I see the reflection of those *promotoras* who led with empathy and strength.

> *Leadership doesn't start with a title; it starts with trust.*

As I grew into leadership roles, my circle of inspiration widened. Mentorship programs reaffirmed that compassion and strategy can coexist. The mentors I met along my journey taught me that representation is more than being seen; it's about using your presence to open doors for others.

My inspiration has evolved alongside my journey. It begins with my parents' sacrifices, grows through community mentorship, and now thrives on legacy. I'm driven by the belief that leadership can be both data-driven and heart-centered—that we can transform healthcare systems without losing the humanity that defines our culture.

When challenges arise, I return to the image of my parents, standing side by side, facing life's uncertainty with courage and faith. Their example reminds me that success is not measured by accolades, but by the lives we touch.

Ultimately, what inspires me is possibility—the possibility that one voice can change a conversation, one leader can change a system, and one generation can lift the next higher than the last. That's why I wanted to write, lead, and serve: to honor my parents' legacy and to help others believe that their stories, too, can shape the future.

THE ADVICE

If I could sit down with my younger self — the first-generation college student filled with ambition and uncertainty — I'd tell her a few things that would have eased the weight she carried.

1. You belong in every room you walk into.

For too long, I questioned whether I was "enough"—smart enough, experienced enough, prepared enough. But belonging isn't something you earn; it's something you affirm. I learned that confidence grows not from perfection, but from purpose. Every voice, especially those shaped by lived experience, brings value. Walk into rooms not as a guest, but as a contributor. You carry the perspective that others don't even know they need.

2. Lead with both data and heart.

In healthcare and in life, I've learned that the most effective change happens when evidence meets empathy. Don't be afraid to be the professional who brings compassion to the table or the advocate who backs it up with numbers. You don't have to choose between being strategic and being soulful; you are strongest when you are both.

3. Turn obstacles into blueprints.

Every rejection, setback, or delay you face is not a closed door—it's an invitation to build your own. When I was rejected from fellowships or jobs, I used my experiences to refine my skills, earn new credentials, and strengthen my purpose. Failure is not the opposite of success; it's the foundation of it. Every challenge teaches you something success never could.

4. Protect your energy like it's sacred—because it is.

Service-driven leaders often give until they are empty. I've learned that boundaries are not barriers; they are acts of self-respect. You can't pour into others if your own cup is dry. Rest, reflection, and self-care are not luxuries; they're leadership tools. I now schedule time for stillness, journaling, and gratitude as intentionally as I schedule meetings.

If there's one shift in mindset I wish I had learned sooner, it's that purpose and peace can coexist. You can chase big goals without losing yourself in the process. You can be ambitious and gentle, decisive and humble, visionary and grounded.

True growth is not about doing more—it's about becoming more aligned with who you are meant to be. For anyone walking a similar journey, especially young Latinas stepping into leadership, I want you to know this: you don't need permission to lead, to dream, or to take up space. The world needs your perspective, your resilience, and your story.

Lean boldly, learn constantly, and never underestimate the power of your authenticity. Because one day, you'll look back and realize you were never becoming someone new—you were simply uncovering who you've been all along.

THE PATH FORWARD

When one Latina rises, we all rise.

As I look ahead, my vision is clear: to build a future where Latinas are not only the heart of their communities but also the architects of the systems that serve them. I want to help create a visible, intentional pipeline where *promotoras de salud* become program directors, where health educators become executives, and where compassion and leadership coexist in every boardroom.

My legacy, I hope, will be measured not by titles or credentials, but by the doors I help open. I want to be remembered as someone who multiplied trust into opportunity for others as much as for myself.

The Latina Equation isn't just my story; it's a model for transformation. When you multiply trust by opportunity, you get empowerment. And when you multiply empowerment by community, you get lasting change.

To every Latina reading this: you are already a leader. Whether you lead a family, a classroom, a clinic, or an organization, your voice carries power. You don't have to wait for permission to step into it. Leadership doesn't begin when you receive a title—it starts the moment you decide your presence matters.

My call to action is simple: **use your story as strategy.** Every challenge you've faced, every barrier you've overcome, and every act of service you've offered—those are credentials the world can't replicate. Share them. Mentor others. Advocate in the rooms you enter. And when those rooms don't exist yet, build them.

The path forward requires all of us. We need Latina leaders in policy, in health systems, in innovation—in every space where decisions about our communities are made. We need to turn representation into reformation, transforming how systems see us, serve us, and include us.

What's next for me is to continue expanding this vision. I plan to strengthen leadership pathways for women in public health, train the next generation of *promotoras* and health educators, and pursue executive roles where I can influence healthcare delivery at the systems level.

But just as importantly, I'll continue mentoring, speaking, and writing—because visibility is power, and storytelling is how we claim it.

To the Latinas coming after me: know that your voice is your vehicle. Use it to question, to create, to connect. You come from a lineage of perseverance and brilliance. The strength you carry is ancestral; it's coded in your DNA.

If my story leaves you with anything, let it be this: your journey is the blueprint someone else is waiting for. By showing up as yourself—fully, boldly, authentically—you become living proof of what's possible.

So keep rising, keep building, and keep believing. The next chapter of our collective story is waiting—and it has your name written all over it.

ABOUT CANDY

Candelaria "Candy" Pahua Oros is a bilingual healthcare leader, health educator, and advocate dedicated to advancing health equity. She serves as a Health educator with the Every Woman Counts program in Northern California at California Health Collaborative, leading breast and cervical cancer prevention initiatives across 16 counties in rural and frontier communities. Candy holds an MBA in Healthcare Administration from Northern Arizona University, a Bachelor's of Science in Health Science from California State University, Chico, a Certified Health Education Specialist (CHES®), and is a Lean Six Sigma Green Belt, bringing expertise in operations, policy, and process improvement. Her consulting work highlights her ability to design innovative, data-driven solutions to reduce preventable hospitalizations. She has been recognized through leadership programs with the Korn Ferry Foundation and the National Association of Latino Healthcare Executives, and she contributes to statewide advisory committees focused on access and workforce equity, such as the Community Health Worker Advisory Committee at the Department of Health Care Access and Information. She volunteers with Soroptimist International of the Americas. This global volunteer organization provides women and girls with access to the education and training they need to achieve economic empowerment, especially those facing significant obstacles. She is also a member of the Hispanic Resource Council of Northern California and collaborates with local and regional agencies for resource management. Passionate about mentoring and systems innovation, Candy envisions a future where every community has access to compassionate, high-quality, and culturally responsive care.

To learn more about and connect with Candy:
LinkedIn: www.linkedin.com/in/candypahua
website: https://candypahua.wixsite.com/portfolio

CLAUDIA CARDOZO

"Self-acceptance was not a discovery for me, it was a return. As I began to honor my deepest values, I came to understand that every struggle had been quietly shaping a gift meant to be shared.."

-   Claudia Cardozo

~ ~ ~

Claudia is an author, TEDx Speaker, and transformational coach who leads with one core conviction: love is a powerful force for change. As the founder of InnateFive, she partners with organizations to elevate leadership, deepen teamwork, and create cultures of true belonging. A Gallup-Certified Strengths Coach and holder of a Diversity & Inclusion Certificate from Cornell University, Claudia is also a Global Listening Intelligence Certified Coach and a Certified Life Coach and Meditation Instructor. Drawing from her experience as a first-generation Colombian immigrant, she advocates for compassionate, inclusive leadership that helps every person feel seen, valued, and empowered. A founding member of the A Loving Organization Consortium and holder of a Diversity & Inclusion Certificate from Cornell University, Claudia's work and her book Love Is the Path invite us to reimagine how we lead, connect, and build a more loving world, starting from within.

~ ~ ~

To the resilient spirit of my younger self, who never gave up seeking a better life, and to every Latina leader who is learning that their deepest power begins with self-compassion.

THE COURAGE TO PAUSE:
A JOURNEY TO LEADING FROM LOVE

THE JOURNEY

When I arrived in the United States at age twenty-five, I carried only five hundred dollars, a suitcase, and a deep purpose in my heart to build a better future for myself and my daughter. Achieving that dream came with an unbearable cost. I had to leave my three-year-old daughter behind in Colombia with her father after our divorce. Leaving her was the single most difficult decision I had ever made, a painful sacrifice that defined those years for both of us. Though I was struggling in many ways, the promise of a new life kept me going.

My first job was rolling burritos and frying tacos at the Providence Place Mall food court while learning English every night at the Lutheran Church across the street, a community of immigrants where I spent some holidays and found support during difficult times.

In 2004, only two years after arriving in the United States and overcoming countless obstacles, I graduated from an Insurance Technician program at Rhode Island College. It was a challenging experience because I was learning insurance terminology while still learning English. However, the idea of pursuing a better job kept me disciplined in my studies. That year, at the end of the program, I celebrated this accomplishment with my daughter present. I remember looking at her as I received my insurance diploma, her eyes full of pride, her smile full of joy, and my heart overflowing.

It wasn't until 2008 that I was able to obtain my daughter's residency to live with me full-time.

Over the years, I built a new life, prioritizing my daughter's education and my career. I moved a few times during her school years, from Pawtucket to Lincoln and then Providence, always seeking the best public schools for her.

Work quickly became a central part of my life. From insurance, I transitioned to economic development, connecting small businesses with statewide resources for seven years. Following that, I spent another seven years in the corporate world as a community development manager for a small local bank. This role allowed me to serve others by teaching financial education and entrepreneurship. In 2017, I started a coaching business.

Over the years, I came to believe my worth was tied to my ability to perform, achieve, and prove that my sacrifices had been worth it. My work, especially in community development, gave me immense meaning and pride. I loved serving people, teaching financial literacy, and helping families find stability. I woke up every morning with a deep sense of purpose.

But in 2021, that sense of purpose began to change in ways I could not ignore. The work I once loved no longer felt the same. The human connection and community service that had always energized me were being replaced by screens, regulations, and spreadsheets.

Simultaneously, my personal life fell apart. My engagement ended, my daughter moved across the country to pursue her career, and I faced health challenges that left me anemic and weak. Suddenly, I was alone, disengaged at work, and questioning the meaning of it all.

Finding myself without purpose plunged me into an existential crisis that forced me to question everything: how I was living, what I valued, and who I had become. Looking within, I recognized how much of my life had been spent trying to fit in, be accepted, and feel valuable, often at the expense of my own well-being. Guilt set in; I felt the weight of having overextended myself in work instead of spending more time with my daughter. Lost, angry at myself, and lacking the spark I once had, I knew something had to change.

I decided I wanted more. I wanted to truly live, to cultivate meaningful relationships, and to reconnect with my roots. I found myself asking a simple but painful question: Why had I forgotten my love for dancing?

In hindsight, that inner shift was the beginning of my rebirth. I took responsibility for the life I had created and decided that if it was my own creation, I could make different choices, ones that granted me a more fulfilling life.

In August of 2022, despite the fear, I chose myself. I walked away from my corporate career and its safety net to dedicate myself to coaching and healing fully. It was a leap of faith. I didn't fully understand back then that this choice would become my greatest turning point, a commitment to authenticity, purpose, and wholehearted service.

THE LEARNINGS

Choosing to step away from my corporate job and fully embrace healing and coaching changed everything for me. My personal journey, along with the privilege of holding space for others, revealed wisdom that could only be learned through experience. This wisdom redefined my understanding of self-worth, leadership, and what it truly means to be human.

It Feels Better to Be Kind Than to Be Right

I learned that we are all doing the best we can with the awareness we have at each moment. This simple understanding helped me develop a deeper compassion for both myself and others. I recognized that my reality was being filtered through my limited beliefs and perceptions, so I shifted my approach to life: I now constantly seek ways to expand my thinking, listening to understand rather than just respond. I learned that it feels much better to be kind than to be right, and that I thrive when I approach the school of life with an open mind and open heart.

It Takes Courage to be Human

I learned that my emotions are an incredible compass, helping me navigate the world with more integrity. I learned to honor my emotions and process them in healthy ways. I learned to feel them in my body and connect with their wisdom. I also realized that vulnerability is not weakness, but courage. By sharing my story and letting others see my imperfect self, I give them permission to be their authentic selves.

Safety Starts Within

I learned that success is measured not by external accolades, but by the quality of our relationships and the peace we feel when our choices align with our core values. While we are all products of our environment, we can make conscious choices to become the best versions of ourselves. My self-limiting thoughts didn't define me; they were merely old versions of myself that I learned to let go of. Most importantly, I realized that I can only create a space of psychological safety for others when I first make it safe for myself, which starts with tuning into my own body and regulating my nervous system, one mindful breath at a time.

> *My self-limiting thoughts didn't define me; they were merely old versions of myself that I learned to let go of.*

THE INSPIRATION

Back in 2022, when I was navigating my darkest moments, God put beautiful souls on my path to help me see the light again. I want to highlight a few of them here.

One of those guiding lights was Ilhiana Rojas. I had always admired her depth of insight, her contagious positive energy, and her genuine desire to serve others. We had worked together on a few projects during my corporate career, so when I needed support, I knew I could trust her to guide me.

She held space for me with such compassion, constantly reminding me that I didn't have to walk this path alone. She encouraged me to reach out, to stay connected, often saying, "Find your tribe." I will never forget those words and the days when her check-ins were the only messages on my phone. Her presence, even through a simple text, made me feel deeply seen and supported.

In the fall of 2022, I embarked on a series of travel experiences that helped me relate to life differently and see parts of myself that were previously hidden.

I reconnected with Juan Antonio, who had left his corporate job a few years before to pursue a dream: creating ULU, Un Latido Universal, a documentary exploring what it means to live a life guided by the heart.

After watching the film, I attended one of his virtual gatherings where he brought together viewers from around the world for spontaneous, heart-led conversations. After just a couple of hours, strangers felt like old friends. It was deeply inspiring.

After a few of these meetings, I decided to sign up for one of his personal transformation programs and embark on a magical 20-day journey to Spain, guided by him.

My walks with Juan Antonio were emotional roller coasters. I often laughed and cried at the same time as he helped me see how tightly I had held onto self-limiting stories that no longer served me, and how I could replace them with more uplifting ones. This emotional work began my journey of experiencing life differently. I learned to pause, savor food with all my senses, and see the world with new eyes.

During the trip, I journaled extensively, which was key to developing more compassion for myself. Through writing, I gained a crucial understanding of my low self-esteem and judgmental tendencies, both toward myself and others. I finally recognized that growing up with an absent father, without a stable home, and living in a cold group home had created the profound emotional instability that fueled these patterns.

Juan Antonio inspired me to accept the pause, embrace the past with gratitude, and step into the present moment with grace.

Another transformative experience came through my friend, Anyi Espinal. We grew closer during the pandemic through her virtual yoga classes, and I later traveled to Casa Bienestar, her sanctuary in the Caribbean mountains of the

I learned that sisterhood acts as a mirror, reflecting our own capacity for self-care.

Dominican Republic, for a private Ayurveda retreat. In that sacred space, I experienced the profound medicine of women healing together. I learned that sisterhood acts as a mirror, reflecting our own capacity for self-care. I returned inspired by Anyi's authentic living and her sacred ability to hold space for me. Her mantra, 'Yo soy mi cura' (I am my own cure), became both a guide and a philosophy I now live by.

In 2023, I traveled to San José del Cabo to attend a spiritual retreat. It was an incredible experience of presence, meditation, and connection with amazing people from all over the world. Nineteen of us still keep in touch through WhatsApp, sharing uplifting messages. What inspired me most was the energy created when hundreds of people gathered in community to meditate. It was unforgettable.

This experience inspired me to become a Meditation Teacher and Life Coach. I now guide others in their practice, helping them look beyond their personal stories and connect with the presence of their own being.

Today, I find inspiration everywhere: in watching bees work in the garden, witnessing a beautiful sunset, or diving into the timeless wisdom of teachers like Don Miguel Ruiz. These moments, both simple and profound, connect me more deeply to the essence of what it means to be alive.

THE ADVICE

After years of chasing external success and losing touch with my inner peace, I've learned that wisdom isn't found in achievement; it's revealed in awareness. Every challenge, heartbreak, and reinvention has been a teacher, guiding me back to myself. These lessons are the truths I would share with my younger self, and with anyone standing at a crossroads, searching for direction and meaning:

1. **Stop Seeking Validation and Start Practicing Compassion** You are not defined by how much you do or how much others approve of you. You are worthy simply because you exist. Success and love are states of being that grow from within.

2. **Redefine Success from Performance to Presence** True success is not about the applause you receive but about the peace you feel. Learn to measure success by your ability to stay aligned with your values, even in the face of uncertainty. Pause often. Breathe deeply. Let your worth come from your being, not your doing.

3. **Build Habits that Anchor You in Awareness** Transformation happens in small, consistent moments. Practice mindfulness using the simple STOP method: Stop, Take a breath, Observe, and Proceed. Pair this with journaling or meditation, and you will begin to respond to life with clarity and intention rather than reacting out of unconscious fear.

4. **Make it Safe for Yourself to Better Connect with Others** One of the biggest lessons I have learned in these last few years is that the relationship we have with ourselves deeply affects our relationships with others. Speak kindly to yourself, set boundaries with love, and honor your emotions without shame. The way you treat yourself sets the tone for how you lead others, whether in your family or in professional settings.

At the heart of it all, growth is not about becoming someone new but remembering who you truly are. These lessons remind me that peace, purpose, and love begin within. Every choice, no matter how small, is an opportunity to return to alignment. When you treat yourself with compassion, lead with awareness, and live with intention, you don't just transform your life; you create the space for others to do the same.

THE PATH FORWARD

Today, I feel full of purpose because I decided to say yes to healing and to love. I am still healing every day; the journey never ends. I even reclaimed my love for dance, and moving my body a few times a week now brings me pure joy.

One of the greatest gifts of this path is the beautiful relationship I have with my daughter today. This bond is now rooted in presence and mutual understanding. I am enjoying fulfilling relationships with family and friends, and I belong to countless tribes, including the A Loving Organization Consortium, a community of heart-centered leaders from around the world who hold space for one another and share best practices to bring love into healthcare and beyond.

My personal journey, paired with my background in coaching and timeless wisdom traditions, has given me the insight and compassion to help individuals gain clarity about their purpose and create more fulfilling lives. It is deeply fulfilling to guide others in finding their purpose and expressing their whole, authentic selves. Through my company, InnateFive, I partner with leaders and teams to cultivate cultures of belonging and psychological safety where people feel seen, valued, and able to bring their whole selves to work.

My own story of workplace disengagement inspired me to write my book, *Love Is the Path*. My hope is that more individuals reconnect with their true selves and sense of purpose, encouraging them to seek and sustain a greater balance in both life and work.

From a place of authenticity and presence, we reconnect with our core values: love, gratitude, compassion, integrity, courage, and the desire to serve. This is the foundation of leading from love, and it creates workplaces where people feel seen, valued, and inspired to contribute their very best.

My choice to live with presence and love is a daily commitment, and some days are undeniably harder than others. When I fall short of my intention, I approach that moment with grace, reminding myself that I did my best and remain grateful for every lesson learned along the way.

My call to you is simple: begin with yourself. Slow down, breathe, and listen to what your heart has been trying to say. When you lead yourself with compassion, you become a catalyst for healing in every space you enter. This is the legacy I hope to leave behind: a world where purpose and compassion coexist, where people work not only to earn a living but to live meaningfully.

Let love guide your path. You are, and have always been, the leader you were waiting for.

ABOUT CLAUDIA

Claudia is a TEDx Speaker, the author of Love Is the Path, and the founder of InnateFive, a consultancy specializing in corporate coaching and workshop facilitation. As a Gallup-Certified Strengths Coach, Global Listening Intelligence Certified Coach, and Certified Life Coach and Meditation Instructor, Claudia takes a holistic approach to personal growth and teamwork, integrating timeless Vedic wisdom to foster deeper well-being, resilience, and purpose.

She brings a unique blend of experience in the private and public sectors, leveraging a vast network to find customized solutions for her clients. As a first-generation Colombian immigrant to the U.S., Claudia draws on her background to advocate for compassionate leadership. She believes that love is a powerful force for creating belonging and helping individuals feel valued, included, and empowered.

Claudia holds a Diversity & Inclusion Certificate from Cornell University and is a founding member of the "A Loving Organization Consortium." Her contributions have been recognized across the community, earning her the Minority Small Business Champion of the Year from the Rhode Island Small Business Administration (2010), the Outstanding Achievement Award from Rhode Island Latino Public Radio (2013), and the Ronald McDonald House Community Service Award (2014).

You can learn more about and connect with Claudia at:

https://www.claudiacardozo.com/
https://www.innatefive.com/
https://www.loveisthepath.org/
https://www.linkedin.com/in/claudiacardozo/
https://www.facebook.com/LoveIsthePath/

DIANA MALDONADO

"There is resounding growth in stillness."

Diana Maldonado

~ ~ ~

Diana Maldonado is a trailblazing Latina whose journey embodies courage, vision, and service. From making history as the first Latina elected to represent Williamson County in the Texas House of Representatives to founding Candidate School—an initiative empowering women to step into leadership and public office with authenticity and confidence—Diana has dedicated her life to creating pathways for others to rise. Her leadership has spanned politics, business, and community impact, holding key leadership roles in Central Texas and as a statewide advocate for Latino youth civic engagement. A global marathon runner and best-selling author, Diana brings to every endeavor the same endurance, focus, and heart that have defined her trailblazing career. Her story is a powerful testament to purpose-driven leadership, resilience, and the limitless potential of Latina women who lead with integrity and vision.

~ ~ ~

In dedication to every Latina who says YES to herself today.

THE GIFT OF PAUSE:
HOW MY SURGERY GAVE ME CLARITY AND ALIGNMENT TO A NEW BEGINNING

THE JOURNEY

As the summer was winding down, there was a change in the air as faint signs were giving way for Fall, a season with an inherent pull to pause to assess the year's career activities and life priorities on a broader scale. The mornings gave way to a stillness in the dark as I opened the blinds, no longer catching the bright summer golden rays that usually glitter through the window screen. The robust cluster of green leaves on the trees were withering into yellow and orange, revealing the intertwined branches and twigs that held them together, as I would do my morning run on the local park trails.

Nature has a subtle way of reminding me to shift my attention to the change around me and join the gentle notes of a symphony as it sends me down a river of reflection between these two seasons. This transitional time is a practice I started a few years back with a self-audit and questions that arise: "Where am I with regards to my work?" "Is what I'm doing relevant to me and others?" I then move into the other concentric circles to include health, community, and culture, a life portfolio of sorts.

In the fast-paced attention economy, with social media platforms and global connectivity at our fingertips, I can easily get caught up in this ubiquitous traffic and quickly lose focus on my goals. This downtime helps me appreciate the ebbs and flows of my career, look back and acknowledge the wins, however small they may be, and take in the surprises that have propelled some tasks far beyond what I had anticipated. It is a time to question the "what" and the "why" of my current priorities as I turn the corner toward the end of the year.

This wasn't always the case. I've spent years losing valuable time, making mistakes, and creating doubt along the way, comparing myself to no avail.

Yet now, I look forward to this refreshingly introspective time to draw out the good stuff amidst the noise and hustle of the work culture and social climate.

What took me deeper into this downtime was an unforeseen surgery for a torn tendon on my right ankle from a recent hiking trip to Colorado in July 2025, folded in with years of running and hiking. (Earlier in the year, I had knee surgery and the odds of having two surgeries in one year was unsettling as it stripped my physical independence away from me.) My schedule came to a screeching standstill as I lingered, looking out the living room window to catch the stillness of the mornings for the next ten days from my couch, which served as my makeshift bed. Being single and living in a two-story house prompted me to work out the logistics for the coming weeks and to make do with as many essentials downstairs during recovery time, with a lot of help from my daughter, Denise, and a handful of nearby friends.

Looking around the living room space, I had to stop and think of every step I would take as I gingerly limped my way to the kitchen, bathroom, and dining area. What one does typically without thought, now took a lot of planning and visioning for me to take the following steps, even if it was only a few feet away! As I pondered this process, it led me to assess my current workflow. Over the past couple of years, I was creating and developing an online program to help women get elected to public office across the nation. Since leaving my time in elected office in 2011, the victory was great, but the experience left me with a mishmash of hard lessons for a Latina to recover from. The process and information needed much improvement if more women like me were to take the plunge and run for office.

Time and time again, women would bend my ear as if sharing a deeply held secret on how to start, thereby validating the need to build this program. I understood firsthand the obstacles a woman faces without relatable figures. How does one ask for money from your family and friends when you are culturally raised not to broach this topic? What are the personal sacrifices a Latina has to make when data says we are paid 54 cents to a white male counterpart? The conviction to see more women like me hold office at all levels of government is what kept me moving forward.

I wasn't immune to the imposter syndrome that crept in the midst of all this excitement. "What if it fails?" All the usual negative scenarios slowly crept in

— the should-haves, could-haves, and would-haves. But I ventured forward, having been battle-tested over the years in my career, the drumbeat for this new idea grew louder. I began to hear a consistent message from friends and colleagues: "When are you going to build your own business? You've helped others grow theirs over the years — now it's time for you to do your own thing!"

As in many Latino upbringings, our culture from prior generations teaches us to stay quiet and not bring attention to ourselves. I was not immune to that philosophy. Do well, but remain under the radar. My parents worked hard to make ends meet, so there was not a lot of advice and guidance, other than the standard character traits of being polite and well-mannered. Quite frankly, these are very important today as well!

When you've been conditioned through exposure from family, culture, and environment to think, act, or feel a certain way all your life, the brain neural pathways take shape and act as your default mode. I grew up with limiting beliefs about money that kept me from leveling up and moving forward for a long time. I had success, but took so many steps to get there..

For me, having a job at all times was my identity – to do good work, prove my worth, and strive to earn an honest day's wage. I had seen my mom struggle to make ends meet, so this left a profound imprint on my sense of worth as a woman. Research shows that girls adopt their money mindset by seeing how their mothers handle money. My mom was always anxious and stressed because she appeared to be running a tad short of making ends meet. Reading more about this was insightful because it turns out that you can rewire your thoughts by incorporating new practices, leaving old stories behind that never belonged to you, and creating new ones.

Back in 2008, I was in the throes of running for public office as a single mother with two kids. I was struggling to pay my household bills while dialing for dollars for my campaign, raising $10,000 in one phone call. I felt conflicted, embarrassed on the personal side of my life as my political life was taking off. For far too long, Latinas were told to work two, maybe three times harder just to get to the start line to compete with someone of mediocre means.

Running for office is one of the most courageous decisions one can make, especially for women, given the high stakes and the inevitable exposure of their personal lives. I used my lived experience to develop the lessons. I was mindful to align with the right individuals and skilled experts. Investing in myself, I hired a contractor to work on marketing, branding and content creation. While that was happening behind the scenes, I was having multiple conversations to bring relatable content. Candidate School was coming into formation. Many times over, I had witnessed other dynamic women take that leap, venturing to launch their businesses with their hard-fought wins. My conversations deepened with women whose conviction and authenticity shone brightly. Building a resource grounded in years of research that equips women with the tools to run with clarity and confidence was the result of the official launch in early 2025.

I was filled with excitement and nervousness, taking on new tasks as I laid a new path ahead of me. Things were gaining traction, albeit with a dust of chaos in the air. I started each day diligently reviewing the uptick in activity on Candidate School. People responded positively to the launch, so I knew it had struck a chord. In between, I went on short runs to let the excitement and adrenaline work their way out and, in turn, spark new ideas.

Yet, I was tugged by my old habits to get on the job search cycle and did what any responsible Latina does – juggle two or more priorities simultaneously! Part of the rationale was that Candidate School required a longer runway to financially support itself and I was self funding my dream project.

I felt like I was balancing on an invisible trapeze line in the job postings I had applied for, as the process was met with the dry, long spells of silence in executive job searches. The lengthy cycles with multiple interview sessions, a list of to-dos, research, and presentations from each one felt like walking a plank, balancing not to fall into the deep waters of regret emails in a competitive market. I had become all too familiar with this competing cadence in prior work opportunities, with my share of wins and losses along the way. As I prepared for each one, my mind would gently wander to Candidate School and envision the impact it could make across our nation if more women held public office, finally bringing the long-overdue parity.

My job interviews were tanking. I struck out three out of three. It became unsettling for me when it struck at the heart of my identity and dignity. There was even a sense of shock and embarrassment. I had carefully prepared, providing the best presentations, and each one slowly gave way to a courteous no. Mind you, each of these was centered on political clout, relationship building, and financial acumen, all of which were part of my DNA of success.

I started to unravel. What would I do financially? Here was the old mindset kicking in (the rewiring of the brain takes work!), Thankfully, I learned about a book, "All the Cool Girls Get Fired" by Laura Brown and Kristina O'Niell, that offers a fresh perspective on job loss. I applied the lessons with my own twist; *all the cool girls don't get hired.* After taking time to absorb these events, I was able to look at the big picture. I had investments that I could tap into prudently and manage the outflow. Having been a financial advisor in a prior career gave me insight to plan for moments like this.

Over the next few weeks, as I continued to heal from my surgery, I began reflecting on the love of labor of my new project and how I could blend my leadership experience to a new role that aligned with Candidate School? I had found myself in positioning these important priorities in opposing energy and that is how the stillness allowed me to realign. I grew deeply curious about the science and psychology that shaped my evolution. I read books, listened to podcasts, and absorbed thoughts and perspectives. I welcomed this shift taking hold inside of me. I realized I was on the cusp of something different — a newfound perspective that I would carry into the next phase of my work.

It then occurred to me that the pause was a gift to a deeper insight of stillness, peace, and gratitude to guide my business and other aspects essential in my life.

During this period, I hit the six-month mark since the launch and pondered all the changes that had occurred, personally and professionally. Those small, consistent actions, like a drip from a water faucet, begin to fill up. I could see the evolution that was transpiring in front of me, including the detour (job search) that thankfully did not work out. I learned to tap deeper into my psyche to get clarity and meaning. I found myself enjoying the pause and letting my ankle heal at its own pace.

I enjoyed the morning birdsong and other sounds that created the subtle hum of the new day unfolding. I got better at maneuvering on my knee scooter, then on crutches, and eventually back to walking. It then occurred to me that the pause was a gift to a deeper insight of stillness, peace, and gratitude to guide my business and other aspects essential in my life.

THE LEARNINGS

What I've learned from my current journey — and will continue to learn — is that life is full of disruptions and changes. It's how we respond to them that shapes our trajectory. We've all heard this before in different ways, but when an event truly hits, it takes on a new shape and meaning that's uniquely yours in that moment.

I never thought the downtime from my surgery would give me such a profound insight as I lay helplessly on the couch, with a feeling of isolation and vulnerability. The stillness was an untapped gift for bringing alignment and coherence in a way I had not yet discovered.

Studies show that about every eighteen months, change finds its way into our lives. Maybe you didn't get the raise, a project didn't work out, or you spent too much time doomscrolling instead of brushing up on a skill — leaving you with a dose of regret along the way. These are the manageable bumps on life's road, giving us space to readjust without too much disruption.

We also experience what research says are lifequakes. This is more like losing a job due to a layoff, being fired, a loss of a family member or close friend, divorce, or a significant illness. These situations take much longer to heal and carry a depth of emotion.

When I had to prepare for both of my surgeries, I was frustrated that everything was slowing me down. I already had my goals planned out, and suddenly had to clear my calendar. One of the most complex parts was giving up my charity bib to run the Boston Marathon — something that had been on my docket for years and would have completed my journey through the six World Marathon Majors, a decade in the making. I also began to worry about my age as the horizon stretched further ahead. Vacations, meetings, and conferences were all canceled for the foreseeable future.

I could have sulked on the couch, complaining and griping (I did a little), it's in our inherent nature to fuss a bit. However, I realized that the Universe was giving me a gift. It opened space for me to create beyond the self-imposed boundaries I had long imposed on myself. It opened space for me to realign my energy and time to my priorities. It opened space for me to identify the small actions that feed my purpose. It opened space for me to say, "It's ok, and even if it's not, it's still ok."

In the midst of this transition, I launched an exciting new venture — *Candidate School* — completed my book, *The Unlikely Candidate: Breaking Barriers to Elected Office and Beyond*, and began coaching women to reach their next level of leadership in public office. Along the way, I met incredible Latinas across the nation through podcasts and virtual meetings, many of whom I now connect with to support one another's endeavors. None of this would have happened without that pause — and the realization of how many gifts it brought me.

THE INSPIRATION

My inspiration comes from my formative years, spent Summer days at the city's public library. Filled with curiosity and imagination, my mind would wander to places beyond the small town of Eagle Pass, where I grew up. I was curious to read about women, fiction, and non-fiction, and how their courage and bravery sparked an interest that I would later embody in my personal and professional life.

I am attracted to the underdog or underestimated because that was my path. Yet a determined woman is another force of inspiration. Women who inspire me are Sonia Sotomayor, Maria Hinojosa, Eva Longoria, America Ferrera, Mel Robbins, Oprah, Malala Yousafzai, and Dolores Huerta, to name a few.

I don't have to go far to tap into kindness and support with friends and like-minded networks such as United Latinas, Poderistas, and Latinas Represent.

At my core, my son, Alex, my daughter, Denise, and my granddaughter, Camila, give me the impetus to be better each day. Shaping a legacy with them and for them is one of the greatest joys!

THE ADVICE

Every chapter of life brings its own lessons, but they don't always arrive in neat, predictable ways. Sometimes, it takes a pause — whether chosen or unexpected — to reveal what truly matters. My own pause reminded me that growth is not always about acceleration; growth also comes in stillness.

As you move through your own journey, here are a few guiding practices that have helped me stay grounded, intentional, and true to purpose.

1. **The way you start your morning determines your day**. This time is sacred as your mind is fresh and pure. Find that one thing or those steps to be part of your flow—meditation, prayer, yoga moves, and opening the window to get fresh air. Over time, you will see how it impacts your week, month, and year! But even if you sit or lie in stillness, do not get your phone and let the flurry of media invade this space. Give yourself at least ten minutes. I usually go thirty minutes to an hour, and I've learned to cherish this time.

2. **Write it down**. Seeing your tasks daily makes you accountable to yourself, and there is discipline in moving them forward. Early in my career, I would "talk" about what I wanted to do, but I realized that I wasn't seeing the outcome. I got tired of talking and decided to jot down thoughts, formalizing them into clear goals and slowly pecking away, seeing the results with this discipline. Have a 90-day contract with yourself. If you miss a day, no problem, just get back to it. Better yet, get an accountability partner!

3. **Be Patient.** Good things take time. In a world of social media comparison, it is easy to get caught up in the wave of being left behind. No one becomes an overnight sensation. The most successful people talk about the long days and nights, even years. Surround yourself with people to support you. Your success is already waiting for you, and with consistent action and commitment, you will shine!

4. **Invest in Yourself.** I am a big proponent of working smart with money because it shapes decisions in business, households, and politics. As a former financial advisor, I have learned to educate

myself continuously so I won't be caught flat-footed. We often shy away from paying for a course or charging a fee for our services, and it minimizes our talent. Bet on yourself and pay yourself first by investing in your 401 (k), business, and services.

5. **Help Others.** There is no greater satisfaction than seeing your talent, knowledge, and generosity multiply as others grow and thrive. As you learn, share. A long time ago, as I was honing skills in leadership, management, operations, and financial acumen, I realized I wanted to share them with whoever was open to receiving them. You don't have to look far to find someone. I learned that their growth is my growth!

Above all, remember that progress doesn't always look like motion. Sometimes the most powerful step you can take is to pause — to listen, to realign, and to let purpose catch up with you. Whether you're writing goals in a notebook, taking a deep breath before the day begins, or lending your wisdom to someone else, every intentional act adds to the life you're creating.

Progress doesn't always look like motion.

Be patient with the process — your path is unfolding exactly as it should.

THE PATH FORWARD

Of late, I have created a *life portfolio* rooted in purpose, success, joy, and the peace that comes with age and wisdom. It helps me refocus my priorities from time to time and reminds me that growth is an ongoing process, not a destination.

Oftentimes, we look for external guideposts to validate our work, only to realize that what we've achieved was never sheer luck — it was alignment, preparation, and grace. I have learned to appreciate, especially in recent years, the synchronicities the universe places in our path.

I've also learned to trust my gut instinct far more and to sit with any unsettling emotions rather than push them away. They say discomfort is data — and

I've found that to be true. Instead of retracting from it, I lean in, curious about what it's trying to teach or reveal.

People often say to look for signs around you, but I'm learning that the most potent signs come from within. They point me toward how I can fully serve others with intention — and in doing so, bring out the best in them.

The pause reminded me that fulfillment doesn't come from speed or certainty, but from listening deeply — to life, to Spirit, and to the wisdom within. That's where clarity lives. That's where purpose takes shape.

As you move forward on your own path, give yourself permission to pause, to reflect, and to trust that your timing is not delayed — it's divine. Each disruption, each quiet season, holds the potential to realign you with something greater. The harvest will come when your soil is tended with intention. Keep cultivating it — with patience, courage, and faith in what's unfolding.

ABOUT DIANA

Diana Maldonado is a best-selling author and trailblazer in Central Texas politics. Her writing draws from a rich tapestry of experiences campaigning, traveling the world, and running marathons — all shaped by her identity as a proud Latina.

Diana made history as the first Latina elected to represent Williamson County in the Texas House of Representatives, where she championed education, business, and community safety. During her tenure, she authored or co-authored 88 bills and was named "Freshman of the Year" by her peers. Prior to that, she served two terms on the Round Rock ISD Board of Trustees, becoming its first Latina president.

Today, Diana continues to empower others through Candidate School, an initiative she founded to prepare women to run for public office with confidence, clarity, and integrity. Her newsletters and training offer the kind of guidance she once wished she had before entering public service.

Outside of her professional work, Diana is a passionate global marathon runner, having completed races in Tokyo, Berlin, London, New York, and Paris. She's an avid traveler, outdoor enthusiast, and proud mother to Alex and Denise. Her greatest joy is spending time with her granddaughter, Camila.

Learn more and connect with Diana:

https://www.dianamaldonado.com/
https://www.candidateschool.info/
https://www.linkedin.com/in/diana-maldonado/
https://www.instagram.com/candidateschool_

DINAMARY HORVATH

"Your difference is your strength—lead with it unapologetically."

-     Dinamary Horvath

~ ~ ~

Dina is the Founder and lead investigator at Maxe Law. Before founding the firm, Dina served as Assistant Corporation Counsel for the City of Hartford and practiced at Jackson Lewis LLP, where she advised employers on a wide range of employment law issues. She went on to lead a regional investigations team at Amazon Logistics, managing 15 investigators across the U.S. East Region and overseeing complex employee relations matters. Dina holds a J.D. from the University of Connecticut School of Law and is licensed to practice in Massachusetts and Connecticut. She holds multiple credentials in employment investigations. Additionally, Dina was featured in the Top 50 Attorneys of 2019 Magazine.

~ ~ ~

For my husband, John Horvath, who saw my potential before I did and planted the seeds of Maxe Law. For Isabella and Sarah, may you always know you are powerful, your voice matters, and your dreams have no limits. And for my parents, whose sacrifices built the foundation for all I've achieved. Esto es por ustedes.

OVERCOMING DOUBT AND DEFINING SUCCESS ON MY TERMS

THE JOURNEY

I grew up in New York as a first-generation Dominican American, watching my parents navigate a new country while maintaining our cultural identity. In our household, education was sacred, as it was the key to opportunities my parents never had.

At Long Island University, I studied International Relations and Political Science, fascinated by how systems of power worked across borders. My master's thesis explored Dominican immigrants in New York City, comparing two generations, my parents and my own. I was studying my own story, trying to understand the invisible barriers and bridges that shaped our community's experience in America. During my sophomore year, I joined a national Latina sorority, La Hermandad de Sigma Iota Alpha, Inc., and became part of a sisterhood that strived towards the expansion of awareness of Latino culture and stood for accomplishments of excellence and education among women. I completed two degrees in four years.

After graduating with my master's, I worked at prestigious law firms in New York City while saving up for law school. The decision to attend law school at the University of Connecticut wasn't just about career ambition. It was about wielding the tools of justice for communities that often-lacked advocates. I concentrated in Employment, Labor, and School Law because I witnessed firsthand how workplace inequities and access to education affected families like mine and those of my sorority sisters. I became an Alvin Pudlin Scholar for advancing the understanding and appreciation of the rights secured by the First Amendment of the Constitution. I also received scholarships from both the Dominican Bar Association and Puerto Rican Bar Association. These recognitions were acknowledgments that I belonged in spaces where I rarely saw people who looked like me.

My career began at Jackson Lewis LLP, a prestigious employment law firm where I was one of 600+ attorneys. I advised employers on discrimination cases, conducted workplace investigations, and developed affirmative action plans. I was good at my work. I was tenacious, analytical, and compassionate, but I also felt the weight of being "the only one" in many rooms. My bilingual skills and cultural competence became unexpected assets, allowing me to connect with witnesses and conduct investigations in ways my colleagues couldn't.

I then served as Assistant Corporation Counsel for the City of Hartford, where I advised on employment matters, policy development, and litigation management for the entire city government. I negotiated labor contracts, drafted ordinances, and trained department heads on employment compliance. The work was meaningful but demanding, with limited resources.

Then came the pivotal moment: I became a mother to Isabella Maxe. Suddenly, the 60-hour work weeks felt impossible. I wanted to be present for her first words, her first steps, her childhood. I did not want to just see photos sent by a nanny. But I also wasn't willing to abandon my professional identity and my commitment to workplace justice.

In 2016, after relocating to Massachusetts, my husband planted the seed, and I did something that terrified and thrilled me. I founded Maxe Law, naming it after my daughter as a daily reminder of why I was building something different. My firm underwent several iterations but ultimately specialized in workplace and Title IX investigations and compliance training. I conduct impartial investigations into discrimination, harassment, retaliation, and misconduct. I am the neutral voice that helps organizations navigate their most sensitive workplace conflicts.

The leap to entrepreneurship was validated when my practice grew steadily. Educational institutions, private employers, and public entities began hiring me for complex investigations. My ability to conduct investigations in both English and Spanish, combined with my deep understanding of both legal frameworks and human dynamics, positioned me as a leader in this specialized field.

In 2020, I took an unexpected turn and joined Amazon as an Employee Relations Investigation Manager. Some questioned why I would leave my successful practice for corporate life. But I saw an opportunity to scale my impact by leading a team of 12 investigators supporting over 22,000 employees across 130+ facilities in North America's East Region. I learned to analyze data trends, mentor investigators, design training programs, and navigate the complexities of one of the world's largest companies.

Those three years at Amazon taught me invaluable lessons about leadership, systems thinking, and the unique challenges of workplace justice at scale. But they also reinforced what I already knew: I am meant to be an entrepreneur, a trainer, a mentor, someone who creates platforms for others rather than operating within someone else's structure.

In 2023, I returned to Maxe Law, bringing with me the insights from managing a large corporate investigation team. Now, I'm not just conducting investigations, I'm also launching training courses for internal workplace investigation teams, sharing the methodologies and best practices I developed over 15+ years. I've also used my experience in serving for five years as a member of the Board of Directors for the Association of Workplace Investigators and served as part-time faculty for their Annual Institute.

Throughout this journey, I have also built a beautiful blended family with my husband, who encouraged me to start my practice, my daughter Isabella, and my stepdaughter Sarah. My parents and in-laws have been my foundation, supporting my unconventional path.

Today, as I look back from my office in Rockport, Massachusetts, I see that every step from that Dominican household in New York to founding Maxe Law was preparation for this moment. I'm not just practicing law; I'm creating a legacy of fairness, justice, and possibility for the next generation.

THE LEARNINGS

The most pivotal challenge I faced wasn't a single dramatic moment, it was the constant internal battle against the belief that I didn't fully belong. In law school, in corporate boardrooms, even in networking events, I often felt like I was translating myself, my experiences, my perspectives, my very identity into something more palatable for predominantly white spaces.

Early in my career at Jackson Lewis, I remember investigating a discrimination case involving a Latina woman who spoke limited English. She was visibly uncomfortable with the male investigator initially assigned. When I stepped in and conducted the interview in Spanish, the relief on her face was palpable. She shared details she had been holding back, and I realized that my bilingualism was not just a skill, it was a form of justice. People deserve to tell their truth in their own language when there is a language barrier. That investigation taught me that what I had considered a challenge in navigating two cultures and two languages was one of my greatest professional assets.

The challenge intensified when I became a mother. The legal profession isn't designed for women who want to be present parents. The unspoken expectation is that someone else raises your children while you bill 2,000+ hours annually. When I was pregnant with Isabella, I watched other women attorneys return from maternity leave exhausted and guilty, missing milestones while trying to prove their commitment hadn't wavered.

I found my inner strength in rejecting that false choice. I would not sacrifice my daughter's childhood or my professional calling. The decision to found Maxe Law in 2016 was my rebellion against a system that demanded I choose. It was terrifying as I turned away from the security of corporate positions, the prestige of big law, and the predictable paycheck. But I was moving toward something more valuable that aligned with my truth, autonomy, presence, and purpose.

My coping mechanism became radical authenticity. Instead of downplaying my Dominican heritage or my motherhood, I centered them. I conducted investigations from my home office, proving that professionalism is not about where you work but the quality of your work. I leaned into my bicultural competence, marketing myself explicitly as someone who could navigate complex cultural dynamics in workplace investigations.

I also deliberately built a support system. My husband became my partner in the truest sense, not only championing my business, but managing household and caregiving responsibilities and celebrating my wins.

Disrupting the status quo came naturally after that. At Amazon, I challenged investigation protocols that failed to account for language barriers, cultural nuances, and implicit bias. I advocated for investigator training that addressed gaps and many that lacked legal compliance. I mentored women of color on my team, explicitly telling them what no one had told me, that our differences are our strength in the workplace.

> *You cannot outrun impostor syndrome, you must reframe it.*

That voice whispering "you don't belong here" must be reframed as it is evidence that you are breaking new ground. Every time I felt out of place, I was exactly where I needed to be, expanding what's possible for me and the Latinas who will come after me.

THE INSPIRATION

There are so many women who lit the path for me.

My mother is my North Star. She immigrated to the United States with dreams bigger than her circumstances, working tirelessly to ensure I had choices she never had. She didn't have a law degree or corporate title, but she taught me the most important lessons that have made me who I am. Watching her navigate systems designed to marginalize her while maintaining her grace and determination showed me what true strength looks like.

When I was struggling in law school, questioning whether I belonged, I thought of her voice: "Tú puedes." You can. Those two words became my mantra in every moment of doubt. During the toughest times, late nights studying for the bar exam while questioning if I'd made the right choice, or the early days of building Maxe Law when clients were scarce, I drew inspiration from the women in my community who had carved paths through even harder circumstances. Women who cleaned offices at night while raising children during the day. Women who learned English at 40 so they could advocate for their families. Women whose names will not appear in history books, but whose resilience built the foundation for my opportunities.

When I received scholarships from the Dominican Bar Association and Puerto Rican Bar Association, it was not just financial support. It was a message to keep going. Those organizations became my professional family, reminding me that I was not alone.

Books also fueled me. I devoured biographies of Justice Sonia Sotomayor, seeing my own immigrant experience reflected in her journey. Reading "In the Time of the Butterflies" by Julia Alvarez connected me to the legacy of Dominican women who fought tyranny. My work in workplace justice felt like an echo of their courage.

But my greatest inspiration arrived when Isabella Maxe was born. Suddenly, my career was not just about my own achievement. It was about modeling possibilities for her. I wanted her to grow up seeing her mother as a business owner, not just an employee. A woman who defined success on her own terms. A Latina who didn't shrink her identity to fit into professional spaces but expanded those spaces to include her whole self.

My stepdaughter Sarah inspires me, too, as I watch her navigate her own journey with confidence, reminding me why women and representation in professional spaces matter. And my husband, who believed in my vision even when I doubted, shows me daily what true partnership looks like.

Today, every time a young Latina attorney reaches out for mentorship, every time I conduct a training session and see someone's eyes light up with understanding, every time I lead an investigation, I'm drawing on the collective strength of all these inspirations. They remind me: this work is bigger than me. It's about creating pathways for the next generation.

THE ADVICE

Before I share the lessons, I wish someone had told me earlier, there is one truth that rises above all others: your heritage is not a barrier, it's your superpower. Everything I had to overcome, my accent, my immigrant story, my cultural values, my commitment to family, became the very foundation of my strength.

Your heritage is not a barrier—it's your superpower

The challenges I faced did not diminish me; they shaped the lens through which I lead, advocate, and build. If the learnings of my journey taught me anything, it's that the qualities the world may try to make you shrink are the ones that will set you apart. When you honor your identity, trust your voice, and refuse to accept limiting narratives, you create a path that is entirely your own. With that truth in mind, here are the four pieces of advice I wish someone had placed in my hands years ago.

1. Your "Different" Is Your Competitive Advantage, Stop Apologizing for It

Looking back, I wasted too much energy trying to assimilate, to sound "less ethnic," to hide the fact that I was navigating code-switching exhaustion. I wish someone had told my younger self: The legal profession doesn't need another lawyer who thinks and sounds like everyone else. It needs YOU with your bicultural lens, your empathy forged from immigrant experiences, your ability to connect across differences.

The shift in mindset that changed everything for me was moving from "How do I fit into this profession?" to "How does this profession need to evolve to include people like me?" That's not arrogance, it's innovation. Stop dimming your light. The legal and corporate worlds need more Latinas who take up space unapologetically.

2. Build Your Career Around Your Values, Not Someone Else's Definition of Success

When I was climbing the corporate ladder, I measured success by titles, salaries, and prestigious firms. But it still didn't provide the sense of satisfaction I was looking for. The pivotal question that changed my trajectory was "What does success mean to ME?"

For me, success meant being present when Isabella woke up. It meant working with mission-driven organizations. It meant saying no to cases that conflicted with my values and yes to opportunities that scared me but aligned with my purpose.

If you are designing your career around someone else's definition of success, whether that's your parents' expectations, societal pressure, or what you think you "should" want, pause. Define success for yourself first. Then build backward from that vision, even if the path looks unconventional.

3. You Cannot Pour from an Empty Cup, Prioritize Rest Without Guilt

As Latinas, we're often raised with the "work harder than everyone" mentality. Our parents sacrificed everything, so we feel we must sacrifice too. But martyrdom isn't a sustainable strategy.

Resting is not lazy, it is strategic. You make better decisions, conduct more thorough investigations, and show up more fully for clients when you are not running on fumes. Give yourself permission to rest. You are not betraying your parents' sacrifices by taking care of yourself. You are honoring them by building something sustainable.

4. Find Your Tribe and Lift as You Climb

Corporate America can be isolating for Latinas. You're often the only one in the room, which means there's no one to celebrate your wins, validate your struggles, or warn you about the landmines ahead.

Actively build your network of Latinas in your field. When I founded the AWI New England Local Circle and joined the Board of Directors, I was not just advancing my career; I was creating the community I wished I had. Now, I mentor young Latina attorneys, making sure they don't navigate these spaces as blindly as I did.

Don't wait until you've "made it" to start mentoring. Share what you learn as you learn it. Bring other women with you. Introduce them to your contacts. Advocate for them in rooms where they're not present. Your success means nothing if the door closes behind you.

The legacy we leave is not measured by individual achievement. It's measured by how many people we empower to achieve alongside us.

THE PATH FORWARD

In this season, I am launching a comprehensive training program for internal workplace investigation teams and an onboarding solution for new investigators—equipping HR professionals and corporate investigators with the tools, methodologies, and ethical frameworks I have developed over 15 years. This work is inspired by my time at Amazon, where I saw firsthand the need for skilled, compassionate investigators who can navigate complex workplace dynamics with cultural competence.

I'm also expanding Maxe Law's reach, partnering with more educational institutions to ensure Title IX investigations are conducted with the rigor and fairness every student deserves. I'm committed to training the next generation of workplace investigators. But beyond my individual practice, my legacy is about amplifying voices, ensuring that every investigation I conduct, every training I deliver, every attorney I mentor contributes to workplaces where fairness isn't aspirational but operational. Where Latinas don't have to choose between authenticity and advancement. Where the little girl from New York, daughter of Dominican immigrants, can see herself in positions of power and purpose.

And for you? Your time is now, step into your power.

To the Latina reading this story right now, feeling the weight of expectations, the pressure to prove yourself, the exhaustion of code-switching: You are enough. Not when you get the promotion, not when you finish the degree, not when you lose the accent, right now, exactly as you are.

The barriers you face are real. Discrimination is real. Implicit bias is real. The gaps in opportunity are real. But so is your power. So is your brilliance. So is your capacity to create change.

My call to you is this: Stop waiting for permission to lead. Stop waiting for the "right time" to start your business, write that book, apply for that position, negotiate that salary. The right time is now. The world does not need you to be perfect. It needs you to be present.

Honor your heritage while building your future. Your roots are not baggage to overcome. They are wisdom to carry forward. The resilience in your DNA, the collective strength of your ancestors, and the cultural richness you embody are strategic advantages in a world desperately in need of diverse perspectives.

Build your career on your terms. You don't have to choose between family and profession. Between authenticity and success. Between your culture and corporate America. Create a third path, one that integrates all of who you are. It will be harder, lonelier, scarier, but it will be yours.

The movement needs you. Not someday. Today. Your story matters. Your perspective is essential. Your leadership is overdue.

Adelante. Let's rise together.

ABOUT DINA

Dina is the Founder and Lead Investigator of Maxe Law, where she brings a depth of experience in employment law, workplace investigations, and employee relations to organizations navigating complex and sensitive workplace issues. Known for her strategic approach and practical insight, Dina has built her practice around helping employers address misconduct, mitigate risk, and foster compliant, equitable workplaces.

Before founding Maxe Law, Dina served as Assistant Corporation Counsel for the City of Hartford, where she advised municipal leadership on employment and labor matters and gained extensive experience working within public-sector legal frameworks. She later practiced at Jackson Lewis LLP, a nationally recognized employment law firm, where she counseled employers across a broad range of industries on workplace compliance, investigations, and employment-related disputes.

Dina went on to lead a regional investigations team at Amazon Logistics, overseeing 13 investigators across the U.S. East Region. In this role, she oversaw high-stakes and complex employee relations matters, including allegations of discrimination, harassment, retaliation, and policy violations.

Dina holds a Juris Doctor from the University of Connecticut School of Law and is licensed to practice law in both Massachusetts and Connecticut. She maintains multiple professional credentials in employment investigations, including certifications from the Association of Workplace Investigators (AWI) and the Massachusetts Commission Against Discrimination (MCAD). Her work and leadership in the field have been recognized nationally, including being named one of the Top 50 Attorneys of 2019.

Through her legal practice, investigations work, and thought leadership, Dina is committed to advancing fair, thorough, and defensible workplace processes. She brings a unique perspective shaped by experience in government, private practice, and in-house leadership, making her a trusted voice for organizations seeking clarity and integrity in employment decision-making.

Learn more and connect with Dina at:
https://www.linkedin.com/in/dinamary/
www.maxelaw.com

DR. EUGENIA FLORES MILLENDER

"From stress and trauma to triumph. Our story is not meant to shrink, but to shine."

- Dr. Eugenia Flores Millender

~ ~ ~

Dr. Eugenia Flores Millender is a visionary psychiatric and mental nurse practitioner-scientist, educator, and global leader transforming the future of mental health care. As Co-Founder and Co-Director of the Center of Population Sciences for Health Empowerment and Assistant Dean for Research at Florida State University's College of Nursing, she pioneers innovative, community-driven approaches that bridge science and humanity. A U.S. Army veteran, TIME CLOSER, and Presidential Leadership Scholar, Dr. Millender's groundbreaking research on the sociocultural roots of stress and trauma has inspired global collaborations across the Americas, and beyond—expanding access to compassionate, evidence-based care. Her story reflects resilience, excellence, and purpose-driven leadership, redefining what it means to heal communities and empower the next generation of changemakers in health and beyond.

~ ~ ~

With deepest gratitude to my family, my community, my friends, mentors, and colleagues—each of you has poured joy, positivity, and unwavering support into my life. And to my grandchildren, the joys of my heart, may this work be a reminder that love, resilience, and purpose are the legacy we carry forward together.

FROM TRAUMA TO TRIUMPH, AND FROM SILENCE TO STRENGTH

THE JOURNEY

I became the person I am today through a journey powered by resilience, fueled by gratitude, and sustained by the strength of my community—family, friends, and countless others who cheered me on, even when life was throwing its best curveballs. My story has had its peaks and valleys (and let's be honest, a few unexpected detours), but every stage, whether joyful or painful, has shaped the woman standing before you today.

I was born and raised in the City of Colón, Panama, where my roots run deep. My mother is from Colón, and my maternal grandfather was Jamaican. My maternal grandmother, from Palmira, Colón, was a guiding force in my childhood. On my maternal side, I am of Afro-Antillean Panamanian heritage. My father came from the Comarca Guna Yala (Isla Digir Dubbu), an Indigenous territory in Panama, and both of my paternal grandparents were also from Guna Yala. On my paternal side, I am of Indigenous Panamanian heritage. This vibrant tapestry of Afro-Caribbean and Indigenous ancestry gave me pride, identity, and an unshakable sense of cultural strength that still carries me today. I carry Colón in my soul—a place where the rhythms of my Jamaican grandfather and the spiritual strength of my Guna Yala ancestors intertwine.

Growing up in Colón, my childhood was joyful, loud, childhood deeply rooted in community—Sunday gatherings with music spilling into the street, neighbors who felt like cousins, and a home where flavors and stories were always present. But even in the midst of that love, my mother carried a vision for something beyond what Panama could offer at the time. When she left to build a better future, I stayed behind, cared for by my grandparents, my father, and my extended family. I was surrounded, protected, and loved, but I also began to understand, even as a young girl, that life was shifting. That was the moment I started growing up faster, watching illness, resilience, and caregiving up close.

At just twelve years old, before leaving Panama, I had the privilege of caring for my grandmother, who lived with severe diabetes. That experience—rooted in love and responsibility—was my first real introduction to caregiving. I didn't know it then, but sitting beside her, tending to her needs, and watching how illness could touch every part of a person's life would ignite a lifelong passion for nursing and healing.

And let me just say this: I was extra spoiled in the best way because I had two fabulous cousins, Mirna and Nidia, who were both nurses, and not just any nurses, the kind who walked in like, "I save lives and look cute doing it." So while I was over here caring for my grandma and acting grown at twelve, I also had these two shining examples of Black Panamanian excellence in scrubs. Watching them, I thought, "Okay, so nursing is smart, powerful, and a little glamorous?" That made it easy to fall in love with nursing. I already had the heart for it, and they showed me what it could look like.

Leaving Panama was a dream in theory and traumatic in practice. One day I'm in Colón, barefoot in the rain, eating good food, surrounded by people who look like me and sound like me — because in Panama we're just Panamanians. And yes, let me say it: I mostly stayed in Colón, so that was my whole world. I know other people had different experiences in Panama, but my Colón was beautiful, loud, and loving, and I had zero reason to go anywhere else.

Then I get to the U.S., and suddenly I'm being asked to pick one box. Excuse me? Pick one? As if my Afro-Antillean, Indigenous, Caribbean, Panamanian self could be squeezed into a single square. To me, checking just one box felt like disowning the others — so I did what any dramatic, identity-protecting Colón girl would do: I checked all the boxes and then wrote extra in the "other" line to explain who I really was.

But of course, filling out a form was the easy part. What was harder was realizing that in the U.S., people treated you differently based on how you looked, how you talked, even how you wore your hair. That was new to me. Back home, I was just Eugenia. Here, I was asked, "Where are you from?" "What are you?" "You speak Spanish?" Really, how did you learn Spanish? So by the time I landed in Brooklyn at twelve, I wasn't just moving — I was learning how to hold on to every piece of me in a place that didn't quite know what to do with all of me. And that's when the real growing up started.

When I arrived in Brooklyn, New York, at twelve, I had to grow up fast. As the oldest child of a single mother working multiple jobs to give us a better life, I quickly learned the true meaning of responsibility. With two younger sisters and a brother from my mother's side, I became the protector of the crew and, on many nights, the family "chef." My early meals were famous but primarily for all the wrong reasons! On my father's side, I was the middle child, my big brother was my protector, and my little sister was my doll.

Those early years in the U.S. taught me sacrifice, empathy, and resilience. They also taught me the deep ache of separation. I still remember missing my sixth-grade graduation because it was the very day I left Panama, my father, and much of my extended family behind. There wasn't much money to make long-distance calls back then, and there were even fewer phones for our family to use. And I hate to date myself, but let's tell the truth — there were no cell phones, no WhatsApp, no FaceTime to stay connected with the people you missed the most. And when there was a chance to call home, trips back to Panama were a luxury we couldn't afford. So not only were the phone calls short and rare, but seeing my family in person was even rarer.

Once we landed in Brooklyn, I did what so many Panamanians before me did: I headed straight for Flatbush with my uncle Papi and my cousins. It was its own Caribbean universe, a place where the food tasted like home, the music stayed loud, Spanish flowed right alongside English, and reggaetón was doing its early, glorious thing. Flatbush and my family let me hold on to Panama while I was trying to make sense of this new idea of "fitting in." But as I moved from girlhood into young womanhood, I realized something important: I didn't need to make myself smaller to belong. I needed to be around people who could handle the whole mosaic of me, the Afro-Antillean, the Indigenous, the Colón girl, the emotional one, the funny one, the "yes, I woke up like this" one.

Then came Marlboro Houses, located in Bensonhurst, Brooklyn— yes, the Projects — part of New York City Housing Authority, the most significant public housing authority in North America. Marlboro was not just an address; it was a training ground. That's where I learned how to stretch a dollar, how to live with very little and still walk with dignity, how to read a room, how to stay focused on the future, and how to push back when the odds weren't in your favor. It was tough, it was scary, but it was also tender. That's where I found friends who became family. People who saw what I was carrying and decided to take it with me. They watched my younger brother and sisters so I could go play basketball, protected my dreams, and stood beside me through the good seasons and the hard ones. They showed up without being asked and stayed even when life got complicated. That's the kind of support I found there. The kind you can call on at any time, steady, and dependable.

And then there was Sheepshead Bay High School's nursing program, my first real doorway into health care. They sent me to Coney Island Hospital for clinicals, and let me tell you, there's nothing like taking the train and a bus across Brooklyn at 15 years old to go be a "nurse in training" to make you grow up fast. That mix: Marlboro's grit, nursing's purpose, childhood friends who kept me grounded, family, and my new love, basketball. That combination kept me focused and, for a while at least, out of trouble. But like many teenagers trying to find their place, I eventually tested a few boundaries. My mother, who has always had an unshakable instinct about her children, saw it immediately. According to her, I was "getting in trouble" and "needed a better environment to thrive." (Translation: Brooklyn was not about to raise her daughter, she was.)

So she made a decision — a hard one for both of us. She moved us again, this time from the Brooklyn that had shaped me to West Palm Beach, Florida, so that I could finish my last year of high school. I won't pretend I was happy about it. I left New York heartbroken, pulled away from friends, rhythm, and the version of myself I was just beginning to understand. But with time, I've come to see what my mother saw: it was one of the best decisions she ever made for me. She was positioning me not just to survive, but to thrive.

When two very different people decide to hear each other — that something new shows up, something that lets you meet in the middle and actually move forward

At seventeen, I thought I was making a clever escape move when I joined the U.S. Army— mostly to get away from home. What I didn't realize was that this "temporary plan" would unlock my entire future. The Army became my classroom for life. The Army taught me how far I could really go. It taught me to push past pain, to think beyond myself, and to find solutions when everything around me said there weren't any. It trained me to do my clearest thinking under pressure, to listen before speaking, to observe what others missed, and to work alongside just about anyone. Those lessons didn't just make me disciplined — they made me adaptable, resilient, and mission-minded. The Army didn't just toughen me up — it sent me out into the world. It put me in rooms, countries, and conversations with people I never would have met otherwise. I had to learn how to work with folks who didn't look like me, talk like me, or think like me, and still get the mission done. It taught me to have hard conversations and, more importantly, to listen to understand instead of listening to criticize. And it's in those moments — when two very different people decide to hear each other — that something new shows up, something that lets you meet in the middle and actually move forward.

While serving, I earned my associate's degree and later started my bachelor's in nursing. That was just the beginning. I never stopped going to school, earning my BSN, MS, and PhD from Florida Atlantic University and continuing advanced studies at Rush University, and additional certifications at the University of Florida, the Wharton School of the University of Pennsylvania, and Harvard Medical School. With every degree and certificate, I wasn't just growing as a person and as a nurse; I was equipping myself to make this world a little better.

What began as a young girl's love for her grandmother became a lifelong calling to bridge the gap between mental and physical health. Early in my nursing career, I saw how stress, trauma, and adversity shape our health—not just emotionally, but physically and how our healthcare systems often fail to see those connections. That realization became the foundation of my research, leadership, and advocacy. As a nurse, I got to do the good stuff, the real, heart-racing, life-on-the-line work. I started in telemetry, then moved into cardiovascular intensive care at Palm Beach Gardens Medical Center, and later into trauma critical care at St. Mary's Medical Center. Every single unit had its own rhythm, its own culture, and its own circle of powerhouse nurses who took me in and said, "This is how we do it."

Those nurses didn't just show me where the supplies were; they taught me the art of nursing, how to walk into a room and know what's wrong before the monitor says it, how to advocate for a patient when no one else is paying attention, how to stay soft with families and steel-strong in a code. I am forever honored to have trained and worked beside those teams. They were excellence in action.

And it wasn't just the nurses. I worked with some outstanding physicians and healthcare professionals who didn't talk down to me — they poured into me. They were the ones saying, "You need to go to grad school. You're not done yet." We had days where we were literally running to save lives, and somehow still laughing at 3 a.m. in the break room. Those years at the bedside were sacred. They made me the nurse — and later the academic — I became.

At Florida Atlantic University, I founded and directed Florida's first nurse-led university community health center to achieve Federally Qualified Health Center Look-Alike designation,an innovation that redefined what nurse-led care could look like. It proved what I've always known: nurses are innovators, leaders, entrepreneurs, and changemakers capable of transforming systems from the ground up.

Today, as Co-Founder and Co-Director of the Center of Population Sciences for Health Empowerment, Assistant Dean for Research, and the Marie Cowart Endowed Professor at Florida State University's College of Nursing, I continue that mission. I do not take lightly that I am one of the very few Afro-Indigenous Latinas from Panama to earn tenure and rise to full professor—a rank most never reach. Fewer than 1% of Latinas hold this title, and for Afro-Indigenous Latinas, the number is even smaller. I am now curious to learn how many Afro-Indigenous Latinas have attained tenure and the rank of full professor—not only in the United States, but globally. If the number is as small as I suspect, I would welcome the opportunity to connect and build community with others who share this path.

My work is for the communities that deserve to be seen, heard, and represented. The awards are not just for me, they are signals to the next generation that they can do it too. And they are reminders to the world that we still have serious work to do to make sure mental health is recognized, funded, and valued as an essential part of health, right alongside physical health. My research examines how stress and trauma influence long-term psychological and physical health, and I focus on translating discoveries into real-world solutions that make mental health care accessible for all.

My work has taken me across the world from the U.S. to Panama, Madagascar, Brazil, and Mexico, where I've collaborated with incredible partners like the Institute of Scientific Research and High Technology Services of Panama (INDICASAT) and the Instituto Conmemorativo

Gorgas. Together, we design sustainable, culturally grounded mental health solutions rooted in community wisdom and local leadership.

In 2023, I was honored to be recognized as a Presidential Leadership Scholar, a fellowship connected to the bipartisan presidential centers of George W. Bush, William J. Clinton, George H.W. Bush, and Lyndon B. Johnson. That experience reminded me that leadership in health is not about politics—it's about humanity.

Through the years, I've secured over $30 million in research funding, but the true measure of success isn't in grants or titles. It's in the lives changed, the communities strengthened, and the young professionals inspired to believe they, too, can make a difference.

Ultimately, my journey taught me to see the best in people and situations, to find belonging even when things felt uncertain, and to honor the wisdom of my ancestors who continue to guide me. Every challenge I faced, every sacrifice I made, and every blessing I received shaped me into who I am today—a nurse, a leader, and a changemaker committed to creating pathways so that others can thrive.

> *Ultimately, my journey taught me to see the best in people and situations, to find belonging even when things felt uncertain, and to honor the wisdom of my ancestors who continue to guide me.*

And for that, I am endlessly thankful.

THE LEARNINGS

Every journey carries its share of hardship—moments that test who we are and what we stand for. Mine has been no exception. Life has placed me in situations that demanded resilience long before I even knew what that word meant. I've faced loss, poverty, and the weight of responsibility at an early age. But within those struggles, I found something powerful: the ability to transform pain into purpose, and to turn every challenge into a lesson in compassion, strength, and faith. Over time, I discovered that my so-called 'negative findings' were teachers in disguise. They showed me what not to repeat and how to try again differently. Because of them, and the wins beside them, I welcome the whole journey; every misstep and breakthrough has shaped who I am today.

The first one etched in my memory was losing my maternal grandmother in Panama. I was a teenager in Brooklyn, New York, and my mother couldn't afford for her and me to travel back to Panama to say our final goodbyes to my grandmother; therefore, she went alone. To this day, I carry the ache of never telling her how much she meant to me. So I do the next best thing: I live in a way that would have made her smile. I speak her name in rooms she never entered, and when I falter, I ask what Eugenia would do. Her steadiness is my compass. The importance of family and community has been my enduring anchor, first taught by my grandmother and strengthened by my mother and those who continue to uplift me. This foundation informs my decisions and drives my commitment to care, equity, and impact. That loss taught me that love and gratitude should never be delayed, and it planted in me a deep respect for the bonds of family and heritage.

Second, growing up in the Marlboro Projects in Brooklyn came with its own weather. I saw domestic violence, crime, the grip of drugs, and the tight margins of poverty. Still, I saw resilience: neighbors linking arms, families sharing what little they had, a community refusing to be defined by its hardest days. There I learned a truth that still guides me: where you live matters, where you go to school matters, and where you get health care matters. Quality or the lack of it, etches itself across a lifetime, shaping health, opportunity, and the odds of future success.

I was lucky to have friends who kept me out of trouble, even when they couldn't always keep themselves out of it. With their steady nudges and a few open doors, I found my way into a school with a nursing program. That program became the first bridge: from survival to service, from watching harm to learning how to heal. It taught me that talent is everywhere, but access is not, and that one good pathway can change a life.

That's the blueprint I carry forward: lead with resilience, center empathy, and build the kinds of schools, clinics, and community ties that turn hard places into launchpads. A zip code should not decide a child's future; when we raise the quality of what surrounds people, we raise the ceiling on what's possible.

Another learning experience took place when a close family member was diagnosed with a mental illness; my path didn't just shift—it clarified. After years in critical care, I saw up close what too many families face: long waits, fragmented services, and care that misses the person behind the symptoms. I stepped toward compassionate, holistic, community-based mental health care because the need was unmistakable. That moment gave me a mission: to fight stigma, educate communities, advocate for those too often unseen, and create healing spaces where people can understand their condition, embrace treatment, and learn to care for themselves. I also learned that families must be equipped, practically and culturally, to become confident caregivers for a loved one living with mental illness. And I made it a point to dismantle the falsehood that mental illness "isn't real," replacing it with a message of dignity, humanity, and hope.

Since then, I've used my voice to design trainings, build partnerships, and shape policies that turn compassion into access—and access into measurable outcomes. I refuse to accept systems that ask people to wait for care; I bring care closer to where they live, learn, work, and heal. Mentorship and financial support from the Substance Abuse and Mental Health Services Administration (SAMHSA) Minority Fellowship Program (MFP) through the American Nurses Association didn't just fund my education; it fueled a mission. First locally, then nationally, and now across borders. I advocate. I educate. I build systems that hold doors open.

This work is anchored by research focused on mental health disparities linked to stress and trauma and their downstream effects on chronic disease. I study how social context shapes risk and resilience, then translate those findings into evidence-based interventions that can be implemented in real settings, not just in journals. My approach integrates community partnership, rigorous evaluation, and continuous quality improvement, so progress is not only felt, it's proven. Recovery is possible. Equity is achievable. And dignity is non-negotiable.

How did I find the strength to overcome all this? Sometimes through grit, sometimes through humor, many times with the support of my village, and often through sheer determination. My strategies were simple but powerful: keep moving forward, lean on community, and never forget where I came from. I challenged systems that made people invisible and pushed back against the notion that one's zip code or circumstances should not define one's destiny.

Now, I see how these experiences have come full circle. They are not scars, they are fuel. They drive me as a nurse scientist, passionate about community engagement, mentorship, and staying connected to my roots in Panama. I carry my knowledge back to my communities, not just to heal, but to inspire and equip others to rise, to lead, and to believe that even from struggle, greatness can grow.

I survived and continue to thrive because of my supportive and extensive family and community. My Village!!! They are my anchor, the ones who keep me grounded and on track. They are also the first to tell me when I'm losing focus, when my work–life balance is slipping, or when I simply need to rest and be cared for. My family is never too far away, and their presence has been a constant source of strength.

These days, boundaries are my love language. "No" is a complete sentence— and I use it when my peace is on the line. I started by saying no to other people; now I'm practicing saying no to **me**: no to overbooking my calendar, no to "just one more email," no to guilt-drenched yeses, and no to 2 a.m. brainstorms that feel urgent but aren't. If it costs me my peace, it's overpriced—even when I'm the one trying to swipe the card.

I keep my balance with simple, consistent rituals: long walks, business audiobooks in my ears, and shameless binges of legal dramas, thrillers, and high-octane action. My calendar even has a standing meeting called "Me"— non-negotiable. I'm no longer auditioning for the role of Everybody's Emergency Contact; I'm choosing where my energy goes so I can show up with intention, not fumes.

Here's the quiet miracle: discipline made my life softer. Every "no" cleared space for a bigger "yes"—to health, to joy, to work that matters. In a world that rewards burnout, I'm choosing a different storyline: I protect my sanity like it pays the mortgage, and when I do say yes, it's purposeful, resourced, and sustainable. That's not selfish; that's how the next chapter gets written.

Another lesson I carry like a thread through every chapter: don't isolate, and don't outrun your own life. My grit, and what some would kindly call a work obsession, helped me get far. Left alone, I could work sixteen, eighteen hours a day, stacking to-do lists like bricks. But my circle never let me disappear into the grind. They know my weakness and keep me honest. "Are you coming, or should we come get you?" they'll text, half-joke, fully serious.

They set the standard for connection in my life, reminding me that community is not a luxury item; it's fuel. I learned early that where I'm from, Panamanians work hard, but we party harder. My mother would host a family gathering every weekend if it were up to her—music up, plates full, stories louder than the playlist. That rhythm refuses to let me forget: joy is as necessary as effort.

So when I start drifting toward the cliff of overwork, my people, my family, my village, pull me back to solid ground, onto a porch, into a kitchen, around a table. They make sure I remember the point of all this striving: to live well, love well, and stay human. The truth is stubborn and straightforward, connection keeps my ambition healthy, and celebration gives my discipline a reason. Left to my own devices, I might work endlessly. Thanks to them, I live entirely. And for that, I am deeply grateful.

In many ways, this support system has empowered me to challenge the status quo. It gave me the courage to push back against silence and stigma, especially around mental health, and to advocate for change within systems not built to serve everyone. My coping strategies and my village's unwavering presence have not only helped me navigate life's challenges but have also shaped me into a leader who believes that well-being, connection, and compassion are at the heart of resilience.

THE INSPIRATION

Inspiration has never been a single moment for me—it has been a thread woven through the lives of people who shaped me, challenged me, and reminded me of what was possible even when life felt impossible. Three people, in particular, have been the guiding lights in my journey: my mother, my mentor, and my father.

My mother was my very first teacher of resilience. I fought her at every step from leaving Panama to starting over in Brooklyn, New York because as a child I could not understand the weight she carried. If you ask her, she'll tell you we're still in spirited negotiations.

Only later did I realize what she was doing: she was building a better life for us, one sacrifice at a time. She was the hardest-working person I have ever known. I remember her on her knees scrubbing hotel floors, or me arriving after school to help her clean extra rooms so we could make ends meet. Later, when she started her own commercial cleaning business, she even "fired" me a few times because, truth be told, I wasn't a very good housekeeper! But those experiences left an imprint. My mother taught me that life is not easy, but you never give up. You do your best, always. And no matter how hard things got, she never lost sight of family. Even when we didn't get along, she instilled in us that family stands together. That lesson still anchors me.

The second person who profoundly shaped me is my academic mentor, Dr. Faye Gary. For more than 20 years, she has seen in me what I could not always see in myself. I remember telling her I wanted to research mental health, and she looked me straight in the eye and said, "You can't do that without clinical skills. You need to understand what mental health is, not just in theory but in practice, so you can truly serve the communities you want to help." That advice changed everything. It pushed me into the clinical world and gave me the foundation to grow into not just a researcher, but a nurse scientist grounded in service. Her mentorship has guided me through every stage of my career, reminding me that excellence is not just about intellect—it is about heart, humility, and staying connected to the people we serve.

Finally, my father gave me the gift of vision. In 2016, while he was ill and before he passed away in Panama, he helped me see the future more clearly. I found myself reflecting on all I had accomplished and all that still needed to be done. In his own quiet way, he reminded me that my talents were not meant to stay confined to one place. He helped me see that my work belonged on an international stage—that the fight against mental health stigma, the push for early intervention, and the effort to break cycles of trauma had to be global. His illness and his wisdom lit the spark for my current journey: to carry what I have learned back to Panama and beyond, so that others can benefit from knowledge, care, and the hope that stigma can be replaced by healing.

Each of these inspirations—my mother's resilience, my mentor's wisdom, and my father's vision—has shaped me into who I am today. They remind me daily that while the road is not easy, it is meaningful. And they fuel my determination to keep moving forward, not just for myself, but for the generations to come.

THE ADVICE

If I could go back and whisper in the ear of my younger self, I would start with this: surround yourself with people who are more intelligent than you, more ambitious than you, and from different walks of life. For too long, I thought my job was to be the one pouring into everyone else, always holding the answers, always carrying the weight. What I didn't realize is that growth comes from letting others pour into you, too —those who challenge your thinking, who brainstorm wild ideas with you, who push you to dream bigger than you thought possible. Some of my best moments have come from sitting in a room where I wasn't the smartest person, but I was willing to listen and learn.

The second piece of advice I would give is to learn the art of being comfortable with discomfort. That's not easy—it feels awkward, even painful at times—but it's the doorway to growth. Trying something new, daring to test out a risky idea, or stepping into a room where you feel out of place can be terrifying. But those moments are often where the magic happens. If you wait for the "perfect time," you'll be waiting forever. Take the calculated risk. Bet on yourself. Every big step I've taken—whether joining the Army at 17, pivoting into mental health nursing, or stepping onto the international stage—came with fear, but also with the knowledge that growth never happens inside the comfort zone.

The third nugget is about trust—trusting yourself, and more specifically, trusting your gut. There were times when I second-guessed myself because someone else was louder or more forceful in the room. I wish I had learned earlier how to articulate my ideas with confidence, to debate my point not with aggression but with clarity and conviction. The loudest voice should not always win. Sometimes, the best idea comes from the quieter voice with the courage to speak up. If I could talk to my younger self, I'd say: trust what you know, and don't shrink just because others take up more space.

Finally, I'd tell myself—and anyone walking a similar path—to invest in habits that continually make you better. For me, at this moment, because I have changed my topics, I'm feeding my mind with podcasts and audiobooks that sharpen both my vision and my leadership skills. I focus on topics such as business strategy, organizational sustainability, international board governance, and philosophy, but I also explore global health, digital transformation, financial stewardship, and the future of the nursing workforce. And of course, how to use artificial intelligence to stay relevant in research. I never stop learning about the art of leading and managing people. These practices not only expand my knowledge but also prepare me to meet the complex demands of leadership with insight, creativity, and purpose.

So my advice is hard-earned but straightforward: find the people who push you to grow, get comfortable with discomfort, trust your instincts, never stop learning, and take care of yourself along the way. Do those things, and you won't just survive the journey—you'll thrive in it.

THE PATH FORWARD

By all accounts, I was not supposed to be here. I checked every box that marked me as "at risk"—at risk of not finishing college, at risk of being trapped in poverty, at risk of being swallowed by the barriers life stacked against me. Yet here I stand, not just surviving, but rising—with a vengeance to be better, to create better, and to inspire better.

My message is simple, but it comes from the depths of my lived experience: your past and your social circumstances are only chapters in your story. They do not define the ending. No matter where you begin, you hold the power to rewrite your path. With tenacity, persistence, and consistency—and with the guidance of inspiring mentors and the unwavering support of family and community—what once felt impossible can, in fact, be achieved. Every obstacle can become a stepping stone, and every challenge an opportunity for growth.

As I reflect on my past and celebrate how far I've come, I know my journey is only beginning. I am committed to taking on the world—not for myself alone, but to show that experiencing stress, trauma, or struggle is not a death sentence. Mental health is real; it is not "fake news." With treatment, healing, and compassion, lives can and do transform. My path forward is clear: to keep breaking barriers, to mentor the next generation, and to leave a legacy of resilience, advocacy, and hope.

I carry a deep calling to illuminate the stories and voices that too often go unseen. For far too long, Afro-Latinas, Afro-Indigenous women, and Panamanian leaders like myself have been underrepresented in the spaces where decisions are made and narratives are shaped. Yet, we are here. We have always been here—brilliant, capable, and integral to the beautiful, diverse fabric of the Latina community. My mission is to make that truth visible and undeniable—to open doors so others can walk through with confidence, pride, and purpose.

I want my journey to remind every woman reading this—especially those who have been overlooked or underestimated—that your identity is not a limitation; it is your power. You are the author of your own story. You can transform misunderstanding into strength, and adversity into wisdom.

So to every Latina reading this: when someone tells you "you can't," when the world tries to shrink your worth or silence your voice, remember this truth—you must believe in yourself every single day, every single moment. Persistence and tenacity are not just words; they are the keys that open doors to your future. Do not let anyone else write your story.

Rise—even when it feels impossible.

Rise with courage, with pride, and with the unshakable knowledge that you, too, can change the world.

ABOUT DR. EUGENIA

Eugenia Flores Millender, Ph.D., RN, PMH-APRN, FAAN, FAANP, is a nationally and internationally recognized nurse scientist, educator, and leader dedicated to transforming mental health care and expanding access to innovative, integrated solutions. She is Co-Founder and Co-Director of the *Center of Population Sciences for Health Empowerment*, Assistant Dean for Research, and Marie Cowart Endowed Professor at Florida State University (FSU) College of Nursing.

Dr. Flores Millender integrates her clinical expertise and research to examine how stress, trauma, and adversity shape long-term psychological and physical health via biological pathways. Her research program is distinguished by community-driven strategies that accelerate the translation of discoveries into meaningful, real-world impact, improving mental health outcomes across all populations.

Her leadership extends across the globe, with collaborations in the U.S., Panama, Madagascar, Brazil, and Mexico. She partners with institutions such as the Institute of Scientific Research and High Technology Services of Panama (INDICASAT) and the Instituto Conmemorativo Gorgas to advance international mental health research and foster sustainable, community-centered solutions.

Before joining FSU, Dr. Millender founded and directed Florida's first nurse-led university health center to achieve Federally Qualified Health Center Look-Alike status at Florida Atlantic University's Christine E. Lynn College of Nursing, an innovation that redefined how nurse-led care could expand access.

She has secured more than $45 million in extramural and intramural funding, including nearly $40 million as Principal Investigator, Multiple Principal Investigator, or site PI, from the National Institutes of Health, U.S. Food and Drug Administration, Substance Abuse and Mental Health Services Administration, Health Resources and Services Administration , state agencies, and major foundations and was recognized in 2023 as a Presidential Leadership Scholar, a prestigious fellowship affiliated with the presidential centers of George W. Bush, William J. Clinton, George H.W. Bush, and Lyndon B. Johnson.

.Her entrepreneurial drive is equally evident. Dr. Millender founded and operated a concierge, community-based, integrated mental health practice that served families with chronic illness, blending innovation, fiscal sustainability, and community engagement. This venture demonstrated her capacity to launch and scale programs that unite clinical service, financial performance, and population health outcomes.

A U.S. Army veteran with six years of honorable service, Dr. Millender brings a disciplined, mission-driven approach to leadership. Her educational pathway mirrors her commitment to continuous growth: BSN, MS, and Ph.D. from Florida Atlantic University; advanced clinical training in psychiatric and mental health nursing at Rush University; precision medicine at the University of Florida; executive leadership at the Wharton School of the University of Pennsylvania; and an artificial intelligence in healthcare certificate from Harvard Medical School.

With a unique ability to unite clinical expertise, entrepreneurship, research innovation, and international partnerships, Dr. Millender is shaping the future of mental health and nursing worldwide.

Research Areas: Stress, Trauma, Mood Disorders, Mental Health, Integrated Care, Sociocultural and Biological Determinants of Health, Community-Driven Translation, Global Health Innovation

You can learn more and connect with Dr. Eugenia Flores Millender at:

www.linkedin.com/in/eugenia-flores-millender

Read more about her work:

Refereed journal articles
Submitted / in press
1. Millender, E. I., Harris, R., Kim, J., Xavier Hall, C., Kelley, M., Winbish-Tompkins, R., Chamber, K., Lowe, J., & Wong, F. (submitted). Differences in hypertension risk by nativity, language, and neighborhood deprivation among a diverse, clinic-based

sample in South Florida. Journal of Community Health. Manuscript submitted for publication.

2. Xavier Hall, C., Meng, Z., Okantey, B., Sabuncu, C., Lane, B., Ramirez Surmeier, L., Sheffler, J., Wong, F., Britton, G., & Millender, E. (submitted). Resilience and social support associated with reduced dementia risk in an examination of biopsychosocial correlates of the Cardiovascular Risk Factors, Aging and Incidence of Dementia (CAIDE) risk score in All of Us. Journal of Aging and Health. Manuscript submitted for publication.

3. Cheung, D., Xavier Hall, C., Okantey, B., Meng, Z., Sabuncu, C., Lane, B., Millender, E. I., Queiroz, A., Hyo Kim, J., Okada, L., Gillespie, A., Simoncin, G., Barile, J., Ma, G., & Wong, F. (in press). Culturally and linguistically adapting a transdiagnostic LGBTQ-affirming cognitive behavioral skills intervention for Vietnamese gay and bisexual men at risk for HIV: Pre-adaptation qualitative interviews. AIDS Care.

Published

1. Khurshid, A., Marin-Velasquez, M., Yaun, K., Ziad Jaber, L., Anairis, & Millender, E. I. (2025). Collaboration as presence: Being relational in research with Indigenous communities. American Educational Research Journal, 1–18. https://doi.org/10.1080/09518398.2025.2571482

2. Tratner, A. E., Oviedo, D. C., Rangel, G. A., Carreira, M. B., Torres-Atencio, I., Millender, E., O'Bryant, S., Villarreal, A. E., & Britton, G. B. (2025). Ethical disclosure of biomarkers for Alzheimer risk in Latin American participants. Geriatric Nursing, 67, 1–10.

3. Oviedo, D. C., Haughbrook, R., Culjat, C., Ladanya Ramirez Surmeier, L., Tratner, A. E., Carreira, M. B., Villarreal, A. E., Harmon, S. L., Batista Ceballos, O. I., Meng, Z., Millender, E., Xavier Hall, C., & Britton, G. B. (2025). Ethical disclosure of biomarkers for Alzheimer risk in Latin American participants. Frontiers in Dementia, 28(4). https://doi.org/10.3389/frdem.2025.1672075

4. Sabuncu, B., Meng, Z., Xavier Hall, C., Taylor, T., Handley, A., Trang, K., Wang, L., Okada, L., Millender, E. I., Gillespie, A., Simoncini, G., Barile, J., Ma, G. X., & Wong, F. Y. (2025). Examining barriers and facilitators to physical activity among a diverse cohort of MSM living with HIV. AIDS and Behavior.

5. Phillips, C. J., Cornelius, J. B., Neira, P. M., Hein, L., Ducar, D., Rose, C. D., Rosa, W. E., Ballout, S., Nagel, D. A., Keepnews, D. M., Flores Millender, E., Neft, M. W., Jablonski, R. A., Murray, T. A., Stamps, D. C., Brous, E., & Keepnews, D. M. (2025). Advancing human rights, health equity, and equitable health policy with LGBTQ+ peoples: An AAN consensus paper. Nursing Outlook, 73(5).

6. Lane, B., Sabuncu, C., Yang, Y., Okantey, B., Campbel, D., Bryant, T.-R., Sorkpor, S., Millender, E., Wong, F., & Xavier Hall, C. (2025). Discrimination and mental health among Black and Latino people living with HIV: Understanding the role of religion and spirituality. AIDS and Behavior. https://doi.org/10.1007/s10461-025-04720-z

7. Lane, B., Millender, E. I., Harris, R. M., Kim, J., Norwak, A., Xavier Hall, C., Pfeiffer, F., Wong, F., Crusto, C. A., & Taylor, J. (2025). Neighborhood deprivation, trauma profiles, coping, and stress prospectively predict depressive symptoms among young African American mothers in the InterGEN Study: A latent class analysis Journal of Racial and Ethnic Health Disparities, 35(1).

8. Cheung, D., Xavier Hall, C., Okantey, B., Meng, Z., Sabuncu, C., Lane, B., Millender, E. I., Queiroz, A., Hyo Kim, J., Okada, L., Gillespie, A., Simoncin, G., Barile, J., Ma, G., & Wong, F. (2025). Mediating roles of social support in lives of MSM living with HIV. Health Psychology.

9. Wang, L., Trang, K., Xavier Hall, C., Zhu, L., Millender, E. I., Sabuncu, C., Barile, J., Ma, G., Gillespie, A., Simoncin, G., & Wong, F. (2025). Subgroups of intersectional stigma, discrimination, and mental health in men who have sex with men. AIDS and Behavior, 29(3), 1011–1027. https://doi.org/10.1007/s10461-024-04583-w

10. Wu, Q., Radey, M., McWey, L., & Millender, E. I. (2025). Within-family processes among safety nets, maternal parenting stress, and child behavioral problems among low-income families: The importance of race and ethnicity. Family Process, 64(1). https://doi.org/10.1111/famp.13056

11. Lowe, J., Millender, E. I., Xavier Hall, C., Wimbish-Cirilo, R., Coker, D., & Kelley, M. (2025). First contact colonial era Native American tribes become visible through the collection of health status data. Lupine Online Journal of Nursing and Health Care. https://doi.org/10.32474/LOJNHC.2025.03.000173

12. Nyembwe, A., Zhao, Y., Millender, E., Hall, K., Caceres, B., Taylor, B., Morrison, M., Prescott, L., Potts-Thompson, S., Aziz, A., Aruleba, F., Crusto, C. A., & Taylor, J. (2025). Perceived discrimination, trauma, mental health and blood pressure outcomes among young African American mothers in the InterGEN Study. Journal of Cardiovascular Nursing, 35(1), 12.

13. Wang, L., Trang, K., Xavier Hall, C., Zhu, L., Millender, E. I., Sabuncu, C., Barile, J., Ma, G., Gillespie, A., Simoncin, G., & Wong, F. (2024). Identifying subgroups of intersectional stigma, discrimination, and the association with mental health outcomes among HIV-positive MSM: Latent class analysis. AIDS and Behavior. https://doi.org/10.1007/s10461-024-04583-w

14. Sabuncu, B., Signorelli, M. C., Evans, D. P., Murgor, J., Millender, E. I., Lane, B., Okantey, B., & Xavier Hall, C. (2024). Partner violence-related safety planning: A systematic review. Journal of Family Violence. https://doi.org/10.1007/s10896-024-00770-4

15. Gabster, A., Diaz Fernandez, F., Pascale, J., Gamba, B., Orillac, A., Moreno, S., Xavier-Hall, C., Millender, E., Frank (Frankie) Wong, Jhangimal, M., Yu Pon, A., Rodriguez-Vargas, C., Arjona-Miranda, D., Fuentes, B., Henostroza, G., & Belen Arauz, A. (2024). Factors associated with self-reported suboptimal antiretroviral adherence and limited retention in care among people living with HIV who attend a large urban ART clinic in Panama City, Panama. PLOS ONE, 19(11), e0311048.

16. Okantey, B., Chenangat Murgor, J., Wong, F., Millender, E. I., & Xavier Hall, C. (2024). How do social work students gain cultural competence, humility, or similar constructs? A systematic review. Journal of Social Work Education. https://doi.org/10.1080/02615479.2024.2409195

17. Wu, Q., Radey, M., McWey, L., & Millender, E. I. (2024). Within-family processes among safety nets, maternal parenting stress, and child behavioral problems among low-income families: The importance of race and ethnicity. Family Process, 64(1), e13056. https://doi.org/10.1111/famp.13056

18. Rangel, G. A., Tratner, A. E., Oviedo, D. C., Villarreal, A. E., Carreira, M. B., Rodriguez-Araña, S., Millender, E. I., Xavier Hall, C., Wong, F., O'Bryant, S., & Britton, G. B. (2024). Depression and plasma pTau181 levels are associated with frailty status in Hispanic community-dwelling older women. Gerontology and Geriatric Medicine, 10, 1–10. https://doi.org/10.1177/23337214241283546

19. Millender, E. I., Radey, M., Wu, Q., & McWey, L. (2024). Exploring the interplay of social safety nets, race, ethnicity, and nativity on psychological distress among low-income mothers. Child Psychiatry & Human Development.

20. Wimbish-Cirilo, R., Lowe, J., Kelley, M., Millender, E., & Liang, H. (2024). A commercial tobacco and alcohol use intervention for urban Native American youth. Archives of Psychiatric Nursing, 4(3), 79–85. https://doi.org/10.1016/j.apnu.2024.06.014

21. Xavier Hall, C., Okantey, B., Meng, Z., Sabuncu, C., Lane, B., Millender, E. I., Queiroz, A. A. F. L. N., Kim, J., Okada, L., Gillepsie, A., Simoncin, G., Barile, J., Ma, G., & Wong, F. (2024). Examining bio-psycho-social predictors of risk for cognitive impairment among a racially diverse sample of men who have sex with men living with HIV. Therapeutic Advances in Infectious Disease, 14, 1–12. https://doi.org/10.1177/20499361241249657

22. Radey, M., Wu, Q., McWey, L., & Millender, E. I. (2024). Instrumental safety net configurations and changes over time among low-income, vulnerable families. American Journal of Orthopsychiatry, 94(3), 339–351. https://doi.org/10.1037/ort0000728

23. Greywolf, C., Lowe, J., Casken, J., Kataoka-Yahiro, M., & Millender, E. (2023). Discrimination, racism, social inequality, and injustice experienced among Native Hawaiians through the lens of historical trauma. International Journal of Sciences: Basic and Applied Research, 69(1), 36–46.

24. Wimbish-Cirilo, R., Lowe, J., Kelley, M., & Millender, E. I. (2023). Talking Circle Intervention among urban Native American youth: A cultural safety research exemplar. Journal of Indigenous Research, 11(1), Article 3.

25. Li, C., Liu, T., Zhang, R., Millender, E. I., Miao, H., Ormsbee, M., Conley, Y., Westbrook, A., Yang, P., Wang, J., & Kelly, T. (2023). The impact of polygenic score on cognitive function decline considering baseline cognitive function, lifestyle behaviors and diabetes among middle-aged and older U.S. adults. Alzheimer's Research & Therapy, 15(196), 1–10. https://doi.org/10.1186/s13195-023-01343-1

26. Millender, E. I., Dickey, S., Ouma, C., Bruneau, D., & Wisdom-Chambers, K. (2022). Addressing disparities by evaluating depression as a predictor of prostate screenings among Black men in a community health clinic. Journal of Community Health, 39(1), 25–39. https://doi.org/10.1080/07370016.2022.2028063

27. Gabster, A., Yu, A., Xavier-Hall, C., Millender, E. I., Wong, F., & Pascale, J. (2022). Dating violence prevalence and risk factors among adolescents (14–19 years) in urban settings in Panama. The Lancet Regional Health – Americas, 10, 100383. https://doi.org/10.1016/j.lana.2022.100383

28. Joiner, T. E., Robinson, M., Robertson, L., Keel, P., Daurio, A. M., Mehra, L. M., & Millender, E. (2022). Ethnoracial status, intersectionality with gender, and psychotherapy utilization, retention, and outcomes. Journal of Consulting and Clinical Psychology. https://doi.org/10.1037/ccp0000726

29. Erausquin, J. T., Sánchez, J., Pon, A. Y., Jhangimal, M., Millender, E. I., Peña, Y., Ng, W., Reina, A., Nakad, C., Quintana, J., Herrera, R., Vistica, G., Pinzón-Espinosa, J., Cabezas-Talavero, G., Katz, J., Pascale, J. M., Rodríguez, F., & Gabster, A. (2022). Sexual and reproductive health and access: Results of a rapid epidemiological assessment among migrant peoples in transit through Darién, Panamá. Frontiers in Reproductive Health, 4, 953979. https://doi.org/10.3389/frph.2022.953979

30. Lowe, J., Millender, E. I., & Best, O. (2022). Talking Circle for Young Adults (TC4YA) intervention: A culturally safe research exemplar. Contemporary Nurse, 58(1), 95–107. https://doi.org/10.1080/10376178.2022.2080087

31. Millender, E. I., Harris, R. M., Barneris, J., Marks, L., Barcelona, V., Wong, F., Crusto, C., & Taylor, J. Y. (2022). The cumulative influence of perceived discrimination, stress, and coping responses on symptoms of depression among young African American mothers. Journal of the American Psychiatric Nurses Association, 28(6), 479–489. https://doi.org/10.1177/10783903221105281

32. Agudelo-Higuita, N., Antonio Suarez, J., Millender, E. I., Garcia-Creighton, E., Francesco Corbisiero, M., Olivo Freites, C., Henao Cordero, J., Kousari, A., Unterborn, R., Marcos, L. A., Henao-Martínez, A. F., Meng, M., Alvarado, Y. W., Nicholls, S. B., Sanchez, J., Rinco, T., Viquez, D., Owen, D., Pascale, J. M., & Gabster, A. (2022). U.S.-bound journey of migrant peoples in transit across Dante's Inferno and Purgatory in the Americas. Travel Medicine and Infectious Disease, 47, 102317. https://doi.org/10.1016/j.tmaid.2022.102317

33. Millender, E. I., Barile, J. P., Barneris, J., Harris, R. M., De Faria, L., Wong, F., Crusto, C. A., & Taylor, J. (2021). Associations between social determinants of health, perceived discrimination, and body mass index on symptoms of depression among young African American mothers. Archives of Psychiatric Nursing, 35(1), 94–101. https://doi.org/10.1016/j.apnu.2020.09.014

34. Dickey, S., Matthews, C., & Millender, E. I. (2020). An exploration of pre- and post-cancer diagnosis and health communication among African American prostate cancer survivors and their families. American Journal of Men's Health, 14(3), 1–15. https://doi.org/10.1177/1557988320927202

35. Millender, E., Valentine, K., Eggenberger, T., Lucier, C., Sandala, H., & Bruneau, D. (2020). Implementing interprofessional collaboration to improve patient outcomes: A caring and social approach to integrated nurse-led community-based care. American Journal of Nursing, 24(1), 39–49. https://doi.org/10.20467/1091-5710.24.1.39

36. Wimbish-Cirilo, R., Lowe, J., & Millender, E. I. (2020). The impact of a substance use intervention among urban Native American youth. Genealogy, 4(3), 79, 2–12.

37. Eggenberger, T., Millender, E., Drowos, J., & Parent, N. (2019). Interprofessional education and practice guides: Developing interprofessional community-based clinical experience. Cogent Medicine, 6(1), 1676582. https://doi.org/10.1080/2331205X.2019.1676582

38. Lowe, J., Wagner, E., Morris, S. L., Thompson, M., Sawant, M., Kelly, M., & Millender, E. I. (2019). Utility of the Native-Reliance theoretical framework, model, and questionnaire. Journal of Cultural Diversity, 26(2), 61–68.

39. Drowos, J. L., Millender, E. I., & Eggenberger, T. (2018). Developing interprofessional skills through clinical care of the underserved using the TeamSTEPPS framework. Society of Teachers of Family Medicine National Family Medicine Clerkship Curriculum. Retrieved from https://www.stfm.org/teachingresources/curriculum/nationalclerkshipcurriculum/overview/

40. Millender, E., & Lowe, J. (2017). Cumulative trauma among Mayas living in Southeast Florida. Journal of Immigrant and Minority Health, 19(3), 598–605. https://doi.org/10.1007/s10903-015-0337-3

41. Drowos, J. L., Eggenberger, T., & Millender, E. (2016). The future health care workforce: Interprofessional education in community settings. Journal of Community and Public Health Nursing, 2(3). https://doi.org/10.4172/jcphn.1000126

42. Millender, E., Lowe, J., & Liehr, P. (2015). What's in a name? Hispanic immigrant-refugee identity crisis: Focus on Mayas. AlterNative: An International Journal of Indigenous Peoples, 11(2), 191–198. https://doi.org/10.1177/117718011501100208

43. Valentine, K., Ordonez, M., & Millender, E. (2014). Transforming practice through embracing caring in nurse-managed centers. International Association of Human Caring Journal, 18(3), 52–64. https://doi.org/10.20467/1091-5710-18.3.52

44. Millender, E. (2012). Acculturation stress among Guatemalan Maya in the United States. Journal of Cultural Diversity, 19(2), 58–64.

45. Millender, E. (2011). Using stories to bridge cultural disparities, one culture at a time. Journal of Continuing Education in Nursing, 42(1), 37–42. https://doi.org/10.3928/00220124-20100901-01

46. Millender, E. (2010). Haiti: A firsthand view. American Journal of Nursing, 110(4), 22. https://doi.org/10.1097/01.NAJ.0000370152.02729.60

47. Millender, E. (2010). Stress experienced by Guatemala-Mayan immigrants. Archives of Psychiatric Nursing, 24(3), 212–214. https://doi.org/10.1016/j.apnu.2009.04.001

48. Millender, E. (2009). Bridging cultural disparities: From practice to research. Southern Online Journal of Nursing Research, 9(2), Supplement.

Invited book chapters

1. Wilson, P., & Millender, E. (2025). Community trauma (Chapter 3). In L. M. Dunphy, J. E. Winland-Brown, D. E. Thomas, & B. Porter (Eds.), Primary Care: The Art and Science of Advanced Practice Nursing (5th ed., pp. 1129–1152). Springer Nature.

2. Millender, E., & Wilson, P. (2025). Generational trauma (Chapter 7). In L. M. Dunphy, J. E. Winland-Brown, D. E. Thomas, & B. Porter (Eds.), Primary Care: The Art and Science of Advanced Practice Nursing (5th ed., pp. 1129–1152). Springer Nature.

3. Millender, E., & Dunphy, L. (2019). Anxiety, stress, and trauma-related disorders (Chapter 68). In L. M. Dunphy, J. E. Winland-Brown, D. E. Thomas, & B. Porter (Eds.), Primary Care: The Art and Science of Advanced Practice Nursing (5th ed., pp. 1129–1152). F. A. Davis.

GABRIELA PARRA

"I am worthy because I am human—everything else is my gift to humanity."

\- Gabriela Parra

~ ~ ~

Gabriela Parra is a trailblazing Chicana attorney, entrepreneur, and advocate whose journey embodies resilience, purpose, and justice in action. As Partner at Layde & Parra S.C. in Wisconsin, she has dedicated her career to defending the rights of immigrants and refugees with compassion, courage, and unwavering integrity. Born to Mexican immigrant parents and raised between Los Angeles and Wisconsin, Gabriela transformed the challenges of cultural isolation and systemic inequities into fuel for empowerment and change. A proud first-generation attorney, she stands among the few Latinas in her field, using her platform to amplify immigrant voices, mentor future leaders, and create spaces where Latin@s can thrive in the full power of their identity and heritage.

~ ~ ~

To my ancestors, my immigrant community, mi familia, and to all Latinos whose resilience, strength, and pride in our roots have carried me through my darkest days.

LA SÚPLICA:
MEANT FOR MORE

THE JOURNEY

In every leader's life, there are moments that demand a choice—crossroads that shape not just what we do, but who we become.

For me, three defining moments changed my trajectory entirely and have led me to where I am today. I didn't choose the circumstances of my birth—where I live, the language I speak, or the struggles I inherited. But I did choose how I responded. I decided whether to listen to that quiet voice that whispers, *"You are meant for more."*

The First Moment: La Súplica

Bang. Bang.

Another shooting echoed down the street. I was seven, maybe eight years old, and what should terrify a child no longer did. It had become background noise—like barking dogs or circling helicopters.

I lived in the San Fernando Valley with my parents, in a neighborhood scarred by poverty and violence. Gang life wasn't something we watched on television—it was what we saw from our front steps. My parents worked long hours, scraping by paycheck to paycheck. Their limited English and immigration status fenced us into a world of constant struggle.

At school, expectations for kids like me were painfully low from the adults. Teachers saw statistics, not potential—another Latina destined to drop out or fall into gang life. The message was clear: dreams like mine didn't belong in the classroom.

I started to believe them.

The gangs offered belonging, loyalty, *familia*—everything I thought I needed. By thirteen, I was drinking, using drugs, skipping school—not because I didn't care, but because I couldn't see a future beyond survival.

And yet, deep down, a small voice refused to die, reminding me I was meant for more.

One day, a local priest stopped me outside the church. "If you pray for fifteen minutes," he said, "I'll give you a rosary—any color you want."

On the surface, it seemed like I didn't care about praying, but I wanted that rosary. Looking back, deep down, I could feel a voice calling out. Although we identified as Catholic, we never went to church, but I did witness my mother's faith—she often prayed to the saints to keep us safe. La Virgencita was a symbol for us, not only in my culture but also in the neighborhood. In hard times, we turned to her for help. I think that is the real reason why I agreed.

Inside that small church in North Hills—the same one that still stands today—I knelt and truly prayed for the first time in my life. Not the memorized kind, but the kind that comes from desperation.

"God," I whispered, "if You're real, please get me out—before this place takes my mind, my body, or my spirit. I know You made me for more, but I don't know how to find it."

Nothing happened that day. But that prayer did its work in ways I couldn't yet see. And as I later learned, God's timing is never ours.

The Second Moment: The Escape

When I was fifteen years old, my parents told me we were moving to Wisconsin. My grandparents had convinced them to relocate for work—and to save me from gang life.

I had never even heard of Wisconsin, yet something inside me stirred. Maybe this was my way out. I knew that if I kept living the life I was living—spending time around some of the most powerful gangs in Los Angeles, constantly exposed to violence, and hearing about young kids being killed in my neighborhood—it was only a matter of time before I would be next. I didn't want to become just another statistic of gang violence.

We moved to Sturgeon Bay, a small, quiet town with no constant sirens or gunshots. For the first time, I could breathe—but that breath came with a new kind of weight.

I was one of the only Latinas in my school. I spoke Spanglish and read at a sixth-grade level when I entered my sophomore year in high school. I didn't understand the small-town white culture, the privilege of having an abundance of financial resources, or the Midwest world I had been dropped into. Some classmates assumed I was a foreign exchange student. Others made racist jokes. Teachers underestimated me again. The isolation was crushing. I thought about dropping out—again.

Then I met Ms. Linda Bauer.

She was an ESL teacher, but for me, she became much more than that. She saw beyond the "gang kid" and the "poor girl" and recognized the young woman fighting to survive. She tutored me after school, listened when I was angry, and reminded me that being Latina was not something to hide—it was something to honor. Ms. Bauer became the first adult in my life who saw my true potential—not just my limitations.

She took me on college tours and helped me fill out applications. When I doubted myself, she believed enough for both of us.

Thanks to her persistence, I enrolled in a local technical college—my first step toward higher education. Beginning higher education with the reading, writing, and comprehension limitations I carried was not easy—but it was mine. From there, I built the confidence to transfer to a four-year college degree and then pursued and earned a law degree.

Ms. Bauer didn't just help me graduate from high school. She taught me to believe I could become something.

The Third Moment: Reclaiming My Voice

Years later, after becoming an attorney, I faced a new kind of battle—not on the streets or in the classroom, but within myself.

I had spent years trying to fit in. As I navigated a predominantly white culture, Latinos and white colleagues told me that assimilation meant success. I softened my accent, mimicked how "successful" people spoke, and dressed conservatively so I wouldn't stand out. I smiled through microaggressions, stayed silent when white colleagues made assumptions, and worked tirelessly to be the "acceptable" version of a Latina professional—polished, agreeable, invisible.

And it broke me.

I had built a life that looked perfect on the outside—but felt hollow within. My silence became a self-made cage. Eventually, my bars collapsed under the weight of pretending, and I fell too. And in that collapse, amid all the assimilation, I discovered something powerful: the only way to lead truly is to live in truth.

I rebuilt myself by discovering who I was again, piece by piece—this time honoring my Spanish accent, my Chicana culture, my Catholic faith, and honoring my ancestors who paved the way for me. I reclaimed my identity as a proud Latina, a daughter of immigrant parents, and a woman of faith.

When I stopped apologizing for who I was, everything changed. My confidence deepened. I began to speak more, share my ideas and views, and call out those who tried to silence my voice. My leadership grew stronger. My purpose as a Latina leader became clear.

Those three moments—my plea, my escape, and my reclaiming of my identity—are the foundation of who I am. They remind me that leadership isn't about power or prestige. It's about courage. It's about walking through fear and still choosing authenticity.

Now, every time I walk into a courtroom, I carry that thirteen-year-old girl from North Hills with me—the one who knelt in a church and prayed for a way out.

I am the product of struggle, of faith, and of second chances.

THE LEARNINGS

Completing a bachelor's degree and eventually law school wasn't easy. In fact, there were moments when it felt completely impossible. Before I could even think about applying to college or dreaming of a legal career, I had to survive circumstances designed to stop me long before then.

As you will see in my battles I have fought over the years to achieve these unreachable spaces, while we cannot control the circumstances we are born into, the limited opportunities we are given, or the many barriers and obstacles placed in our paths, we *can* control how we respond to them—and that response shapes our future. We can choose to sit in resentment over the obstacles before us, or we can push through them and keep moving forward.

My first battle wasn't academic—it was survival. It was making sure I didn't fall into the traps that surrounded me: joining a gang, dropping out of high school, or becoming another statistic in a system that rarely expects success from people like me.

For instance, when I received a very poor grade in college—after spending hours on the assignment and visiting the writing lab multiple times—those thoughts that I didn't belong there came back even louder. And I would begin to question my worth. It took everything in me to hold on to the quiet belief that I was created for something more. I had to trust that my circumstances did not define my potential, even when the world around me insisted otherwise. That inner voice, though small and sometimes hard to hear, kept reminding me that there was more to life than the limited options laid out before me.

It's challenging to keep your faith when everything around you points in one direction—poverty, struggle, and limitation. People will label you based on your background, your accent, and your neighborhood. They will tell you who you are before you've had a chance to decide for yourself. Through it all, I had to protect the small light inside me. Even when it dimmed, I refused to let it go out.

Eventually, the opportunities I created in pursuit of my goals let me step into new environments—ones that gave me a fighting chance. But starting over came with its own challenges. I graduated from high school, reading at about a sixth-grade level. In college, I had to teach myself how to truly read, write, and comprehend. I spent countless hours in tutoring centers, rewriting essays late into the night, and giving up weekends just to catch up to everyone else. I often felt behind, but I refused to give up.

Even as I began to improve academically, I faced a new mountain: figuring out how to get into law school. When you grow up with limited opportunities, you learn quickly that you have to work twice as hard to get half as far. It was not fair, but it's a truth I had to accept early on. I learned that my success wouldn't come from privilege or access—it would come from persistence.

For a long time, I believed my struggles reflected my intelligence or ability. I thought something was wrong with me because everything seemed harder. It took years to unlearn that mindset. I eventually realized that some people simply start with more resources—family support, financial stability, mentors, and networks that open doors. I didn't have those things, but I did have something powerful: determination and a deep faith that my effort would lead somewhere meaningful.

My journey was filled with battles of every kind. I escaped gang life only to confront new forms of violence—racism and systemic barriers that followed me through school and into the legal profession. Each step forward seemed to come with its own set of walls to climb. But I kept climbing.

When I started thinking about law school, I didn't know any attorneys. I didn't know where to apply or how to prepare. I didn't have the money for prep courses or consultants, and I had no one to guide me through the process. I was alone. What I did have was my grit and resilience. I told myself that if others had done it, so could I. I studied late at night, worked multiple jobs, and prayed for opportunities to move me forward.

Somehow, they came—one at a time, like stepping stones across a wide river I wasn't sure I could cross. When I walked into the legal field, it felt like stepping into another world. I entered a profession where less than three percent of attorneys in the United States are Latinas. Instead of discouraging, this lack of representation fueled me. I knew that my presence mattered— that every room I entered, every case I touched, every person, young and old, who saw me in this role could begin to imagine new possibilities for themselves.

I learned that representation isn't just about numbers—it's about breaking cycles and expanding possibilities. My path to becoming an attorney was not traditional or easy, but it was real, and it was mine. It was forged through faith, persistence, and an unshakable belief that my story, with all its imperfections and detours, had value.

When I look back now, I see not just the struggles but also the strength they brought. Every obstacle, every failure, every moment of doubt became part of the foundation I stand on today. My journey is proof that even when the odds are stacked against you, your light—no matter how dim—can still guide you through the darkness.

THE INSPIRATION

For me, inspiration arrived quietly—through ordinary moments that hold extraordinary power. I was able to stay present, recognize those divine nudges that plant seeds of possibility long before they bloom.

When I was twelve years old, I sat in the auditorium at Sepulveda Middle School, and a former gang member came to speak. He had left gang life behind and gone on to graduate from college at Harvard. I don't remember his name, but I remember how his story sparked something open inside me. For the first time, I thought—maybe I can be more than what my neighborhood offered me. That day, a seed was planted in me.

Looking back, I realize that the single act of kindness from a Catholic priest watered that seed. That small and unassuming moment became a source of inspiration that carried me through every season of doubt. It reminded me that faith often begins not with certainty, but with surrender.

Two years later, I was on my way from North Hills, California, to Sturgeon Bay, Wisconsin—thousands of miles from the chaos I knew. I didn't realize it at the time, but that prayer had been answered.

Just when I was ready to give up—feeling stupid and alone because I couldn't keep up in school—Ms. Linda Bauer walked into my life. She was more than a teacher; she was light. She told me there was nothing wrong with me—that I wasn't broken, I just hadn't been given the right tools yet. Her belief became my anchor. She showed me that once given an opportunity, I could achieve anything.

Mentors appeared at every stage of my life. They saw potential in me long before I saw it myself. They reminded me of the promise I made at twelve, when I whispered, "I'm going to be an attorney." That dream had gone silent, buried beneath fear and survival, but their encouragement helped me unearth it again. With their guidance, I pushed past doubt and applied to law school.

One of the most transformative chapters came when I became an entrepreneur. I never planned to start a business—I didn't think I had what it took. Then came my business partner, someone willing to take a chance on me while taking a chance on himself. Together, we built Layde & Parra, S.C., an immigration law firm that serves and uplifts immigrant families and their children.

I had no business background, no mentors in entrepreneurship. It was terrifying. I gave up a steady paycheck, health insurance, and stability while being the family's leading provider. But sometimes the greatest blessings are hidden behind the scariest risks. I learned that faith doesn't erase fear—it gives you courage to move forward despite it.

Even after building a successful firm, I faced a new challenge—reclaiming my voice as a Latina leader. There were moments when I felt like an imposter, afraid my *Latinidad* wouldn't be accepted. I questioned whether my Spanish accent, my Chicana culture, or my story belonged in the spaces I was now leading.

Once again, mentors appeared—strong, unapologetic leaders who reminded me that I didn't need to shrink to lead. They showed me that my identity wasn't something to hide; it was my greatest strength. My accent, my culture, my story—they weren't barriers. They were my foundation.

When I finally stepped fully into who I was—unapologetically Latina, unapologetically me—I flourished. Each of these people—some who crossed my path briefly, others who stayed for years—played a part in my becoming. They were mirrors reflecting the parts of myself I couldn't yet see.

Because of them, I stand here today not just as an attorney or business owner, but as a woman of faith who believes in the power of community and second chances.

Inspiration doesn't always arrive in grand moments. Sometimes it's a stranger's story, a teacher's faith, or a whispered prayer in the dark. Each one plants a seed that, with courage and grace, grows into purpose.

THE ADVICE

Looking back, there are so many things I wish I could whisper to my younger self—truths that would have made the road a little less heavy. Over the years, as I've stepped into rooms I once thought were unreachable, I've collected small lessons—nuggets of wisdom born from both pain and perseverance. These are the reminders I now carry with me.

Visualize It

Dream big, even when your world feels small. If you can't see your goal, it's almost impossible to reach it. Before I ever became an attorney, I spent nights lying awake, imagining it all—walking across the graduation stage, holding my law degree, standing in a courtroom speaking up for families like mine.

Visualization became my lifeline. It gave shape to the impossible. The more I pictured it, the more it began to feel real. When you see your dream clearly enough, your heart starts moving toward it, even before your feet know the way. Don't be afraid to write down those bold, ambitious goals. Look at yourself in the mirror each day and remind yourself that no matter how extraordinary that dream may seem, it is within your reach.

Break It Down

Big dreams can feel like mountains. When you stare at the peak, it can paralyze you. The secret is to look for the next step instead. Every small victory matters—the test you pass, the paper you rewrite, the email you finally send. Every single one counts.

And along the way, remember that no one climbs alone. You will need people—mentors, friends, familia, and believers who see your light when you can't. Having a plan matters, but having a community will keep you alive within it. Without them, the weight of the dream can crush you. With them, it becomes bearable.

Embrace the Setbacks

Setbacks will come, often at the worst times. When life knocks you down—and it will—you'll have a choice: to stay there or to get up slower, wiser, softer. Resilience isn't about never breaking. It's about learning how to bend without losing yourself.

There will be nights when you doubt everything—your worth, your path, your strength. You'll want to give up. In those moments, let yourself feel the ache. Cry if you must. Then get back up. Growth happens right there—in the quiet space between falling apart and starting again.

Grit: The Fire Within

Talent will open some doors, but grit will keep them open. You must know your why—the reason that burns deep enough to carry you through when everything else falls apart.

I didn't have privilege or connections. What I had was hunger. That hunger became my strength. It turned my fear into focus, my struggle into skill, my pain into purpose.

Hard work matters, but hard work with heart—that's what changes everything.

Connection and Community

Hard work might get you noticed, but connection sustains you. Don't be afraid to reach out, to ask questions, to learn from those who've walked before you. Success grows faster when it grows in community.

You must also be intentional about choosing the people you surround yourself with. Had I continued spending time with friends involved in gangs, it would have only been a matter of time before I joined one myself. Instead, I chose to surround myself with people who are successful, who think big, who speak my name even when I am not in the room, and who support me when I am at my lowest. There are many individuals—including within our Latino *comunidad*—who will bring you down when you are already struggling.

And I must admit, I would not have a successful business or be able to balance motherhood had I not chosen the right partner—someone who understood my ambitions and quietly supported me from behind as I pursued them.

> *Walk into every room knowing you belong—not because someone told you so, but because your story carved the way for you to stand there.*

But through it all, never trade your *Latinidad* for acceptance. For years, I dimmed my light to fit in. I softened my voice, my culture, my edges—believing it made me more "professional." But our *Latinidad* is not something to hide. It's our power. It carries our ancestors' prayers, their faith, their fire.

Walk into every room knowing you belong—not because someone told you so, but because your story carved the way for you to stand there.

Leave the Door Open

When you finally reach the spaces that once felt out of reach, leave the door open. Hold it wide for the next Latina who's still finding her way.

There's no greater joy than watching another woman rise because you shared your map, your time, or your faith in her. That's how we honor those who came before us—and those who prayed for us before we even knew how to pray for ourselves.

Remember Your Worth

There will be times when you question your worth. You'll push yourself to exhaustion, believing your value is measured by how much you do, how hard you work, and how much you give. That's a dangerous lie.

You are not the hours you work or the titles you earn. You are worthy simply because you exist. When you forget that, look in the mirror and say it out loud:

"Yo soy chingona. Yo valgo. Yo podré."

You are powerful. You are capable. You belong.

And just like that little girl from North Hills—you are still leading, still shining, still becoming everything you once dared to imagine.

THE PATH FORWARD

I still have so much to accomplish. And at a time when my comunidad is under attack, I have never felt a stronger calling to fight back—to challenge the systems that continue to hold us back despite our countless contributions.

I will continue mentoring others, lifting as I climb, and advocating fiercely for the respect and acknowledgment our comunidad deserves. I want Latinas to know that we don't reach positions of power because everything was handed to us. We get there because we refuse to give up—even when we have nothing but faith, grit, and determination to keep going.

I want to be remembered as a Latina who opened doors and fought with courage and conviction—for justice, for equity, for belonging. And when my time here is done, I hope my legacy is this: that every Latin@ who reads my story believes—deep in their bones—that they are capable of greatness. That they belong everywhere.

> *I want to be remembered as a Latina who opened doors and fought with courage and conviction—for justice, for equity, for belonging*

Because we are not guests in this country's story. We are the authors of its future.

We are not defined by our circumstances but by how we choose to respond to them. Your limitations do not define you—your choices do. Keep your eyes on the prize and your heart anchored in purpose. The road may be difficult, but if you refuse to let your circumstances confine you, you will rise into the greatness you were always meant for.

Let go of resentment. Say no when you need to. Embrace the setbacks. Lead with authenticity.

Because when you show up as your full, unapologetic self, you open the door wider for every Latina who comes after you.

We owe it to ourselves—and to our ancestors who paved the way—to keep pushing forward, no matter how hard the road may be. Our stories are proof that when we rise, we lift generations with us.

ABOUT GABRIELA

Gabriela Parra is a dedicated immigration attorney, business owner, and partner at Layde & Parra S.C. in Milwaukee, Wisconsin. With over nine years of experience in immigration law, she provides strategic and compassionate representation to immigrants and refugees navigating some of the most complex legal processes. Known for her meticulous preparation, proactive approach, and creative problem-solving, Gabriela is committed to advocating for her clients with diligence and integrity.

Gabriela's story is deeply rooted in her Chicana identity. Born to Mexican immigrants in Los Angeles, she came of age in the San Fernando Valley during the 1990s—a time when her community was heavily impacted by gang violence, drive-by shootings, and an education system that often discouraged Latino youth from aspiring beyond survival. At a young age, she witnessed firsthand how structural inequities and low expectations worked to limit opportunities for students like her.

When her family relocated to Sturgeon Bay, Wisconsin, a predominantly white neighborhood, the landscape changed, but the barriers persisted. Though she no longer faced the dangers of street violence, she encountered systemic discrimination, cultural isolation, and the reality of being one of the only Latinas in her classrooms. Those experiences instilled in her both resilience and a clear understanding of how deeply inequity can shape lives. Instead of deterring her, these challenges fueled her determination to push forward, pursue higher education, and break into a field where Latinas represent about 3% of attorneys in the United States.

Gabriela earned her Juris Doctor, cum laude, from the University of Wisconsin Law School. She views her professional achievements not simply as personal milestones but as a testament to her parents' sacrifices and the countless barriers she overcame. Her legal career is an extension of her lived experience—driven by a passion to dismantle systemic inequities, amplify immigrant voices, and advocate for policies that create lasting opportunities for underrepresented communities.

Gabriela holds a long-term vision that Latin@s will live in a world where they see their culture, language, and community as a beautiful treasure, and where they can enter every space feeling safe and empowered in their full Latinidad. She is passionate about mentoring others and helping them reclaim their voices as leaders in their communities.

You can learn more and connect with Gabriela at:

Parrg09@gmail.com
https://laydeimmigration.com/
https://www.linkedin.com/in/gabriela-parra-9b312779/

MILAGROS HELENA CARRASQUEL

"Courage isn't loud – it's the quiet decision to move forward."

- Milagros Helena Carrasquel

~ ~ ~

.M. Helena Carrasquel is a strategic connector, intentional leader, and visionary bridge-builder who transforms complexity into clarity and purpose. With more than 20 years of cross-industry experience—from international business and HR to program management and AI strategy—she has dedicated her career to creating people-first cultures where teams feel seen, supported, and empowered to excel. A Latina leader fluent in both systems and human behavior, Helena has guided multinational organizations through high-impact initiatives across technology, risk, learning, and global operations, always grounding her work in empathy and excellence. Today, as Senior Director of AI Operations and Strategy, she continues to champion growth, advocacy, and visibility for the Latina community—using her voice, her expertise, and her deep commitment to collective success to open doors and elevate those who follow.

~ ~ ~

For Antonio, who stands beside me with quiet strength, love, and care. For Ana Helena, so that she always knows her voice and her dreams have a place in this world - to always walk with courage, curiosity, and joy. And to my mentors, Sharon and Mercedes, thank you for opening the door and keeping it open.

LEADING WITH ALIGNMENT: REDEFINING SUCCESS WITH COURAGE AND HEART

THE JOURNEY

As it often happens in life, we seek what we lacked as children. For me, that was stability and roots. That search shaped every decision I've made, personally and professionally.

In many Latin families, there's a deep sense of belonging — generations living close, shared meals, the comfort of presence. My experience was different. My parents' divorce changed everything overnight. What had once felt secure disappeared. One moment, I was surrounded by family; the next, I was in a small apartment with my mother and two siblings, trying to make sense of a world that felt unrecognizable.

Not long after, my mother and I moved to the United States. I was twelve, didn't speak the language, and had no idea what starting over meant. It was both exciting and disorienting. I was curious about this new world, but underneath it all, I carried a quiet sense of displacement. I understood, even then, that opportunity and instability could coexist.

A year later, things got harder. My mother faced financial struggles and sold everything we owned, including our home. When she remarried, we moved again to another state — another world. Soon after, our landlord changed his mind about renting to us, and we had two days to leave. In the chaos, I stayed with my stepfather's family friends. I don't remember much about them, but I remember their kindness — and the moment I promised myself I would never again live in that kind of uncertainty. That night, I understood something that has stayed with me since: stability doesn't happen by chance. It takes intention and effort.

I learned survival skills early. The lesson my grandmother taught me — keep going, no matter what — became my anchor. From a young age, I knew what

I wanted and, more importantly, what I didn't. I wanted to build a life that felt steady, where security and fulfillment weren't opposites. I tried to rely on myself. And I understood no one would hand me that.

That realization gave me focus. I became independent as soon as I could. Every decision — from education to career — followed one principle: build a foundation I could stand on. It wasn't easy or linear, but it gave me direction. Over time, that pursuit of stability evolved into something bigger — the desire to create it not just for myself but for others.

Throughout that journey, I've been shaped by my proverbial village — people who appeared at the right time. I don't believe in coincidence. I believe people show up when they're meant to. My uncle and aunt gave me a glimpse of what a grounded, loving home could feel like. My cousin made me laugh when I needed it most, reminding me that joy is its own kind of resilience.

My career was never linear. In college, I admired the people who knew exactly what they wanted to study or who had a clear vision of the path ahead. I wasn't one of them. I chose International Business because it felt broad enough to help me figure things out as I went. I did well academically, but when graduation came, finding my first job proved more challenging than expected. Eventually, through a series of fortunate events, I landed a role. It wasn't the flashy consulting or banking job many of my peers were celebrating, but it was with a reputable global company that taught me the realities of the working world.

Like many young professionals, that transition was hard—the pace, the expectations, the pressure — all new. Still, I kept moving forward. I earned more responsibility, shifting from managing logistics for car parts to representing an elite tire brand across the Caribbean and LATAM. I knew nothing about tires — not even how to change one — but I embraced the challenge. I traveled extensively, learned quickly, and did well. Still, I knew I didn't want a long-term career in sales.

Then came an unexpected call from the recruiter who had placed me in my first job. Another global company wanted to interview me. The role was similar in function but on a bigger scale: new commodity, distribution leadership, and a team. I went through a demanding interview process and, against the odds, got the job. I knew I wasn't entirely ready for it — but I took it anyway. My boss set a high bar and became a model for the kind of leader I would always look for. Unfortunately, he was reassigned shortly after I joined. Overnight, the ground beneath me shifted.

Things deteriorated quickly. I started feeling sick every morning before work. Meetings were hostile, shouting was normal, and the culture was deeply toxic. No amount of preparation, strategy, or effort made a difference. Eventually, I reached my limit. With no plan and only the clarity that I needed to protect myself, I resigned. Looking back, I know nothing I could have done would have changed the outcome — but at the time, it felt like failure, and I carried that weight for years.

After that, I tried entrepreneurship. My timing couldn't have been worse — it was the beginning of the 2008 financial crisis. That period taught me another layer of self-reliance and a realistic understanding of what it means to carry the full responsibility of earning your own paycheck. I hustled, worked hard, and still couldn't build the stability I needed. Ultimately, I accepted a low-level temp position at a trade association, managing event registrations. It was humbling, but it was also what I needed. I made the role my own, was hired full-time, and eventually led operations. It restored my confidence. But after five years — and after my daughter was born — I knew I was selling myself short by staying.

What I needed was a reinvention, not another job. I began to explore what had always interested me seriously: the intersection of process and human behavior. Graduate school emerged as a way to pivot from international business into HR and Organizational Development. I found a program in a different city, uprooted my family, and began a journey that stretched me to my limits: raising a three-year-old, studying full-time, and learning an entirely new domain.

Halfway through the program, I landed a graduate internship — I was the oldest in the cohort, which felt strange at first — but it was in Talent Management, focusing on organizational culture, exactly what I had hoped for. I worked hard and earned a full-time offer. It felt like a breakthrough, though I later realized the role wasn't a long-term fit. It lived too much in theory for someone who craved execution.

That realization led me to the field that finally brought everything together: Project Management. It became clear that my broad and diverse background — logistics, sales, operations, OD, culture work, and lived leadership experience — gave me a unique advantage. As David Epstein describes in *Range*, I could connect dots that others didn't see. I could speak both the language of systems and the language of people.

Project Management became my sweet spot. I thrived. I grew. I earned my PMP. I was promoted three times. I began leading cross-functional programs and eventually technology portfolios — a space I had never worked in, but once again, I learned quickly. My ability to translate between technologists and the business became invaluable, especially as AI began reshaping the world.

Those opportunities opened doors I didn't even know existed. Today, I lead strategy for a key technology area, working with exceptional teams and doing work that directly impacts people across the organization. It took many pivots, failures, reinventions, and leaps of faith to get here. But every step — even the hardest ones — expanded the path beneath my feet.

Looking back, the final turning points in my career were made possible by the mentors who walked with me through those transitions into Talent Management and, later, into Project Management. They saw capabilities in me that I hadn't yet recognized in myself — a strategic mind, an ability to connect people and processes, a natural inclination for leadership. Their belief created the space for me to believe in myself again. They challenged me, advocated for me, and reminded me that reinvention isn't just possible — it's powerful. Their support helped me step into roles I once questioned my readiness for, and ultimately into a career where I could fully own my strengths, my voice, and my potential. They are a defining part of who I am today.

THE LEARNINGS

In the summer of 2025, I was forced to stop running on autopilot. Life invited me to rise to the moment, and I accepted.

An accident—one wrong step out of the house—forced a complete stop. Multiple fractures in my right leg, followed by surgery, plates, screws, a wheelchair, crutches, and a long stretch of stillness. I had broken down, figuratively and literally. In the ambulance, I cried harder than I had in years, not from pain, but from acceptance. I had been burned out for a long time, moving through life as if momentum alone could hold me together.

I remember saying to myself, I got the message. It wasn't subtle. I had built my life around control, around doing, around maintaining a version of "fine" that looked successful but felt hollow. The illusion of safety — the idea that I could manage my way through anything if I worked hard enough — was gone.

When I learned I'd need surgery, I felt both relief and panic. Relief because I finally had a legitimate reason to stop; panic because stopping meant facing myself. The first wave of grief came when I realized our long-awaited summer trip was gone. It was symbolic — the one thing my family and I had been holding onto was suddenly off the table. I didn't want a life that only felt good in rare, future moments.

So, I stopped. I let the anger and frustration come without softening them. I let myself feel disappointed. Then I asked, quietly but seriously: How do I want to live through this? I could keep spiraling through stress, guilt, and overthinking, or I could sit with what was real — no judgment, no performance.

Recovery gave me time — the one resource I had been trading away without thought. In that time, I saw how much of my life had been driven by fear of slowing down. I started writing what I was learning, not as affirmations or lessons, but as reminders to myself:

- Life doesn't ask for permission. It unfolds whether we're ready or not. Resisting it only adds more frustration.
- Control is an illusion. My instinct to plan and predict everything was keeping me from experiencing anything.
- I don't have to know everything. Curiosity works better than certainty.
- Exploration counts as progress. Not every decision needs an outcome attached to it.

- Perfection isn't the point. I had spent years chasing an ideal version of performance that never arrived.
- Not everything deserves 100%. Some things just need enough.
- Closure is healthy. I learned to recognize when something has run its course — a project, a role, even a version of myself.
- Wishful thinking hides fear. "It would be nice if..." had become my way of avoiding commitment. Rebuilding my sense of yes, I can start with small, grounded action.
- Letting go of "should." Most of my stress came from trying to meet invisible expectations. Replacing "should" with "choose" changed everything.
- Rest is not indulgence. It's where clarity starts.
- I am not alone. Asking for help doesn't make me less capable; it makes me more connected.
- Anger can be useful. It can burn through denial if you let it.
- Toxic positivity is still denial. Pretending everything is fine is not the same as being resilient.
- Gratitude is a recalibration. It brings me back to what's working, not what's missing.

Those months stripped me down to essentials. I had to accept that my old ways of operating — overthinking, overworking, overcontrolling — were not signs of strength. They were coping mechanisms. Letting them go felt like losing parts of my identity, but it made space for something steadier: self-trust.

Rest is not indulgence. It's where clarity starts.

I began therapy again, not to fix myself but to understand my patterns. I started paying attention to the difference between doing something out of fear and doing it out of alignment. I learned to pause before reacting. To ask: What would feel honest right now?

The experience didn't make me a different person; it made me a more accurate one. I stopped mistaking exhaustion for achievement. I began to see rest, reflection, and honesty as forms of strength — not luxuries, but necessities.

By the time I could walk again, I wasn't the same. Not because my leg had healed, but because I had. I no longer needed life to be predictable. I just needed it to be real.

THE INSPIRATION

I come from a large extended family led by strong women. At the center was my grandmother — the person who shaped my understanding of strength, dignity, and perseverance. I grew up with her, and to this day, more than a decade after she passed, I still dream about her often. It's hard to describe how close we were. She was my constant, my grounding force.

Her life was not easy. She lost her mother when she was very young and grew up in a difficult household with a stepmother she described, at times, as "evil." As soon as she was old enough, she left. She married my grandfather by power of attorney and escaped in the middle of the night with a single bag. She left behind her home, her family, and the only world she knew. I think that moment defined her — she made a decision that her life would not be dictated by circumstance.

She didn't talk much about those years, but looking back, I believe that experience built the foundation of her character. She learned that life keeps moving forward, and so must you. Complaining or waiting for things to change was never an option for her. That belief — that you just keep going — became her way of living and the example she set for all of us.

Together, my grandparents built a pharmaceutical business that grew into a successful enterprise and eventually expanded into the food industry. They worked hard, but they also gave back. My mother remembers how people would line up outside their home after my grandfather passed away, just to pay their respects. They had helped many in the community — providing jobs, paying for education, supporting small businesses, and assisting families in making ends meet. For them, success meant having enough to help others.

My grandfather's death at fifty-five changed everything. He died of leukemia right as the business was expanding. His passing devastated my grandmother, but she found a way to keep going. She leaned on the strength she had carried since childhood — the same determination that had gotten her through every difficult moment before. My uncles stepped in to run the company, but she remained involved. That business ended up supporting our extended family for more than a generation.

To me, she wasn't a businesswoman or community figure — she was Abuelita. Nothing in our family happened without her knowing or having a say. She was only five-foot-three, but she had a presence that filled the room. People often said she carried herself with the elegance of a queen, and in many ways, she did. When she entered the dining room, no one sat until she sat. It wasn't out of fear — it was out of respect.

I was the youngest of twenty-five grandchildren. By the time I came along, she was in her seventies, and from the beginning, we were inseparable. After my parents divorced when I was six, she became my safe place. When my mother and I moved to the U.S., I still spent every summer with her until well into my thirties. Those summers were my anchor — a reminder of where I came from and who I wanted to be.

As a teenager, I would join her at the rosary teas she hosted with her friends. I was the youngest person there by at least fifty years, but I loved going. I enjoyed listening to their stories and watching how they interacted. My grandmother was different in that setting — softer, more playful — and it made me appreciate her even more. I think she secretly liked that I went, too. I could tell she was proud to have me there.

Leadership starts at home — in how you care for people, how you show up, and how you take responsibility when things go wrong – and right.

Looking back, I realize how much I learned from simply being around her. She never used the word "leadership," but she practiced it every day. She taught me that leadership starts at home — in how you care for people, how you show up, and how you take responsibility when things go wrong —and when they go right. She taught me that resilience isn't about being unshakable; it's about finding your footing again after life knocks you down.

She also showed me that influence doesn't have to be loud. Her authority came from how she treated others — direct but fair, firm but kind. She understood that people remember how you make them feel. I didn't know it then, but those lessons would later guide me in how I lead teams, navigate challenges, and show up for others.

She passed away at 111, still sharp and active. I wasn't able to be with her physically, but the beautiful soul that was her nurse, Myriam, called to let me know the time had come. I stepped out of a meeting at work to take the call. "She can hear you," she said. I took a deep breath and told her, "Abuelita, soy yo. I want you to know that I am the person I am today because of you. We're all okay. You can rest now."

That was the last time I spoke to her. I didn't cry right away. I held it together — the way she taught me to — but in the quiet moments after, I understood that her lessons would live on through me.

Everything I know about perseverance, grace under pressure, and leading with both empathy and conviction traces back to her. She shaped not only the way I see leadership but also how I understand purpose. She believed our responsibility was to lift others as we move forward. That belief has guided me through every phase of my life — as a daughter, a wife and mother, a professional, and a leader.

Her story isn't just part of my history; it's the foundation of who I am. And while I didn't set out to be an "empowering changemaker," I realize now that the example she set — her courage, her work ethic, her quiet influence — planted that seed long ago.

Another source of inspiration was a mentor who helped me confront the most brutal truth — that sometimes the biggest obstacle isn't circumstance, it's ourselves. She pushed me to see beyond the patterns that held me back and to understand that self-awareness, not perfection, is the growth path. Another cousin showed me the importance of self-care, and that strength lies in authenticity — in the courage to face who we are becoming.

And through it all, I've had one constant: a dear friend I met when I was six, who became family in every sense. She lives with honesty and heart and always appears when I need her most — often before I realize it. Her ability to evolve, to face life with courage and humor, continues to inspire me every day.

These powerful Latinas, and many others, have been quiet architects in my life. They remind me that strength doesn't mean doing everything alone — it means allowing others to stand beside you. Their presence reinforced what I learned long ago: stability isn't a place; it's a state of being, built one honest, deliberate choice at a time.

THE ADVICE

If there's one thing life has taught me, it's that the path is rarely straightforward. And that's not a flaw — it's the point. Growth doesn't happen in straight lines; it occurs in the moments we allow ourselves to take a turn we didn't plan for.

Safety can be comforting, but it can also keep us small. That can make change feel like failure, when in truth, it's often the invitation we need most. There can be many right paths. Being open to them requires courage — the kind that comes from trusting yourself enough to start again. Sometimes you recognize you're ready for a new direction; other times you move forward simply because staying where you are no longer fits. Either way, movement is growth.

That said, while the path can twist and change, direction matters. You don't need to know every step ahead, but it helps to have a sense of what "your north" looks like — a general idea of the life you want to build. A destination gives purpose to progress. Without it, the journey can feel endless, and what once felt like resilience can become exhaustion. I've learned that having a target isn't about control; it's about clarity. It allows you to say no to what's misaligned and yes to what feels true.

It's also crucial to know when it's time to exit survival mode. Many of us, especially those who've faced instability, learn to operate from a constant state of alertness. It helps us endure — but it can quietly become the only way we know how to exist. After a while, the habit of surviving takes over the ability to live. The shift comes when you choose to move from survival to intention — to live not just to get through the day, but to shape it consciously.

If I could tell my younger self one thing, it would be to accept all of herself sooner — the good, the bad, the messy, the proud. We spend so much time editing ourselves to fit expectations that we forget wholeness comes from integration, not perfection. Ignoring the parts of ourselves we dislike only gives them more power. What defines us isn't the sum of our traits, but the choices we make about how to use them. Self-acceptance isn't complacency; it's clarity.

I would also tell her that the people around you matter more than you think — and that they will change. Who you surround yourself with in one season might not belong in the next, and that's okay. Growth naturally redefines connection. The right people won't compete with your evolution; they'll challenge and celebrate it.

Trusting your gut is another skill that deserves protection. It's easy to lose touch with intuition when surrounded by noise, expectations, or hierarchy. But that quiet inner voice — the one that nudges you toward or away from something — rarely lies. It's the wisdom you earn from lived experience. Whenever I've ignored it, I've paid the price. Whenever I've honored it, things have aligned in ways logic couldn't predict.

And to any woman stepping into leadership or navigating complex environments, remember this: confidence is a muscle. You build it by using it, even when it trembles. Nurture your strong, assertive voice. If someone is uncomfortable with it, that discomfort is theirs, not yours. There will always be bullies — in schoolyards, boardrooms, and sometimes behind polished titles. The best way to disarm them is not by matching their energy, but by standing firm in yours. Kindness and composure confuse the unkind. Authentic confidence disarms those who rely on intimidation.

I've learned that courage isn't the absence of fear; it's the decision to move anyway. The difference between those who stay still and those who grow isn't certainty — it's the willingness to take the next step, whether the ground ahead is known or not.

Over time, you learn that power doesn't mean dominance — it implies ownership. Ownership of your time, your story, your choices, your mistakes, and your growth. You learn to stop waiting for permission to be yourself.

So my advice is this: stay curious, stay grounded, and stay kind — especially to yourself. Life will ask you to shed versions of yourself you once thought were permanent. Let it. You'll find that what's left isn't less of you, but the truest version you were always meant to be.

THE PATH FORWARD

I'm currently walking a new path — one I had been preparing for, consciously and unconsciously, for years. It's a path defined not by expectation but by choice. I'm aiming to realize my potential without fear, and to give myself permission to design this next chapter from a place of strength, generosity, and advocacy — for myself and for others.

For a long time, I defined success by achievement — by outcomes, recognition, and delivery. Today, I define it by alignment: doing meaningful work that lifts others and expands access to opportunity. My purpose is shifting from "how far can I go" to "how many can I bring with me."

If there's one thing my journey has taught me, it's that growth is not linear, and strength doesn't always look like endurance. Sometimes, it is pausing, recalibrating, and permitting yourself to start again. The path to fulfillment isn't about perfection or constant motion — it's about self-awareness and intentional choice. Success built on external expectations eventually collapses, but success built on authenticity and courage becomes sustainable.

I want my story to remind other Latinas that their power doesn't come from proving themselves — it comes from being themselves. Our stories matter not because they're perfect, but because they're real. Each of us carries a collection of experiences, lessons, and contradictions that, when shared, can open doors for others. We can't control where we start, but we can decide how we show up and what we create along the way.

My call to action is simple: permit yourself. Allow yourself to take up space, to evolve, to start over, to rest, to lead, and to dream audaciously. The world benefits when Latinas stop asking for permission to exist in full color.

What's next for me is about amplification — of impact, of community, of voice. I'm focused on creating environments where others can rise: building pathways for leadership, advocating for inclusion, and mentoring those navigating their own turning points. I want to help redefine what leadership looks like — to prove that empathy, strategy, and humanity are not competing forces but the foundation of sustainable success.

The legacy I hope to leave isn't a list of accomplishments. It's the ripple effect of encouragement — women who feel seen, supported, and capable of designing their own futures. I want my journey to serve as proof that you can build stability without losing curiosity, lead with conviction without losing compassion, and chase growth without losing yourself.

So, to every Latina reading this: keep moving toward what calls you, even if the path isn't clear. You don't need to have everything figured out to take the next step. Trust yourself enough to move, even when the outcome isn't guaranteed. That's where transformation begins — not in knowing, but in choosing. The courage to take that next step — in faith, in truth, in your own voice — is the legacy we all leave behind.

ABOUT HELENA

M. HELENA CARRASQUEL is a strategic connector and intentional leader, fluent in bridging ideas and people by translating complexity into practical steps that drive successful results. With more than 20 years of cross-industry experience, she is dedicated to fostering people-first cultures where individuals and teams feel valued, supported, and empowered to thrive.

Helena began her career with a B.B.A. in International Business, managing logistics and operations for multinational corporations across the Caribbean and Latin American markets. Born in Caracas, Venezuela, Helena later moved to the United States in 1989. She completed her early education in Ohio and Tennessee, attended college in Louisiana, and began her professional career in Florida. Ultimately, she settled in Charlotte, North Carolina—together, these experiences shaped her adaptability, perspective, and leadership approach. Inspired to bridge process with human behavior, she earned a Master of Science in Organization Development and transitioned into HR at a Fortune 100 financial services firm. She later advanced into Program Management, earning her PMP® and leading high impact programs in technology, risk and compliance, learning, and pay and transition portfolios with cross-functional and multi-country teams—gaining critical insight into what drives successful deliveries.

Today, as Sr. Director for AI Operations and Strategy, Helena continues to be a strategic connector, finding pathways to create and share valuable learned insights, experiences, and collective knowledge, all with the purpose of fostering growth, advocacy, visibility, opportunities and success for the Latina Community.

To learn more and connect with Helena at:

www.linkedin.com/in/helena-carrasquel-pmp

DR. LAURA PRIETULA

"Every decision is an act of legacy."

- Dr. Laura Prietula

~ ~ ~

Dr. Laura Prietula is a visionary technology and leadership catalyst whose 30-year career bridges innovation, transformation, and human-centered leadership. A global educator, executive coach, and champion for women in STEM, she has empowered countless emerging and senior leaders to navigate complexity with clarity, courage, and purpose. Her work spans Fortune 100 companies and one of the largest health technology modernization initiatives in the United States, where she leads mission-driven solutions that strengthen communities and improve lives. With a gift for creating psychologically safe spaces, Laura helps individuals align values, identity, and action—unlocking presence, resilience, and authentic leadership. Her journey reflects a deep commitment to shaping the future of technology and guiding the next generation to lead boldly, inclusively, and with unwavering integrity.

~ ~ ~

To my sister, who demonstrates selflessness and love every day.
To my brother who cares beyond limits.
To my parents, who taught me how to love and live freely.
To my husband, who has given me wings and propelled my flight.
To my kids for their unparalleled love and for being my inspiration.
To my extended family for always supporting me.
To my ancestors who have shown us how to live.
To future leaders: be fearless, bold, and passionate. The world is waiting for your light.
For those who rise with purpose and lead with heart —
may your courage inspire action, your legacy begin today,
and your work always serve the good of humanity.

LEADING FOR THE LOVE OF PEOPLE: LEGACY AS A DAILY PRACTICE

THE JOURNEY

I was born and raised in Mexico City, surrounded by love, laughter, and learning. My dad was a surgeon, and my mom worked in nuclear medicine. They both loved what they did, and they always said that education was the only inheritance no one could ever take away from us. In our home, learning was part of daily life—just like dinner around the table or the smell of coffee in the morning.

We went to American and British schools, took piano and art lessons, and spent our afternoons in gymnastics or karate. My parents believed in structure, and also in curiosity. They wanted us to understand the world through people and experiences, not just textbooks. Before we traveled abroad, my dad would say, "You must know your own country first." So while some of my friends were visiting Disneyland, I was exploring Chichén Itzá, walking through ancient ruins, and learning the stories behind every stone. Those trips taught me that to understand people, you must first understand where you come from. Understanding our roots gives strength to our wings.

My grandmothers were both matriarchs in their own ways. My dad's mother believed in discipline and precision. She even had desks at home for us during the summers—no playing until a math workbook was done. My mom's mother taught in the open air of Mexico City's markets. She would take us to buy fruit and vegetables, showing us how to choose the best, how to talk to people, and how to negotiate fairly and with respect. From her, I learned that empathy and discernment can go hand in hand.

And then there was our family "sport"—people watching. We would sit together and observe, inventing stories about the people walking by. My parents would ask, "What do you think this person might need today?" or "Where do you think they're going?" They rarely asked "why." To them, "why" sounded too judgmental. They believed "what," "where," and "when" opened the door to curiosity. That minor distinction shaped how I see the world. I learned that asking the right questions is not about finding fault—it is about understanding.

My sister has always been my loudest cheerleader, my first call for any celebration or challenge. My brother, my quiet anchor—we lived together through college and even started a company side by side. We share the same belief that love is the most enduring currency. Together, we can face anything.

My life has been one of privilege—not of wealth, but of grounding. Growing up in Mexico, I saw corruption and classism woven into the fabric of daily life. But within our family, we built a different world—one based on honesty, unity, and purpose. My parents taught us that fairness and kindness were choices, even when the world did not always reflect them.

Those lessons became our compass. We learned how to navigate complexity without losing compassion, how to rise above without looking away. We learned to observe, to think strategically, and to act with purpose. We understood early that strength does not come from confrontation—it comes from discernment. I learned to read people and situations before reacting, and to approach every decision with both courage and care. That combination became my foundation for leading boldly and wisely—curiosity anchored in integrity.

That anchoring in love also gave me the courage to make one of the boldest decisions of my life. I left my country, my friends, my family, my job, and the lifestyle I knew to be with the love of my life. It was a leap of faith—one grounded in everything I had been taught about trust, resilience, and partnership. More than thirty years later, that choice remains one of the best I have ever made. It taught me that courage can be quiet and strategic; it is not about defiance but about choosing alignment with what matters most. That choice became my first true act of leadership—the leadership of self through conviction, clarity, and love.

That foundation gave me the confidence to take bold steps later in life, to analyze before acting, to ask questions before deciding, and to trust my instincts when stepping into the unknown. It became the rhythm of who I am—curious, courageous, and deeply human. Every role I have taken, every culture I have embraced, and every challenge I have faced has been guided by those early lessons. Education opens doors, empathy builds bridges, and love—always—keeps us steady through it all.

The seed of my professional journey was planted in middle school, when I began tutoring elementary students in science. I found joy in helping others understand something new—it was my first glimpse of how knowledge can empower. By junior high, I was teaching English to senior executives at a pharmaceutical company in Mexico, helping them communicate more effectively with their international colleagues. And by high school, I was competing—and winning—national awards in mathematics and other subjects, realizing that curiosity and discipline could take me far. These experiences shaped how I would approach my professional career later on: with a deep belief that learning, communication, and human connection can transform lives. It taught me that hierarchy and titles are not what prove our worth - our talents, skills, soul, and our making are what prove who we are and what we bring to the table. I focus on bringing "who I am" to "what I do." I need to respect and love myself first, just as we had to discover our own country (Mexico) before we went exploring elsewhere. Knowing who you are helps you embody and embrace yourself fully and shines throughout your life.

During college, my professional career officially began. I joined one of the top four global consulting firms and later worked across supply chain, manufacturing, and technology, covering industries as diverse as steel, cement, glass, and automotive. My curiosity drew me toward solving complex problems and leading through change. I never searched for a "job for a woman" or a "job for a Hispanic." I looked for roles where my mind, skills, and values fit. I learned that courage is not always loud; sometimes it is the quiet determination to enter spaces others might hesitate to enter and to deliver excellence that speaks for itself.

As my career progressed, I realized I was consistently drawn to the edges of innovation—places where technology, people, and possibility collide. Whether it was early bedside computing, XML and CCOW before they were mainstream, or preparing healthcare systems for Y2K, I gravitated toward problems that required courage, clarity, and experimentation. Being an immigrant and often the "only Latina in the room" sharpened my ability to see around corners. I learned to assess risks quickly, ask questions others were afraid to ask, and bring people together around new ideas. Innovation did not intimidate me; complacency did. I am known to consistently challenge people, make them uncomfortable with being normal. I love being weird.

After my son was born, everything in my life shifted. When he was only two weeks old, he became ill and required hospitalization and surgery. In that moment, my professional ambition did not disappear—it simply reframed itself. My focus changed. My purpose expanded. Loving and protecting my family became the center of my life, and with that clarity, I chose to trade my business career for a stay-at-home career. Those years were not a step back; they were a deliberate investment in what mattered most. I was learning a different form of leadership—one rooted in care, presence, intuition, and the quiet strength of nurturing others.

A few years later, a friend came to visit, and I invited her for dinner. What began as a simple meal became an unexpected job interview, and eventually, a job offer. I have always believed that God places me where I am needed most, and this moment felt purposeful. After careful reflection, I accepted the opportunity to join the federal government. That decision opened the door to the next significant chapter of my career—and to a deeper calling to serve at a national scale.

After nearly fifteen years in federal service, I made a choice that surprised many: I stepped away. I had led major system-of-systems transformations at the Department of Veterans Affairs (VA), served at the behest of the VA Secretary, and guided teams through recovery efforts after Hurricane Katrina and Superstorm Sandy. People sought my counsel, my leadership, and my ability to stabilize complexity. And yet, internally, I felt a truth rising: **I was no longer learning.** I was delivering results at an elevated level, but my own growth had plateaued. My curiosity—my lifelong compass—was telling me it was time to evolve.

Returning to the private sector reignited something in me. In two years, I built a new division from the ground up and increased profit by 78%. It was energizing to create again, to innovate, to stretch. Even then, VA continued to seek my support. I realized I wanted to be part of the envisioned transformation, so I returned—this time with a deeper understanding of what I needed to thrive.

That clarity led me to pursue my doctorate. The decision had nothing to do with collecting degrees or claiming a title. It was about learning, relevance, and refusing complacency. It was a promise I made to myself—to invest in my mind with the same intensity that my parents invested in my education, and never become obsolete.

THE LEARNINGS

Pursuing my doctorate became my commitment to continual growth, intellectual rigor, and staying prepared for the challenges ahead. Always keep learning. Always keep evolving.

The process demanded focus, resilience, quiet courage, and the ability to carry both ambition and vulnerability. As a Latina immigrant, earning that degree carried emotional weight. It affirmed that I belonged in spaces where decisions shape systems, organizations, and futures.

One of my most formative experiences came when a Senior Vice President for Information Technology at a healthcare organization invited me to join his team as a senior assistant. That role placed me at the heart of the organization's digital transformation. We implemented bedside computing in a dialysis unit when most hospitals were still operating on paper. Physicians could approve verbal orders from home over dial-up connections using clunky tokens, and we were experimenting with XML and CCOW long before they became standard. That experience awakened my lifelong fascination with emerging technology—what I now call leading and leaning forward.

My rise into federal leadership became the bridge between every lesson learned along the way. Leading modernization for one of the largest healthcare systems in the world has been a profound responsibility and honor —one grounded in service. Federal leadership requires a steady hand, a clear mind, and a deep respect for people whose lives are directly impacted by your decisions. I often reflect on my journey from Mexico to the USA, and I see a common thread: the courage to start, the discipline to adapt, and the love of people that anchors every choice I make.

Progress demands courage—leading at the edge of innovation requires both boldness and discipline. Being strategic about risk means asking, *What can we learn from this?* Instead of *What if it fails?*

It also taught me one of the most important lessons of leadership: if you tell people it is acceptable to fail, you must also design the infrastructure that allows them to recover. Declaring "it is safe to fail" without creating systems of support is not empowerment—it is neglect. Building that failure infrastructure became a cornerstone of how I lead. It means being bold, but not careless; visionary, yet grounded in structure.

Life reminded me that courage takes many forms. I faced another profound test—breast cancer. My mother and my nephew both passed away from cancer, so the diagnosis carried emotional weight that words cannot describe. I survived, but the experience forever changed my lens on life. It taught me that every day is a gift, and that living fully means aligning your actions with who you are. Professionally, that realization became simple and powerful: love what you do and do what you love. There is no time to spend on work that lacks meaning. I choose roles that reflect my values, challenge my intellect, and allow me to serve others.

Across decades, industries, and titles, the pattern has remained the same—learn, adapt, grow, and lead with empathy. Transformation is not a destination; it is a mindset. We live, we learn, we lead, we grow, and above all, we do it for the love of people.

THE INSPIRATION

I often say that I am a compilation of the people I have met—my soul, a kaleidoscope of colors shaped by every interaction, every story, and every act of kindness or courage I have witnessed. My inspiration comes from people—those close to me and those I have admired from afar—who have chosen to live authentically and lead with purpose.

The most significant sources of inspiration in my life have always been my family. My parents modeled integrity, discipline, and compassion. My sister and brother remind me that unconditional love is strength, not softness. My husband and children keep me grounded, teaching me that love must always be at the center of everything I do. Their laughter, resilience, and quiet support fuel me more than any title or accolade ever could.

That early example of integrity and authenticity shaped what I admire in others. I am drawn to people who live with honesty, courage, and a deep sense of purpose—whether in art, leadership, or everyday life. I have long admired artists like Frida Kahlo, who turned pain into beauty and vulnerability into power; Nelson Mandela, whose grace and forgiveness redefined leadership and humanity; and performers like Stevie Wonder, Tina Turner, Boy George, Cyndi Lauper, Simply Red, Prince, and David Bowie, who showed us that individuality is art and authenticity is freedom. They lived without apology—celebrating difference and reminding us that expression itself can be an act of courage.

They were willing to act boldly in the face of uncertainty. They remind me that leadership—whether on a stage, in a community, or within an organization—is not about playing it safe; it is about moving forward with intention, even when the outcome is unknown.

Beyond their creativity, what fascinates me is the human mind—the choices we make, the contradictions we live with, and the stories we tell to make sense of them. I have always loved puzzles, mysteries, and narratives that challenge how we see the world. I am drawn to Agatha Christie's novels and the sharp mind of her Hercule Poirot, to the complexity of television shows like *Criminal Minds*, and to documentaries about mysteries or long-lost treasures. Whether it is a pirate's hidden map or a series exploring the psychology of a criminal, I watch to imagine what it was like to live in their time, to think as they thought, and to understand the layers of human behavior. For me, curiosity is not passive—it is strategic. It is how I connect, analyze, and grow.

There is a moment in every leader's life when the weight of responsibility becomes clear—not as a burden, but as a calling. One of those moments happened to me during a visit to a Department of Defense (DoD) installation. As a member of the Senior Executive Service, my military officer equivalent would be a General. I do not focus on titles, yet I carry the responsibility with deep respect.

When I arrived, DoD officials welcomed me and rang the bell to signal that a senior official was on-site. The executive conference room was arranged in a U-shape, with the emblems of every branch of service displayed on the walls. Beyond the table were rows of additional seats—those "not at the table," yet still essential to the mission.

When the meeting ended, a man seated in the middle of the left row walked straight toward me with purpose. His expression was serious, almost urgent.

"Ma'am," he began, "I want to thank you for inviting me to this meeting."

I smiled and replied, "You are always invited to these meetings," and I started to add something about how we are all one team when he gently interrupted.

He took a steadying breath and said, "I…really wanted to thank you for letting me see what someone who looks like me can aspire to become." He was Hispanic.

His words reached directly into my heart. I was momentarily speechless. A wave of humility, strength, and responsibility filled me. In that instant, I understood that leadership is not about the seat at the table—it is about the possibility you represent to someone else.

I offered to mentor him right then and there. It felt natural. It felt right. It felt like a purpose.

He accepted with gratitude, and over time, I watched him grow into his own leadership—lifting others, shaping his teams, and becoming the example he once needed to see.

That experience reaffirmed something I hold as truth:

> We have an impact every single day—whether we notice it or not.
> Whether we intend it or not.
> Someone is always watching.
> Someone is always learning.
> Someone is finding courage through our choices.
> Own that influence.
> Live it with purpose.
> Pass it on with love.

For every story that exposes the complexity of the human mind, there are others that celebrate its beauty and simplicity. There is one I often carry in my heart about a Mexican artisan who made her living weaving baskets. One day, a tourist offered to buy her entire inventory at once. To his surprise, she refused. When he asked why, she explained that weaving baskets and selling them allowed her to share her story and connect with many people. Selling them all at once would mean sharing her story with only one person. Her words stayed with me. She gave her work meaning and purpose—it was never about the sale; it was about the connection.

That same search for meaning and connection guides my work today. I seek value in everything I do and strive to create impact that endures beyond the moment. I aspire to be a transcendental leader—someone whose influence continues through others long after the conversation ends. If even one person is positively changed by my words, my work, or my presence, then my purpose has been fulfilled.

THE ADVICE

As I reflect on my journey, I see a pattern—curiosity, courage, and care working together. None of my steps were accidental; they were intentional, guided by purpose and a belief that growth happens when thought and action meet. These are the ideas I return to again and again—the ones I share with students, teams, and leaders navigating change.

Lead boldly, but with clarity.

Boldness is not volume; it is vision with direction. I have learned that strength shows up in preparation, in how we ask questions, and in how we listen before deciding. Every meaningful transformation requires a moment when someone says, "Let's try." Lead with that courage, but pair it with empathy, foresight, and accountability.

Stay in motion through learning.

Learning is my constant. Degrees, mentors, mistakes—all of them shaped me. Investing in your own growth is not a luxury; it is leadership hygiene. Curiosity keeps you relevant, and reflection keeps you grounded.

Do meaningful work, fully present.

Work is not just a job—it is an extension of who we are. Target environments and projects that align with your values and energy. When you engage with purpose, excellence follows naturally. If the work does not challenge or fulfill you, redesign it or move on. Life is too short for misaligned effort.

Curiosity keeps you relevant, and reflection keeps you grounded

Design for recovery, not perfection.

Innovation lives in experimentation. I believe in building what I call a *failure infrastructure*—systems that help people learn safely, adapt quickly, and try again. Leaders do not eliminate mistakes; they create environments where mistakes become data, not defeat.

Lead for the love of people.

Everything begins and ends with people. Technology changes, organizations evolve, but humanity remains constant. See others. Hear them. Lift them. Leadership is not about being followed; it is about leaving others stronger than when they met you.

Growth, for me, has never been a straight line—it has been a rhythm of reflection, learning, and action. I often take quiet moments at the start or end of the day to ask, *What did I learn today? What did I give?* That practice keeps me grounded, intentional, and grateful for the opportunity to lead and serve.

THE PATH FORWARD

I believe we leave our legacy every day—not thirty years from now, not when we retire, and certainly not when we are gone. Legacy lives in our choices, our tone, our empathy, our follow-through, and our service to each other. It is present in how we show up, how we listen, and how we lift others.

Legacy lives in our choices, our tone, our empathy, our follow-through, and our service to each other.

Every interaction is an opportunity to make a difference. It doesn't require a stage or a title; it requires intention. What did you do today to change someone's life positively? Did you mentor a colleague, offer encouragement, or create space for another voice to be heard? Those are the quiet moments that shape who we are and how we are remembered.

I often say that every decision is an act of legacy. It's more than a statement—it's a philosophy of intentional leadership. It reflects the discipline to think strategically, the courage to act decisively, the vision to see beyond the moment, and the empathy to recognize that every choice leaves an imprint on others.

To me, leadership is not about control or recognition—it is about helping others find their own strength and voice. You can be both analytical and kind, bold and grounded, decisive and deeply human. True transformation begins from within, by knowing yourself and aligning your actions with that truth.

I have always been driven by connection—the belief that every achievement is built on both courage and community. From an early age, I learned to see people—not just their titles or circumstances, but their essence, their effort, and their humanity. That practice shaped how I lead and how I live.

I celebrate accomplishments and failures; however, I take special care in celebrating connections. Accomplishments may fade with time, failures will come and go, but nurtured connections endure. They continue to grow, to inspire, and to strengthen the fabric that holds us together.

My call to you—especially to every Latina reading this—is to lead courageously and compassionately in your own sphere of influence. Take the time to know yourself deeply, invest in your growth, and stand firm in your values. Do not wait for permission to act or for conditions to be perfect. The moment to lead is always now.

Be the person who notices others. The one who listens fully. The one who gives credit generously. The one who believes that love, when paired with strategy and discipline, can transform any organization, any team, any life.

We each have the power to create impact—one thoughtful decision, one kind conversation, one bold step at a time. Legacy is not something we leave behind; it is something we live—each day, through the love we give and the people we lift.

ABOUT DR. LAURA

Dr. Laura Prietula is a technology and leadership catalyst who inspires individuals and organizations to navigate complexity with purpose and confidence. With over 30 years of experience across the public and private sectors, she blends executive and career coaching with deep expertise in digital transformation, personal branding, and organizational leadership.

A committed advocate for women in leadership and STEM, Laura has helped countless young women grow into bold, impactful leaders—opening doors, building trust, and encouraging them to shape the future of technology with courage and authenticity. She believes that inclusive leadership is not just an aspiration, but a responsibility.

As a coach and advisor, Laura empowers emerging and senior leaders to align values, identity, and action—developing clarity, presence, and resilience. She creates psychologically safe spaces where individuals and teams can explore their leadership identity, embrace change, and unlock their full potential.

In her public service career, she leads one of the largest health technology modernization initiatives in the United States, driving large-scale, mission-critical technical solutions that improve lives and strengthen communities. She has also guided Fortune 100 organizations through business-aligned technology evolution across healthcare, finance, and manufacturing.

Laura also serves as a global visiting faculty member, teaching digital transformation, analytics, and leadership at top-tier institutions around the world. Her work is driven by a deep commitment to shaping the next generation of leaders—equipping them with the insight, agility, and values needed to lead wisely in a rapidly changing world.

She holds credentials from the International Coaching Federation (ICF), the European Mentoring and Coaching Council (EMCC), PROSCI (Change Management), and the Program Management Institute (PgMP and PMP).

You can learn more and connect with Laura at:

www.linkedin.com/in/LauraPrietula
www.SeldonAdvisors.com
Laura@SeldonAdvisors.com

LETICIA CORONADO-PADILLA

"Becoming is not a single moment; it is the quiet courage within you that whispers even in darkness, to keep becoming."

- Leticia Coronado-Padilla

~ ~ ~

Leticia Padilla is a seasoned financial strategist and entrepreneur whose 25+ year career reflects unwavering resilience, vision, and dedication to empowering others through financial excellence. As Founder of Real Finance Group LLC, she has become a trusted advisor to business owners and nonprofits, helping them strengthen operations, drive growth, and achieve long-term sustainability. A proud DePaul University alumna with advanced degrees and certifications in accounting, finance, and entrepreneurship, Leticia blends deep technical expertise with a heart for service. Her journey is a powerful example of how perseverance, integrity, and purpose-driven leadership can transform challenges into opportunities—and build lasting impact across communities and industries.

~ ~ ~

This is dedicated to my little sister, Helen Coronado, and every woman who has a dream and has faced personal challenges and feeling unseen, unheard, or unworthy; to remind them they are valuable, capable, and enough.

BECOMING –
FROM SURVIVAL TO PURPOSE BY RESCUING MYSELF

THE JOURNEY

My journey began long before I understood what the word "journey" even meant. My first journey actually started in 1974, when my mother made the brave decision to leave her parents and siblings behind in central Mexico and immigrate to the United States. I was only six months old when she carried me across the border, chasing the hope of a better life. She didn't have much, just faith, determination, and seven children who depended on her strength.

By 1978, my parents had separated, and my mother was left to raise us on her own through the hardships of the 1970s and 80s. I watched her fight every day against poverty and exhaustion, holding our family together through sheer willpower. The challenges she faced were painful to witness; her sacrifices often felt unbearable, but she somehow found ways to keep us fed, sheltered, and safe. Her resourcefulness became our survival.

As a child, I watched her dreams quietly fade away. The woman who once had her own hopes and ambitions replaced them with a single goal: to make sure her children could live the American dream. She gave up on herself so ours could exist. Those years left an imprint on me. I grew up knowing that I had a responsibility to make her sacrifices count.

By the time I reached high school, I had already made a silent promise to myself and to her that I would not disappoint her. I decided I wouldn't have children until I could stand on my own two feet, buy a home where she could live comfortably, and build a career that would allow her to retire from the factory work that had worn her down for years.

As the second-youngest of seven, I found myself in a unique position when all my older siblings moved out to start their own families. I was the one left behind to help my mother with the bills and watch over her. At that time, I was attending college full-time and working full-time as an accountant. The weight of responsibility was heavy, but it also taught me independence, resilience, and discipline. Yet, I still wanted to become a good daughter.

My mother eventually became a grandmother to more than twenty grandchildren, her once small family expanding into a legacy she had built through her endurance. I was the last to leave her home, marrying at twenty-six. It was a bittersweet milestone—one that marked both my independence and the end of the start of my own dreams.

College was a defining chapter in my life. My dream is to become an actual college student. While working toward my bachelor's degree, it was never easy juggling a full-time job and evening classes, but I was determined to finish — one course, one year at a time including summers. Education became my lifeline, the one thing that could promise a future of stability and freedom.

Growing up, I had seen too many women trapped in unhappy marriages, unable to leave because they were financially dependent on a spouse. I promised myself that it would never be my story. I didn't just want to survive; I wanted to thrive — to live with purpose and to become someone others could look up to.

I had dreams, but at that time, I had no roadmap, no mentors, no real friends, no resources, no confidence, and no money. What I did have was a deep desire to make something of myself. My motivation came from the few people who believed in me: my finance teacher, but especially, my oldest friend of 26 years, Jason Chan. We were colleagues when he first told me I had potential for greatness. I couldn't see it myself, but our friendship passed the test of time. His support, encouragement, friendship, and advice have helped me for the last 26 years. Those simple words of encouragement stayed with me.

What kept me going was remembering how, as a young child, I watched my mother work two or three jobs at a time for $2.50 to $3.00 an hour — a powerful reminder of why I needed to keep moving forward. Her sacrifices and my supporters' faith in me were the quiet voices that carried me through the toughest moments, especially when self-doubt whispered that I wasn't enough. I knew exactly what I didn't want my life to become, and that clarity kept my mind steady and my determination strong.

Looking back, I realize that my journey wasn't just about escaping poverty or fulfilling a daughter's promise. It was about becoming the woman my mother had unknowingly raised me to be – a woman who stands tall in the face of adversity, who doesn't give up, and who believes that resilience is inherited through love and sacrifice.

Every struggle, every long night of work and study, every moment of uncertainty built the foundation of the life I live today. My journey began with a mother's courage to cross borders and a daughter's determination to honor that sacrifice. The lessons I learned in those early years, responsibility, hard work, and gratitude, became the pillars of my character. And realizing I deserved happiness too.

And as I write this now, I can't help but cry. The emotions are heavy, but also full of pride and disbelief at how far I've come. From a six-month-old child brought across a border with nothing but hope, to the smart, stronger 52-year-old woman I am today, I have carried my mother's strength every step of the way.

As I look back, I see that every chapter of my life has been both a blessing and a lesson. Some of my most challenging moments came not from what life handed me, but from the choices I made along the way. I've learned that when something no longer serves us, we must have the courage to pivot, walk away, or face our fears to realign with our old and new purposes and move forward. We have to, we must be unapologetic. Life is fragile and fleeting, and none of us is promised tomorrow. We are all living on borrowed time, and what matters most is how we use it, how we rise, adapt, and continue becoming the best version of ourselves. I have lived several versions of myself, and that was just the beginning.

THE LEARNINGS

Life has a way of forcing us to look in the mirror when we least expect it. For me, the most pivotal struggles, the ones that broke me open and shaped who I became, were also the most painful. Those times taught me that bad things will happen, people will hurt us, and sometimes we unknowingly attract the wrong ones because we forget our own worth.

After earning my bachelor's degree, I married an architect named Rick Vasquez in 2000, someone I had met very young during my undergraduate years and dated for seven years. I believed at the time it was the natural next step in life. It was the timeline also embedded in my head by society and my culture. All my young life, I stayed straight to follow the rules, expectations, laws, and to fit in with America's family narrative. Instead, it became the hardest lesson of all.

My marriage turned into a trap, a life shared with a narcissist who sought control, belittled, and isolated me. His dream of being a big shot with a big house and fancy car meant he needed a double-income household. He resented my ambition, my ongoing career success, and my determination to keep building skills, learning, and growing. I see now that he was intimidated by my growth.

After we married and I began pursuing my master's degree, the insults and degradation started. The physical attacks followed, and his true colors became unmistakably clear. Over the years, his words slowly chipped away at my confidence and my self-worth. He made me believe I was stupid, unworthy of love, and undeserving of the dreams I aspired to. I didn't see it at first; I just kept trying to stay safe long enough to finish my degree and leave. I thought that if I stayed out of sight, I could go before it was too late.

No one knew what was happening. His family had no idea, and mine only knew we argued because I sometimes left the house for days at a time to escape on a weekend. He warned me that if I ever told his family about the brutal abuse or showed them my bruises, he would kill me. I believed him after learning of other stories of this coming true. This all the while the story of the murder of Laci Peterson on the news. To this day, the dentists asked what happened to my jaw. Around this family and his friends, he was a completely different person—charming, composed, and adored. In their eyes, he could do no wrong. We all should learn to recognize those narcissistic behaviors in relationships.

Meanwhile, in October of 2006, tragedy struck and shattered everything I thought I knew about pain, faith, and the meaning of life. My youngest sister,

Helen Coronado—so beautiful, a wonderful mom, full of life, with her own ambitions and dreams—was killed in a crossfire between rival gangs while simply walking down the street. It was all over the news. I resented how the coverage reduced her to a statistic.

At the hospital, I received the official news, and the earth disappeared beneath my feet. I remember feeling as though something inside me cracked—deeper than I knew my soul could go. My mind froze to protect itself from reality. My heart couldn't connect to my mind. My heart crumbled.

I remember it all — the funeral, the court hearings, showing up at work and at home — yet through it all, something kept tugging at me: "Hey, something's wrong here." A small voice inside is urging me to wake up. Someone once told me I was living on autopilot, and they were right. I went through the motions of life, but inside I was completely numb.

In the chaos of grief, I turned to Rick for comfort. During our time of "reconciling," I asked him for support to attend counseling with me, hoping to find healing in the marriage together. Instead, counseling revealed his betrayal, multiple affairs that had been hidden behind my back. My suspicions were real. His promises of stopping the abuse were fake. My grieving angered him because it took attention away from him, so he continued to assault me.

The emotional and physical abuse, the infidelity, and the constant belittling became unbearable. One day, when I truly feared for my life and felt all my energy drain away, something shifted. I began planning my escape—quickly, quietly, determined to reclaim the woman I had lost and to save the inner child who had vowed never to become this.

I finally called the police the moment I felt the last bit of denial fall away, and I saw the truth of my situation. Once that call was made, I knew I had to run. I kept thinking that once his family found out, his threats would become reality. I decided to leave and file for divorce—because he didn't even know how. Thankfully, my best friend Phil Langenderfer and his wife introduced me to a family lawyer who helped me execute the divorce fast. Phil and his wife were my rock during this new life transition into becoming single again and moved to my 1st apartment and helped furnish my new space living single with a TV and microwave. I remain forever grateful for both of them.

I moved out on the 1 year anniversary of my sister's death in October. Alone for the first time, I finally began to mourn—not just her death, but the life I had lost, the weight the trauma of a terrifying marriage had placed on me. Yet beneath the grief, there was relief and gratitude that I had escaped. I also carried the sorrow of all the time I had wasted trying to fix what could never be fixed. My siblings and I grieved separately, each of us holding our pain in silence. Thoughts of suicide lingered on my mind for a few years. It took nearly three years before I could say my sister's name or drive near the block where it happened, without breaking down.

When I finally allowed myself to feel again, I realized that time had moved on without me. My birthday came and went. Seasons changed. But I was still trapped in the past, living through memories that no longer served me. Healing became my full-time job. I started rebuilding slowly, reconnecting with friends, changed jobs to remove memories, finding new communities, and allowing moments of joy to reenter my life. I found a new environment to grow.

It had taken me almost ten years to make peace with those events, the ex-husband, his lack of remorse, and the loss of my little sister and the boys who killed her. I forgave them all, not because they deserved it, but because I needed to free myself from the weight of anger and guilt. Forgiveness was my way of surviving. I even forgave myself for being afraid to disappoint others, for staying too long, for not holding him accountable for the scars he left.

Forgiveness doesn't erase the past, but it allows space for the future. It taught me that healing doesn't mean forgetting; it means remembering without letting the pain define you. These experiences forced me to rebuild other parts of myself; to remember the woman I promised my younger self I would become. There is another part of me that is aware of needing healing or becoming better, and that alone is a journey.

Through every heartbreak and every loss, I learned the most profound truth: *I am my own rescue.* I learned that strength doesn't always roar; it sometimes whispers, *keep going, you've come this far to quit.* I learned that life would test us repeatedly, but every test is an invitation to grow, pivot, and realign. And above all, I learned that even in the darkest moments, there is still light, and that light is within me.

Awareness of the years of pain and healing taught me that every ending carries the seed of a new beginning. Through loss, betrayal, and forgiveness, I learned to see life differently, to understand that even broken pieces can form something beautiful when we choose to rebuild. Those lessons didn't just change how I lived; they changed how I saw myself. From that point on, inspiration came not from what I endured but from what I became, and the people and purpose that gave my story new meaning.

THE INSPIRATION

There came a point when the pain I carried became too heavy to bear. I had experienced loss so deep it nearly broke me. But even in that darkness, I knew I wasn't a selfish person—I couldn't let down the people who loved me, especially my mother and the sister whose life was taken too soon. So, I made an agreement with myself: I would live with purpose, for them and for me. I promised that their sacrifices and love would not be in vain.

Through those dark years, day by day, I pulled myself out of depression. There was no quick fix, no overnight transformation, just small, intentional steps toward freedom from pain and loneliness. I focused on caring for myself the way I deserved, no longer leaving my happiness or worth in anyone else's hands.

The strength of my mother, the same woman who had once carried me across borders in the middle of the night and through every storm, became the foundation I stood on when I needed to find my own. I decided to become who I was meant to be.

After years of mourning, I began to feel life return to me. I started laughing again, making new friends, and rediscovering joy in small things. I was living independently and beginning to feel whole for the first time. Then, life surprised me once again, but this time, with love.

I was lucky to love again. I met my now-husband, Oscar Padilla, a kind and patient soul who helped me continue healing from my past. He was gentle and understanding, and he never judged me for the scars I carried. For the first time in my life, I felt truly seen. He loved every part of me, the good, the bad, and the parts I was still working on. Our connection brought light into places I thought would always stay dark.

We have been married for 15 years. Our marriage, like all things worth having, has had its challenges, but it has been grounded in love, patience, and faith. We dreamed of having children, but by the time we met, I was already 40. Doctors warned that pregnancy would be too dangerous, so we accepted our role as the best aunt and uncle possible. We traveled, laughed, and embraced life with the youthful freedom we didn't have when we were younger.

Yet, even with all the blessings around us, we still felt an emptiness, something missing from our hearts. Then, one day, life gave us the greatest gift in the most unexpected way. During a visit to the hospital to see my niece, we met a 12-year-old boy under DCFS state care. He was sick, didn't speak English, and had no family by his side. Oscar and I instantly felt a connection.

Without hesitation, we volunteered to foster him, beginning the long process of interviews, training, and navigating the system to bring him home. He was our missing piece, the son we didn't know we were waiting for. Coincidentally, he was born in 2006, the same year I lost my sister. That realization felt divine, as if life had come full circle. My purpose had found me.

Overnight, I became a mother, nurse, teacher, therapist, social worker, and advocate. Our days were filled with medical appointments, dialysis training, and late-night praying. But every challenge was worth it. After years of healing, we had finally built a family rooted in love, compassion, and second chances.

Today, he is our son in every way, officially adopted, healthy, and thriving. He carries our name and fills our home with laughter and curiosity, even at 19 years old. His story is still being written, but through him, I've discovered the deepest form of love and purpose. He saved me as much as I saved him.

Becoming a surprise-mommy changed everything; I became a different person again. As I watched my son navigate his own identity and the challenges of growing up after such a difficult start, I realized I needed to model strength, purpose, and possibility. I wanted him to see that even when life hands you change and uncertainty, you can still build something meaningful. That belief ignited the mindset to become my own boss, to create a business that reflected my values, gave me the flexibility to be the mother he needed, and showed him that with resilience and faith, he, too, could achieve his dreams.

Becoming a mother awakened something powerful inside me—a new drive that reached beyond my own healing. Watching my son navigate his identity, face change, and find his place in the world reminds me of my own journey. I realized that the best way to guide him was to model strength, purpose, and perseverance. I wanted him to see firsthand that no matter where you start, you can build a meaningful life with faith, hard work, and courage.

That realization became the foundation for my next chapter: becoming a business owner. I wanted to create something that allowed me to provide for my family, serve my community, and teach my son the value of independence and integrity. I knew I could no longer settle for just surviving; I wanted to build something lasting, a legacy to inspire him to follow his own dreams.

In 2021, I founded Real Finance Group LLC, an accounting firm dedicated to helping small businesses and nonprofits build strong fiscal foundations. I didn't start it with a grand plan — I started it with a purpose: to change how people see their finances — not as a source of fear, but as a path to freedom.

Building my own firm and becoming a business owner was more than entrepreneurship — it was reclaiming my voice. Every part of my life has taught me something vital: resilience from my mother, empathy from loss, and courage from survival. Those lessons became the heart of my business. I wanted to help others create clarity where there was confusion, integrity where there was uncertainty, and confidence where there was fear — so my clients could develop a healthy financial mindset, too.

As my firm grew, so did my mission. Working with small business owners and nonprofit leaders reminded me of my younger self, determined but uncertain, passionate but struggling to see their own value. Through Real Finance Group, I discovered that my true gift wasn't just balancing numbers — it was teaching others to understand their story through their finances. I call it *financial storytelling*. By teaching and coaching business owners as they learn the ropes of building their own operations, I'm able to add real value to their growth.

Looking back on my career, I realize that my journey to becoming a respected financial professional — and the best and highest version of myself — started long before I founded Real Finance Group. It began in high school. I still remember when a teacher told me I would be nothing — "just another pregnant Latina teenager who wouldn't graduate". I carried those words with me for years, through every sideways glance when I stepped outside the city, through every stereotype that tried to box me in.

At first, I wanted to prove everyone wrong — to show that I could be just as intelligent and capable as anyone else. But over time, I learned that proving myself to others didn't matter. I was working hard for my mother, my sister, myself, and now my son. That became my actual reason for building something of my own.

Another turning point was realizing that, after decades of employment, I had been living small by performing the roles others expected of me instead of being who I truly was. In every organization I worked in, I felt confined by politics, limited growth, and unprepared leaders. I had ideas, vision, and heart, but when I tried to bring innovation or efficiency, I was silenced or pushed aside.

My last employee-experience made the decision clear. I worked under a leader whose management style was controlling and dismissive, narcissistic, creating an environment where ideas were stifled and collaboration was discouraged. The atmosphere was heavy — no laughter, no conversation, only quiet compliance. I left within a week, determined never again to let anyone define my worth or limit my potential.

That's when I chose to help organizations from the outside, serving nonprofits and small businesses with honesty, integrity, and transparency. Selecting to work with leaders who are serious about leading the business with the same values. I wanted my clients to know I would always be honest with them through both the good and the difficult. Many consultants sugarcoat the truth, but people deserve clarity. They need to feel both the urgency of their challenges and the pride of real progress. I focus on the educational and coaching side of my new plans, offering workshops, virtual seminars, and coaching for startups to help them build a stronger financial mindset and realize their dreams.

That belief became the foundation of my company's name: **Real Finance Group LLC.** *Real* because authenticity is my promise; *Group* because I dreamed of building a team that shares that same trust and integrity to grow with my business.

Starting my business was thirty years in the making; I just didn't know back in high school that accounting would be the path. My degrees became tools, but it was my life experience that truly built me. Working across nonprofits, private companies, and corporate offices taught me what people really need when they seek financial help: compassion, understanding, and a safe place to ask questions without judgment.

THE ADVICE

Everyone's path is a little zigzagged, just like mine. And when someone chooses me to help them, I don't take that lightly. I see it as an honorable chance to help them succeed, feel seen, and know they are not alone. My old feelings still get triggered, and I might feel vulnerable if my client isn't happy or if I didn't get the new client. Those old feelings of not being good enough still sometimes show up, which makes me want to run away.

If I could offer advice to my younger self, or to anyone who has lived through pain, loss, or reinvention, it would be this: be kind to yourself. You are not behind; you are becoming. Every choice, even the wrong ones, can be redirected toward growth if you take action to make something better out of them. Don't wait for the perfect time to start over; healing begins the moment you decide you deserve better.

Happiness doesn't come from perfection; it comes from peace.

It's okay to cry, to fall apart, and to rebuild again. The key is never to stop moving forward and staying on the path to who you really are. Happiness doesn't come from perfection; it comes from peace. Be proud of what you've done, even if it didn't go as planned. If a bad decision took you off course, balance it with a better one tomorrow.

One of the most important lessons I've learned over fifty years is to stay true to yourself. I'm a work in progress, still. Stop pleasing others, stop living under judgment, and stop shrinking to fit. I used to carry the weight of others' expectations, the voices that told me I wasn't enough. But now, I know my worth.

In the past year, I've had the blessing of working with a mentor, **Carolyn Litton** of *The Vision Project*, who became my transformational guide. Through her coaching and our work in quantum thinking, meditation, and energy flow, I finally understood how to align my thoughts with my vision and true self. Carolyn helped me confirm what I always knew deep down but had been taught to suppress: my intuition, my power, and my voice. She guided me through breaking the invisible walls built around me, and in doing so, she helped me rescue the little girl inside, to bring out my authentic and highest self, the one who feared the future but never stopped dreaming.

The habits that changed my life are simple, but powerful: practicing gratitude every day, setting clear intentions, protecting my peace, and choosing joy even on the hardest days. Reading, spending time alone, and reflecting on the books and people's stories that shaped me, along with working with mentors like Carolyn, and those friends who stuck by me, strengthened my mindset and renewed my faith in myself.

For anyone who relates to even one part of my story, know this: your journey is not over, and your story is still being written. You can fall and rise again. You can rebuild your life and identity at any age, in any circumstance. I invite you to continue following my story in my next book, where I'll share more of the lessons, tools, and breakthroughs that helped me reclaim my purpose.

You can rebuild your life and identity at any age, in any circumstance

Because after everything, I've learned that living authentically, being honest with yourself and others, is the ultimate freedom. And that, more than anything, is the purpose behind everything I do.

THE PATH FORWARD

Transformation is not a single moment; it is the quiet decision to keep becoming. Every choice, every hardship, every leap of faith has led me to this place of clarity. I used to think transformation meant changing who I was, but I now understand it is about returning to who I have always been.

My journey taught me that healing is not linear; it bends, pauses, and restarts, but it always moves forward. Through heartbreak, rebuilding, and rediscovery, I learned that purpose comes when you honor the lessons life gives you and use them to light someone else's path.

Today, my mission is no longer only about financial management or entrepreneurship; it's about transformation through integrity and being the highest version of yourself. Whether I am helping a small-business owner understand their numbers, guiding a nonprofit to sustain its mission, or mentoring someone searching for direction, I want people to feel empowered to take ownership of their story. The same courage that helped me start over can live in anyone willing to take the first step.

Through **Real Finance Group LLC**, my purpose has evolved into something greater than myself. The success of the people I work with, client or not, is about building relationships rooted in trust, patience, transparency, and long-term partnership, because real success is sustained through collaboration. I am now a board member of three organizations, and it is a passion of mine. I strive to stand side-by-side with clients, celebrating their progress and guiding them through challenges with honesty and compassion. When we build together, we grow together. Ears and minds need to be open during the whole journey.

If my story resonates with you, if you're ready to rebuild your business, your finances, or your confidence, let's connect. Whether through coaching, CFO services, or nonprofit guidance, I welcome the opportunity to partner with those who want to create stability, clarity, and long-term growth. Together, we can transform uncertainty into strategy and purpose into measurable success.

As I move forward, my focus remains on serving with authenticity, mentoring others to rise, and continuing to share my story so that others can find courage in theirs. Transformation is an ongoing journey, a daily act of choosing faith over fear, integrity over image, and love over doubt.

To the reader who sees pieces of your own story in mine: this is your invitation. Don't wait for perfect timing; begin where you are. You are worthy of peace, stability, and success. Start small if you must, but start. Trust your instincts, stay true to your values, and keep building toward the life you envision. Every setback can become the foundation for your comeback.

So, here's my call to you: live boldly, lead with heart, and never stop becoming. Your purpose is waiting for you, just as mine was waiting for me. And when you're ready, I'll be here to guide, collaborate, and build something real together.

I have written this first part of my story, to continue healing and becoming who I'm meant to be and my hope is that as you read these pages, you understand and are therefore inspired to act because you are NOT alone. I want you to know that no dream is too late, no story too complicated, and no past too heavy to transform. Growth begins when we choose to believe that we are enough.

I give credit for my growth to the blessings of being surrounded by true friends from the last 26 years who stuck by me, believed in me and my vision for my business and encouraged me to keep going. I especially thank my amazing husband and son for trusting and understanding my crazy ideas, hobbies, passions, practicing many new sports and having patience during long hours of work and still creating space for me to take vacation trips alone and be more becoming.

ABOUT LETICIA

Leticia Padilla's professional journey spans over 25+ years of hands-on leadership in progressive accounting and financial management. A proud graduate of DePaul University, Leticia earned her Bachelor of Science in Administration with a minor in Finance, followed by a Master of Accounting & Financial Management from Keller Graduate School of Management. Her background includes Certifications in tax preparation, Non-Profit Accounting, Entrepreneurship Program and Notary services, Leticia has continuously expanded her skill set, adding immense value to those she serves. Her academic achievements laid a solid foundation for her expansive career.

Leticia's expertise stretches across various sectors, significantly deepening her understanding and enabling her to offer robust support to business owners and nonprofit organizations, enhancing their operational efficiencies and financial integrity. She has faced and overcome numerous challenges throughout her career, each one fortifying her resilience and deepening her commitment to her clients' success.

Her passion for nurturing growth in businesses, through her own accounting firm, Real Finance Group LLC, has driven her to build an extensive network and forge strategic partnerships with other professionals, providing her clients with essential tools and resources. This has proven particularly beneficial in supporting startups with their business development, helping them to navigate the complexities of financial management and strategic planning.

Leticia Padilla stands as a testament to enduring strength and expertise in the ever-evolving field of financial management.

Learn more and connect with Leticia at:

https://leticiapadilla.com/
www.realfinancegroup.com
info@realfinancegroup.com

MASSIEL PAOLA EVERSLEY

"You don't have to wait for permission to live a life of no regrets"

-    Massiel Paola Eversley

~ ~ ~

Massiel P. Eversley is a Dominican-born, Boston-raised nurse executive, coach, author, and transformational leader whose career embodies courage, innovation, and heart-centered impact. With nearly two decades of experience leading large-scale change in healthcare from the nation's top-ranked pediatric hospital, to a world renowned Harvard-affiliated academic medical center, and now in her current role as Associate Chief Nursing Officer for Ambulatory Care within one of Massachusetts' most trusted regional health systems, she has reimagined care models, elevated nursing leadership, and championed equity for patients and care providers alike. A certified coach and award-winning leader, Massiel has also stepped boldly into entrepreneurship and authorship, founding wellness and leadership ventures and writing The Magic Inside, a bilingual children's book celebrating culture, resilience, and inner strength. Passionate about elevating women and diverse leaders, she continues to create spaces where others can rise, lead boldly, and live without regrets, building a legacy of empowerment, healing, and transformation.

~ ~ ~

To my mother, Olga.
To my daughter, Mia.
To my amigas.
And to every woman who needs a
reminder that she can keep going.

May these pages guide you back to the
strength, resilience, and possibility that
have always lived within you.

TRUST YOUR OWN TIMING: THE ALCHEMY OF BECOMING

THE JOURNEY

My entrance into this world was a miracle. During her pregnancy with me, my mother fell ill and was placed on bed rest after threats of miscarriage. Still, I held on. In divine timing, I was born in the Dominican Republic under the Caribbean sun in a military hospital; the very same one where my mother served as a physician.

I've heard stories of her working long night shifts, nurses taking turns watching over me, or bringing me to her between patients so she could feed me. Looking back, it feels almost destined that my earliest days were spent surrounded by healers. I see it as a foreshadowing of the path I would one day choose.

I was educated early through Montessori-style methods, learning to read and write at a young age and advancing to third grade by age six. Respect and formality, always softened by love, were the expectations in our home. We were taught to respect our elders, to *"Besar la mano"* (ask for their blessing) upon arrival, and to use "usted," never "tú," when addressing them. I grew up surrounded by strong-willed women who were defying the expectations of a patriarchal time.

My parents made sure my older brother and I had everything they could offer. Their roles as government officials taught me pride, discipline, and the pursuit of excellence. These were virtues my mother lived by, and my father demanded. Those early lessons heightened my self-awareness and my instinct to meet expectations, even when they felt heavy.

Today, nostalgia for the island stirs up memories I can't quite recreate in the U.S. The soft breeze on the drive along *El Malecón*, merengue floating through the warm night air, the moonlight's reflection sparkling on the

Caribbean Sea, and the joy of visiting my primos. Those moments felt like pure magic, the kind only the island can create.

My family's journey to the United States began with my uncle, who traveled often and encouraged my mother to consider the move. He believed that while life in the Dominican Republic was good, the U.S. offered broader opportunities for her and for her children's future. My mother resisted for years, frequently visiting but never intending to leave home. Everything changed when my father and brother traveled to the U.S., initially staying temporarily, but soon enamored by the possibilities for a better life. On her deathbed, my grandmother insisted that my mother promise she would keep our family together by moving. With an approved two-year military leave, we moved to Boston, Massachusetts, when I was six and never moved back. Witnessing her keep her promise without wavering taught me, at a young age, what it means to honor your word, even when the path ahead is uncertain.

Our first years in the U.S. were not as smooth as the television made life look. When we went to obtain official identification, we were told our names were too long. My family always addressed me by my middle name, Paola. I loved the creative, affectionate varieties they would conjure. *Paolita* was always my favorite. I painfully dropped my maternal last name, making it feel as if, upon arrival, we were told to leave part of our identity at the door.

The first year brought constant change. Attending several schools, temporary arrangements, transitional housing, and unfamiliar foods made everything feel foreign. I would cry many mornings upon waking as I was reminded we now lived in a foreign place. During meals, while others were excited to try new foods, I would often refuse to eat anything foreign to make my resistance to change known to all.

At school, the administrators felt I was too young for third grade, and that it was best I learn English with children my age in first grade. A multi-year plan to have me skip grades never came to fruition due to frequent moves. One positive was that Boston Public Schools gave me access to bilingual education and diverse teachers, which made all the transitions a bit more tolerable over the year and a half it took me to pick up English while preserving my Spanish.

These experiences taught me adaptability before I even knew the word. Fortunately, we soon found a faith community that welcomed us, opened its doors, and helped my mother access resources. She enrolled in English classes to improve her fluency, since most of what she knew came from medical textbooks. After some research, she realized that practicing as a physician would be too complex, so she enrolled in nursing school as soon as she could to get us back on our feet. Looking back, I see how that circle of women from her church became our lifeline, carrying us forward when we needed it most. For that, I will always be thankful.

Growing up in Boston, I was surrounded by a vibrant mix of cultures and languages that reflected the city's growing diversity. Holidays and summers were spent visiting family in New York, which always felt like a return to our roots. In middle and high school, I attended an exam school that expanded my world. I had the benefits of a curriculum that taught African American History, a science teacher who allowed a project on lucid dreaming and even learned that the military is not for me through JROTC. Those years taught me that education isn't just about achievement; it's about awakening to who you are.

At home, I lived between two worlds. Saturday mornings were filled with the rhythms of Juan Luis Guerra's *Ojalá Que Llueva Café*, and evenings ended with shows like *In Living Color* or *The Arsenio Hall Show*. Over time, conversations with my brother naturally shifted from Spanish to Spanglish. I participated in *El Reinado Anacaona*. A pageant part of Boston's Dominican Cultural Festival, where I reconnected with my roots by learning traditional *baile folklórico* and studying the legacy of inspiring Dominican women like *Las Hermanas Mirabal*. Life was now a reflection of how I had started to release the grip of resistance, allowing the cultures to intertwine.

I learned that opportunities don't simply appear; you must create them. One summer, at sixteen, while my parents were out of town, I got my first job at a pharmacy, despite my mother's insistence that I shouldn't work yet. That experience sparked something in me, the realization that I had agency, that I could shape my own path. From then on, I sought opportunities that piqued my interest, like summer internships, youth programs, and community initiatives.

When it came time for college, moving away wasn't something my parents believed in. I started at UMass Boston as a psychology major while living at home. After a few classes, I realized something was missing. I didn't feel the same passion I saw in my mother when she spoke about caring for her patients, now as a Women's Health Nurse Practitioner.

Eventually, my parents agreed to let me transfer to Northeastern University and live on campus just fifteen minutes away. It wasn't far, but it meant freedom and trust, the start of learning to live on my own terms. During orientation, I realized I didn't just want to study behavior; I wanted to make a difference. Nursing felt like the obvious choice.

I quickly realized healthcare wasn't as diverse as I had imagined. I thought of my mother, brilliant and beloved by her patients, yet critiqued for her accent in performance reviews. I remembered how comforting it is to be understood in your own language, and I felt an immediate responsibility to make healthcare more inclusive.

I noticed there were many nursing students but few opportunities, so I planned to pursue co-ops that differed from my peers' experiences. I was placed in settings where I experienced rich clinical learning, though not without social challenges. I learned that some environments can be isolating for new nurses and students when a supervisor said I "might not be a fit for nursing."

At times, the weight of exclusion would make my presence feel like a quiet rebellion. Yet I persisted and kept showing up. This only deepened the compassion I brought to caring for my patients. It also gave me hope that one day I would help create cultures where every nurse feels seen, supported, and valued.

Early in my nursing career, I found myself at Boston Children's Hospital, where my love for the profession was restored. I loved that I was able to leverage my bilingual skills during the many home visits and see the relief on the families' faces when their nurse looked like them. In that role, I learned that nursing's impact truly touches lives, reaching far beyond the bedside into the community, patient advocacy, and publications.

In many ways, I feel like leadership chose me. I was recruited for a Director role that required my rare blend of experience and language skills. I was immediately sold when I realized I could make a meaningful difference as a leader. Once in the role, a nurse asked how I got it. "Did you get your role here because your parents work here?" This brought memories of being mistaken for the assistant or phlebotomist, not the nurse. At that moment, I prepared myself to be underestimated and let my results speak for themselves.

I took on stretch assignments and was promoted to Regional and Senior roles with increasing levels of responsibility, with the aim of remaining close to the populations I felt needed me most. My philosophy as a leader was that staff should reflect the patient population they serve to improve outcomes. I could see the ripple effects of my actions as a leader positively affecting patient care. My experiences from learning resilience as a child to finding my voice in nursing had actually been preparing me for leadership all along.

THE LEARNINGS

In my twenties, I pursued my Master of Jurisprudence in Health Law at Loyola University Law School. I wanted to be at the forefront, or as we say in the Dominican Republic, *"Alante, Alante"* exploring the business and legal dimensions of a rapidly changing healthcare system.

Soon, the weight of work and motherhood became too heavy to carry. By day, I was everything to my daughter, and by night, I studied into the early hours, surviving on little sleep. Eventually, my body gave in. A cascade of health issues followed, and when western medicine failed to restore my balance, I turned to a herbalist who changed my life. She created a holistic plan that helped me heal. We uncovered a gluten and dairy intolerance, likely rooted in my early shift away from natural foods when we arrived in the U.S.

That experience taught me that our bodies are wise. They whisper before they scream and make us stop in our tracks. It's up to us to slow down, listen, and act. Over time, honoring my body, listening to what it needs, and mindful nutrition have become a way of life. Some may see it as discipline; I see it as my love language.

A few years later, I anticipated the arrival of my second child. I imagined a smooth, natural birth and had it all planned in my mind. After hours of labor in the hospital, something went wrong, purging all illusions of a perfect birth. Within moments of starting an epidural, I felt my body become weak, my voice slipping, my breath fading. The room blurred, voices echoed, and I heard my name and a code being called in the distance.

I believe what kept me connected to this life is the love I felt for my family at that moment. When I came back into awareness, I was then rushed into an emergency cesarean. It was both deeply traumatic and soul-stirring. It awakened something deep within me. This near-death experience reminded me of the fragility of life, the sacredness of every breath, and made me evaluate who was really in the driver's seat of my life. I wondered at what point other people's agendas became my own. It reminded me of my need to feel a sense of purpose in all I do.

With my third child, I faced unexpected postpartum challenges that left me searching for ways to restore my health and energy. Knowing I would have to return to work, I began researching how to heal the body after birth and quickly realized I wasn't alone since so many women struggled to feel nourished, strong, and whole again.

What stood out to me was learning that women of color have a significantly higher risk of maternal and postpartum complications, regardless of education and income. I remembered how I, too, was part of that collective experience with hospital re-admissions for complications after going home with my babies. I wanted to do something to remedy these realities since they felt so disempowering.

Most products marketed for the postpartum period were filled with ingredients that didn't align with my values or nutritional needs. I thought of all the mothers I could empower by creating a healing product not available on the market. I partnered with experts to formulate a vegan all-in-one postpartum and lactation protein powder – a product designed to help women heal, nourish, and thrive.

Around the same time, the COVID-19 pandemic halted everything. As a Regional Director overseeing several primary care clinics, I was tasked with leading large-scale recruitment efforts and business operations for a newly formed hotline. The moment called for both compassion and clarity. My prior training in Jean Watson's Caritas Coach Education Program, rooted in the Theory of Human Caring, gave me the foundation to lead from empathy. To better support my seven nurse managers during this uncertainty, I took it a step further: I pursued an executive coaching certification and trained as a Positive Intelligence coach, focusing on mental fitness and mindset transformation. It opened my eyes to the possibility of future entrepreneurial pursuits.

Once work stabilized and the world began to settle into its "new normal," I revisited my supplement business and began developing a leadership curriculum centered on authenticity and purpose. I couldn't shake the pull toward entrepreneurship. I needed to bet on myself and at least one person to believe in my idea. With my husband's support, I made a bold decision: I resigned from my secure position and gave myself six months to see where the journey would lead.

I joined a startup accelerator focused on social impact, positioning my supplement company as a mission-driven venture. I was hiring contractors, approving websites, marketing on social media, pitching to investors, and applying for grants, all while consulting and running coaching cohorts grounded in authentic leadership. By month four, reality set in: less than two percent of venture capital funding goes to women, and even fewer dollars reach women of color. If I wanted this dream to thrive, I would have to bootstrap it myself and return to work to help fund its growth.

Two years later, I transitioned into my current executive role as Associate Chief Nursing Officer, overseeing multiple ambulatory sites across specialties and locations. It's a role that demands both strategic vision and emotional endurance, setting the direction for the practice of nursing, with a focus on role clarity, high reliability, quality and staff well-being. The lessons I once learned about empathy, resilience, and authenticity now serve as my compass as I lead teams through constant change.

With new demands on my energy, I began to reassess my business. I had to confront a hard truth. Despite being an award-winning entrepreneur, recognized for innovation and achieving many milestones, the venture had taken a lot from me and now required more than I could give. Without a whole team to sustain its growth and amid politically charged boycotts that disrupted sales and manufacturing, I knew it was time. After five dedicated years, I made the difficult decision to retire from the business, my first "baby", and grant myself the freedom to course-correct.

I've learned that we all move through seasons, each with its own purpose, lessons, and eventual ending. That season of my life had run its course. I no longer wrestle with the what-ifs or should-haves because I went all in. I followed my excitement, let my creativity bloom, and gave everything I had to the vision. There were highs and lows, moments of triumph and tears, and I allowed myself to feel them all. Embracing the raw, human emotions that leaders often suppress, but that true transformation quietly requires.

I walk away from that chapter with what I call an experiential MBA and, most importantly, with choice. I can take the lessons, apply them differently next time, and grow wiser from them. I don't carry shame in its ending; I carry pride in having tried. I helped mothers take charge of their postpartum healing, raised awareness, and sparked conversations that mattered. Now, I move forward with gratitude knowing that endings aren't failures, they're invitations to begin again, this time with more profound wisdom and even more heart. I carry with me the confidence that creativity and leadership can coexist, that alignment is the new definition of success, and that the courage to give yourself the space to choose differently is its own kind of victory.

THE INSPIRATION

My most significant sources of inspiration have always been my mother and my children. They represent the generations before and after me, each shaping who I am in profound ways.

My mother's story and the wisdom of our ancestors have been my compass. Born in the final years of a dictatorship, she became an Air Force physician in the Dominican Republic at a time when few women held respected positions in that field. She led with courage in places where women's voices were rarely heard, and later, when we immigrated to the United States, she reinvented herself gracefully. Watching her rebuild her life from the ground up taught me that true resilience isn't about never falling, it's about rising each time with greater wisdom, humility, and faith. Her strength continues to inspire me at every stage of my life.

My children have become my mirrors; the inspiration they give me is a reminder of my purpose and my power. During college and into early adulthood, poetry became my outlet. I read and wrote to untangle my emotions and give them shape. But motherhood transformed that creative impulse into something more profound. When my daughter was young, I dreamed of writing children's books that would show her the world through my eyes. I made a quiet promise to myself: if the inspiration was there and the opportunity ever came, I would follow it.

One day, after a swim lesson in which he never made it into the water, my youngest son sat quietly in the back seat, afraid to try again. On the drive home, I told him about the magic he had inside, that with belief and practice, he could do anything! That moment stayed with me. I knew I had to capture it. What began as a car ride conversation became a manuscript, and eventually a bilingual children's book I wrote: *The Magic Inside / La Magia de Adentro: A Story of Inner Power*. My encouragement to every child who needs a reminder of the magic that whispers within them.

Looking back, I realize writing was never just a form of expression; it was a form of transformation. It became my way of alchemizing emotion into energy, turning pain into purpose, doubt into drive, and reflection into strength. My children remind me every day to believe in my own magic. My mother taught me how to honor it. Together, they continue to inspire how I lead, create, and live, with courage, compassion, and no regrets.

Beyond the people who shaped me, certain books found me at just the right moments, like mentors guiding my evolution. *The Alchemist by Paulo Coelho* reminded me to trust divine timing and the unfolding of my own journey. That the path of seeking in the end transforms the seeker. *Illusions: The Adventures of a Reluctant Messiah, by Richard Bach,* taught me that we are both students and teachers in this classroom of life, and that our beliefs shape the reality we live. It helped me see that every challenge is an opportunity to rewrite my story and reclaim our power. We are not bound by fate but by the choices we make in co-creating with reality. *No Ego by Cy Wakeman* grounded those lessons, reminding me that leadership begins with personal accountability and that peace and progress depend on the energy we choose to bring into every situation. *Crucial Conversations by Kerry Patterson and colleagues* offered me the language to communicate with clarity and compassion, especially in moments that mattered most. Lastly, I recommend *Create Your Best Year One Day at a Time* by *Clara Angelina Diaz,* a book I'm proud to have co-authored. It offers a gentle, poetic approach to turning daily intentions into a purposeful and meaningful life.

Together, these books shaped the way I live and lead. They reminded me that true alignment doesn't come from getting everything right; it comes from staying rooted in who you are while remaining open to growth.

THE ADVICE

If I could sit with my younger self or anyone standing at a crossroads, I would begin with this:

Get to know your true self. Not the titles or roles you play, but the soul underneath it all. Explore your beliefs, values, and triggers. Once you understand them, decide what you deserve and what you will no longer accept. The relationship you have with yourself sets the tone for every other relationship you will ever have.

Remember, life moves in seasons. There will be times to bloom, to rest, to release, and to start again. Changing your mind doesn't mean you've failed; it means you're evolving. When something ends, look for the gift it leaves behind. You either learn the lesson, or life will lovingly repeat it until you do.

Release the grip of regret. Regret keeps you looking backward, replaying scenes that can no longer be rewritten. It convinces you the past holds more power than the present, when in truth, the future is happening *now*. A clean slate full of possibilities. Honor who you were, even when you didn't know better. You were learning. Honor who you're becoming, because you are using those lessons to rise higher. Growth requires letting go of what could have been. When you choose presence over punishment, the past transforms into wisdom, and the future opens its doors.

Protect your inner voice. Don't internalize the words of those who underestimate or misunderstand you. The loudest critic often becomes the one in your own mind. Soften the voices with compassion. Thank it for trying to keep you safe and for giving you reassurance that you can create safety while still growing. You are not what others project onto you; most people are too caught in their own fears to see you truly.

Choose your battles wisely. Measure your energy, not your ego. Some things are better observed than absorbed. The more you learn to observe without reacting, the more peace you'll find. Once you can see the bigger picture, focus your energy on what creates lasting impact, not on what simply drains you.

Focus your energy where it creates lasting impact, not where it simply drains you.

Make stillness a daily habit. Meditation is freedom. Don't get lost in the rush of the daily grind. Create space for silence, imagination, and regeneration. The tranquility you cultivate within becomes the clarity you carry into the world. In that stillness, you'll realize that your power has never been about doing more; it's about *being aligned* with who you truly are.

THE PATH FORWARD

To every woman standing at the edge of change, understand that you are allowed to evolve. You can co-create with the universe and write your own story without apology. Reinvention is not failure; it's evolution in real time.

We've been taught that success means walking a predetermined path, smiling through sacrifice, and believing stability equals safety. But the truth is, success looks different for every woman. Some lead organizations, others nurture families, and many do both while creating something entirely new. You don't have to choose between intellect and intuition, logic and love, or leadership and softness. You can be all of it and still be you.

If you've ever felt you did everything "right" and still sensed something more was waiting for you, that's your intuition calling. Listen. That whisper isn't doubt; it's direction. You are allowed to want more and to receive it safely, without guilt or regret. It's about trusting your inner compass, even when the world doesn't understand your direction.

Every lesson, emotion, and experience holds wisdom if you let it. Move in the direction of your curiosity, your excitement, your peace. Read, love, explore, and consider new perspectives. Let each season of your life teach you something new about who you are and who you're becoming.

> *That's how growth happens: one breath, one lesson, one act of courage at a time.*

Release the need to get it right and stay open to possibility, while having compassion for the parts of you that are still learning. That's how growth happens: one breath, one lesson, one act of courage at a time.

Because your life isn't meant to be lived by someone else's blueprint, it's meant to be written boldly, softly, and entirely by you. The world doesn't need more copies. It requires more originals, more magic, more *you*.

As for me, my next chapter is about continuing to listen to my intuition, acting on my passions, and expressing my creativity in new and exciting ways; by writing, leading, pursuing my doctorate, and continuing to get to know all the layers of me. I trust that I am a child of God, of Source, and of the Stars, and that the universe is always conspiring in my favor.

I hope, as you read this, you remember:

The universe is conspiring in your favor, too; just trust and allow.

ABOUT MASSIEL

Massiel P. Eversley is a Dominican-born, Boston-raised nurse executive, author, coach, and transformational leader with nearly two decades of experience advancing equity, redesigning care models, and leading large-scale change across complex healthcare systems. Rooted in her heritage and guided by purpose, she is known for blending strategy, authenticity, and vision to create meaningful, lasting impact.

Her work has strengthened public health programs for vulnerable children, elevated nursing leadership across academic and community settings, and helped shape new standards for ambulatory care. Today, she serves as Associate Chief Nursing Officer for Ambulatory Care at a leading regional health system, where she continues her mission to advance equity, leadership development, and system transformation in healthcare.

Massiel earned her Bachelor of Science in Nursing from Northeastern University and her Master of Jurisprudence in Health Law from Loyola University Chicago School of Law. She is a Board-Certified Nurse Executive, Certified Professional Coach, and is currently pursuing her Doctor of Nursing Practice degree at the University of New Hampshire. She was recently appointed President-Elect of the National Association of Hispanic Nurses, Greater Boston Chapter, aligning her leadership journey with her passion for advocacy, mentorship, and community engagement.

Her leadership and vision have been recognized nationally, including honors such as Northeastern University's Women Who Empower Innovator Award, the Excellence in Nursing Award from the New England Region of the Black Nurses Association, and the Brigham and Women's Hospital Internal Medicine Residency Nursing Award for service and commitment to patient care. Her work has also been featured on CNN, highlighted within HarvardX global coursework on building effective healthcare teams, and shared through conversations on leadership resilience within academic medical centers.

An entrepreneur at heart, Massiel previously founded Nisus Life, a wellness brand dedicated to simplifying postpartum health, and Next Level Pivot, a healthcare consulting and executive leadership coaching firm supporting rising and underrepresented leaders. She now draws on those experiences as an author and thought leader, expanding her impact through storytelling and advocacy. Her newest bilingual children's book, *The Magic Inside*, celebrates culture, resilience, and the power within every child.

As a Latina leader, Massiel is deeply committed to elevating voices, creating pathways for women in leadership, and inspiring the next generation to live boldly and without regret. A proud wife and mother of three, she continues to build spaces where women and diverse leaders can thrive, leaving a legacy rooted in empowerment, innovation, and purpose.

You can learn more and connect with Massiel at:

https://www.linkedin.com/in/massieleversley/
MassielEversley@gmail.com

You can find her books:

https://MassielEversley.com

DR. MELISSA RAMIREZ

"One step at a time — de poquito a poquito — because where there's a will, there's a way."

\- Melissa Ramirez

~ ~ ~

Dr. Melissa Ramirez is a trailblazing organic chemist, scholar, and advocate whose journey embodies brilliance, resilience, and the transformative power of representation in STEM. A first-generation Latina scientist with roots in Guanajuato, Mexico, she has trained at some of the nation's most prestigious institutions—UPenn, UCLA, and Caltech—earning competitive fellowships and producing groundbreaking research at the intersection of synthetic and computational chemistry. Now leading her own research program at the University of Minnesota, Melissa is advancing innovative solutions in organic synthesis to improve human health while championing cultural change in academia. Through her #LatinXMentorFirst movement and community leadership, she is redefining what it means to succeed in science—lifting voices, opening doors, and paving the way for the next generation of Latinx scientists to step into their power.

~ ~ ~

For my niece, Camila Romero. I am so proud of the person you are becoming; I'll be there every step of the way. Y para mis papás, Guadalupe y Ramiro Ramirez. Gracias por todo los sacrificios que hicieron para que yo pudiera.

DE POQUITO A POQUITO:
TURNING PERSEVERANCE INTO PURPOSE

THE JOURNEY

I became the empowering changemaker I am today by watching my resilient parents work hard to create a better future for my sisters and me despite facing a series of health challenges, and by struggling with a sense of belonging from a young age.

To provide some background, my parents were both born on a rancho called Botija in Guanajuato, Mexico. My dad is the oldest of ten siblings and grew up in poverty. He didn't get an education past second grade, starting work at age nine as a shepherd and field worker. He immigrated to Pasadena, California, at age sixteen after years of physical abuse by his mother. He worked sixteen-hour shifts, five days a week, at a restaurant local to Caltech (i.e., Burger Continental) for thirty years, later becoming a dining hall attendant at NASA's Jet Propulsion Laboratory and Caltech's Browne Dining Hall. In his forties, he was diagnosed with narcolepsy, a chronic neurological condition that affects the brain's sleep-wake cycle. His diagnosis changed his life and my entire family's. Additionally, my dad deals with diabetes, arthritis, and high blood pressure.

My mother immigrated to the U.S. with my dad and immediately began working as a caregiver for the elderly. She grew up as the youngest of eight siblings and, like my father, did not get an education past the second grade. She also worked as a housekeeper in the undergraduate dorms at Caltech for a short time. Even though my parents didn't understand what an Ivy League university was or the hexagons (cyclohexane molecules) that I drew, they taught me to be independent and to create a future for myself rather than settle for less. Like my dad, she also deals with diabetes, which she was diagnosed with in her forties.

Despite their lack of formal education, my parents fostered my curiosity by encouraging me to ask questions and to be authentic and vulnerable as I pursued my dreams. These values shape my determination to create safe spaces for students from historically excluded backgrounds as they navigate higher education.

One of the earliest pivotal moments in my journey happened in third grade, when I asked my parents if I could join the Girl Scouts. It was one of the first decisions I made for myself—something that pushed me out of my comfort zone and that my parents didn't fully understand but still supported. Until then, the only extracurricular activity I had participated in was swimming lessons at the local community center. My parents didn't often sign us up for extracurriculars because they had limited time and money, and there were three of us; I am one of three daughters—my younger sister Vanessa is a year younger, and my older sister Faviola (or Favi) is nine years older. My mom worked as hard as my dad, balancing her full-time job at a retirement home with her role as a mother.

In eighth grade, I was first exposed to the idea of college. I attended Marshall Fundamental School, a predominantly Hispanic, low-income school from sixth through twelfth grade. I first learned about college when Maribel Dominguez, a counselor at Marshall, gave a presentation on the Puente Program in English class. Puente is an academic and community leadership program that aims to increase the number of underrepresented students who enroll in four-year colleges and universities. I joined Puente in ninth grade and through Puente, I learned what college was and also took on leadership roles despite my limited sense of belonging and my timid nature.

The program gave me a sense of community and opportunities to volunteer and give back in Pasadena and Los Angeles County. I was pretty quiet when I first joined, but I pushed myself to take leadership roles and eventually became Puente president during my senior year. It helped me develop the confidence to take leadership roles in other college prep and service-focused student groups at Marshall, including Unidos and Associated Student Body. It also gave me the courage to start playing sports; I joined the volleyball and cross country teams while at Marshall.

I took advantage of every opportunity that Puente offered—from community service to college-preparation workshops—to craft the best college application I could. As a first-generation college student with no one in my family having attended a four-year university, Puente gave me guidance and connection. Lastly, Puente also introduced me to two of my closest friends and *hermanas*, Elizabeth Palma and Jasmin Diaz, who remain an important part of my life and support system today.

Moving across the country to complete my undergraduate studies at the University of Pennsylvania in 2012 was another pivotal moment in my journey. I was awarded a Gates Millennium Scholarship and an ACS Scholar Program Scholarship, and was selected as a QuestBridge Finalist during my senior year of high school. I chose to attend UPenn instead of UC Berkeley, where I had been selected as a Posse Scholarship Finalist. It was a major decision—my parents wanted me to stay in California, but I knew I had to take this leap.

Attending UPenn for my undergraduate studies taught me resourcefulness. I had struggled with anxiety in high school and was taking medication for it. I began therapy a few months before moving across the country. I had never spent more than a month away from my family, which was very tight-knit. I left for Pennsylvania in July 2012 to attend two summer programs: the Africana Summer Institute and the Penn Pre-Freshman Program (PFP). I knew I'd be homesick and needed extra time to adjust, so I took advantage of these summer programs, even if it meant leaving California earlier. Initially, I wasn't invited to participate in the PFP, but I called UPenn's La Casa Latina and successfully advocated for myself to be selected for the Program.

That experience—learning to speak up for myself and ask for what I needed—became a through line in my story. Thus, my journey has been defined by pairing determination with self-advocacy.

THE LEARNINGS

After graduating from UPenn in 2016, I took a month off before beginning graduate school at UCLA. Completing my PhD in organic chemistry was a defining chapter that taught me what I was capable of, both personally and scientifically. Initially, I thought I would join an organic synthesis group, but during rotations, I discovered that I was also interested in computational chemistry while working in the laboratory of Professor Ken Houk, a well-known computational organic chemist.

In December 2016, I asked Professors Neil Garg and Ken Houk if I could join their laboratories as a joint student in organic synthesis and computational chemistry, beginning a challenging but rewarding new journey. Being part of two research groups—spanning two different disciplines—pushed me to my limits. Tuesdays stand out vividly: my workday started at 8 or 9 a.m. and often didn't end until after 9 p.m., following a 3–6 p.m. Houk group meeting. I was constantly running a reaction, a calculation, or analyzing results for one lab or the other.

> *My intuition consistently told me that I was going to open doors for others in my community in the long run, so long as I stayed true to myself and held onto my purpose.*

There were many moments when I felt like I wasn't good enough. Communicating to two scientific audiences required a new skill set, and I often worried I wasn't meeting expectations in either space. I also avoided mentioning that I went home on weekends to spend time with family or attend events like baby showers or quinceañeras. I didn't want to give the impression that I wasn't working hard enough. Yet, those small acts of choosing connection helped sustain me. They reminded me that being a scientist didn't mean sacrificing my humanity. They also reminded me to keep perspective: struggling to solve a problem in the lab or not feeling "good enough" in science were minimal challenges compared to the challenges my parents, for example, faced, so I could have the opportunity. My intuition consistently told me I would open doors for others in my community in the long run, so long as I stayed true to myself and held on to my purpose.

In 2021, I completed my PhD, secured a postdoctoral research position at Caltech, and was awarded my first two fellowships by Caltech and the National Science Foundation. Winning these two fellowships was especially momentous because they funded my own research ideas. They proved that I was not only a scientist but a capable and innovative one. I would complete my postdoctoral studies (analogous to a medical residency) back in my hometown. Returning to Caltech as a postdoc from 2021 to 2024 brought my academic journey full circle. My parents had once worked "blue-collar" jobs on Caltech's campus—now I was conducting cutting-edge research there. I made sure to give back to my community during my time at Caltech. For example, I was a speaker for the Caltech Science Journeys Seminar Series, where I shared my journey in science and my research in organic chemistry to an audience of approximately 800 students and teachers from the Pasadena Unified School District. I also organized and participated in science outreach at Marshall Fundamental High School, the local public high school that I previously attended, as well as McKinley Middle School and Octavia Butler Magnet Middle School in PUSD.

During my third year at Caltech, I applied for faculty positions at research-intensive, or R1 institutions. The application process for faculty positions was grueling, but it showed me what I was capable of. At each of my interviews, I carried a note in my pocket that read "Soy chingona." I pulled this note out during restroom breaks as a reminder to myself that everything I do is bigger than me and that I've already "been paid for," as Maya Angelou said. More specifically, Maya Angelou has previously shared:

"You've been paid for by people who never even saw your face. Your mother's mother, your father's father. And so it behooves you to prepare yourself so you can pay for someone else yet to come. Whose name you'll never know. You just keep the good thing going."

Moving to Minnesota in 2025 to start my own research lab marked another major transition. It was both exciting and challenging; I started my own research program at the University of Minnesota Twin Cities as an assistant professor of chemistry, and I also bought my first home. My parents didn't fully understand what I was doing with work, and the sadness of my moving away was especially hard for my mom. In that moment, I was reminded of the importance of holding space for both my emotions and those of the people I love.

Starting a lab from scratch and leading a research team for the first time was no small feat—it required constant learning, adaptability, and giving myself grace. To keep myself grounded, I decided to train for my first marathon. In July 2025, I signed up for the Twin Cities Marathon in Minneapolis and Saint Paul with only two and a half months to train. I did it to prove to myself that I can always figure things out, that I have agency, and that I can choose how I show up.

That summer, I found community in new places—joining the Callejeros Run Club, led by Latinos in Comunidad, as well as Ambition Run Club and November Project Minneapolis. These groups gave me friendship, motivation, and a sense of belonging in a new city.

Crossing the marathon finish line at a pace of 9:08 minutes per mile was one of the most empowering moments of my life. It reminded me that I am capable of anything I commit to—with intention, heart, and discipline. Two months later, I completed my second marathon in Hawaii. This was the Honolulu Marathon in December 2025. I completed the marathon at a pace of 9:11 minutes per mile, of which I was especially proud, given the challenge of running in humid and sunny weather.

Each stage of my life has shown me that growth happens in motion—through change, challenge, and courage. My journey has been about expanding what's possible for myself and for others who come after me. I carry my parents' sacrifices, my community's resilience, and my own determination as fuel for everything I do next.

> *Growth happens in motion—through change, challenge, and courage.*

THE INSPIRATION

My mom is my best friend and role model. I look up to her for the immense love she gives my sisters, my dad, and me. She taught me to be independent and to create a future for myself. Furthermore, from my mom, I learned how to value what I have and to be grateful for the opportunities that I am given and the people who have helped me along the way.

My mom showed me the importance of hard work and taking action towards building a better future for myself. I am a go-getter because of her. Even when she's a bit reserved, she always makes me feel loved. She didn't always know the right thing to say, but she let me be me. As I grow older, I turn to my mom more and more for advice, knowing there is truth in the wisdom she passes down to me.

My dad is my hero. One of my most special memories as a kid is my dad letting me pick any book from the Scholastic book order, no matter how much it cost. My mom, being the money manager, always wanted me to pick the $1 book, but my dad let me pick any. He would let us stop by the Book Fair during Open House, and he was the one who bought me my very expensive Girl Scouts book and green vest in the third grade.

My dad was diagnosed with narcolepsy when I was in fifth grade. This changed my dad's life. My dad's diagnosis occurred at a late stage in his condition. I remember trips to Tijuana, Mexico, for my dad's neurology appointments and medication because he did not have health insurance at the time. This posed a significant financial burden on my family. Still, despite our family's limited finances, my dad supported me in everything academic. Although he experienced emotional and physical pain throughout his life, he always pushed forward, and his efforts ultimately allowed my sisters and me to have better opportunities than he ever had. He passed down his strong sense of curiosity and enthusiasm for learning to me; I can always count on him to update me on something new he learned on the Discovery Channel or National Geographic.

I am thankful to my dad for nurturing my love for learning and my fascination with the world around us (this later translated into a passion for chemistry!). I am also grateful to my dad for reminding me about the importance of leading from the heart. One of the most important things he did for me was let me feel my feelings. He encouraged me to express myself without fear or shame about how I felt. My dad made me feel seen starting at a young age.

I think that by reminding me to be humble while also making me feel seen, he fostered in me a quiet yet ever-present sense of self-love and self-compassion. He helped me recognize that every life experience is something we can learn from, and that, over time, we can learn from the hard feelings and challenges we face.

Three other people who have been important mentors to me through their books and podcast interviews are Michelle Obama, Viola Davis, and Stacey Abrams. Stacey Abrams's book *Minority Leader: How to Lead from the Outside and Make Real Change* motivated me to go for it in pursuing a career in academia. I read this book at a turning point in my journey, right after completing my PhD at UCLA. Through this book, I gave myself permission to dream big and to write my story.

Michelle Obama's books *Becoming* and *The Light We Carry*, along with her *Light Podcast*, have also pushed me to live authentically by aiming high. Lastly, Viola Davis's *Finding Me* has helped me learn how to love myself and embrace every part of who I am.

THE ADVICE

My biggest advice is to stay true to yourself. Think deeply about your values and make decisions based on them. Staying true to yourself will mean that not everyone will like you—and that is okay! Being liked by everyone probably means that you are playing the likability game.

Instead, always search for people whose values align with yours because they will lift you up and help you see your strengths and power. In staying true to yourself, don't gaslight yourself when it comes to the things that matter to you; validate yourself.

Seeing yourself clearly is more important than having it all figured out. To me, "seeing yourself clearly" means having a strong sense of self-worth. This means you can see how valuable you are, including all the imperfections you bring. Those imperfections are what allow you to lift others up or problem-solve in a way that stands out. The strength and resilience needed to figure things out will come when you have a strong sense of self-worth.

There is no such thing as perfect timing. You either do or you don't—you either take action or you don't. A quote from Barack Obama that resonates strongly with me is this: "Change will not come if we wait for some other person, or if we wait for some other time. We are the ones we've been waiting for. We are the change that we seek."

I truly believe that taking action builds confidence and that action fuels motivation. We cannot wait to have the confidence and motivation to act on what matters most. We just have to go for it and learn at every step.

Do not wait for joy—find some way to experience it every day. For me, it means finding joy even in the smallest, most everyday experiences. This can include enjoying my cup of Nespresso coffee in the morning, the flowers I get myself during my weekly Trader Joe's trip, or the view of the sun rising over the icy Mississippi River as I drive home from my 6:15 a.m. HIIT workout during the Minnesota winter.

Joy can also mean making time to meet a friend for dinner or simply giving myself permission to rest on the couch. This year, marathon training has brought a new kind of joy into my life as I've had the chance to meet new run club friends to train with.

Be resourceful! All the tools are laid out for you—and if they're not, then all the doors are waiting to be knocked on. Having that mindset will help you overcome and overcome and overcome. Shooting all the shots is important to living a purposeful life that's bigger than you and in service of others.

THE PATH FORWARD

I am inspired to help other Latinas and women recognize that they matter — that they have agency, and that fully embracing who they are is a powerful driving force for change. Living an intentional and authentic life can transform not only our own paths but also the communities around us.

My deepest desire is to encourage them to pursue their dreams, regardless of their backgrounds or the obstacles they may face. I want them to lean into courage and self-love, to aim high while working alongside fear — not against it.

Because fear never truly goes away. It's always present. But growth and transformation happen when we face the "scariest," most anxiety-inducing parts of life head-on. That's where we discover just how much strength, resilience, and brilliance we truly hold within us.

For me, this means that I'm holding onto the beauty of self-actualization. Life has consistently shown me that there is much more than I can even picture for myself. Continuing to foster my curiosity by integrating my wide range of interests, such as my interests in organic synthesis, chemical biology, computational chemistry, social justice, running, and lifting, into my work and life is critical to me. There are so many parts of me that I am excited to realize and take power in. I hope to help others realize they, too, are worthy of their dreams and that they have the power to define themselves.

ABOUT DR. MELISSA

Melissa Ramirez is an organic chemist and change-maker.

She was born in Los Angeles, CA, and is a proud first-generation Latina in science with roots in Guanajuato, Mexico. Melissa obtained her B.A. in chemistry at the University of Pennsylvania in 2016. While at UPenn, she was a Questbridge Scholar and received scholarships through the Gates Millennium Program and American Chemical Society Scholars Program. After completion of her undergraduate studies, Melissa obtained her Ph.D. in organic chemistry at the University of California, Los Angeles (UCLA). At UCLA, Melissa was trained as a computational and synthetic organic chemist in the laboratories of Professors Ken Houk and Neil Garg. Her PhD research centered on investigating the reactivity of strained cyclic intermediates and the mechanism of pericyclic reactions for complex molecule synthesis. Following her doctoral studies, Melissa joined the laboratory of Professor Brian Stoltz as a Caltech Presidential Postdoctoral Scholar, NSF MPS-Ascend Fellow, and NIH K99/R00 MOSAIC Scholar. Her postdoctoral research focused on enantioselective Ni catalysis using a combination of experiments and computations.

Melissa launched her independent career in the Department of Chemistry at the University of Minnesota Twin Cities in 2025. Her research program centers on solving challenges in the areas of organic synthesis using a combined experimental and computational approach to advance human health. Outside of the laboratory, Melissa is passionate about changing the culture of academic research laboratories and increasing the number of Latinx-identifying individuals pursuing careers in science. Her efforts include leading #LatinXMentorFirst, an initiative that unites faculty members in the Latinx community to advocate for a mentee-centered research environment that embraces everyone's unique roots and serving as a *Poderistas* Power Squad member.

You can learn more about and connect with Melissa at:
Personal Website: www.m-ramirez.com
LinkedIn https://www.linkedin.com/in/melissa-ramirez-ph-d-833a08243/
Instagram @dr.melissaramirez

MONICA POIRIER

"Get uncomfortable and do something that scares you."

\-   Monica (Gutierrez) Poirier

~ ~ ~

Monica Poirier is a transformative people leader, strategist, and advocate whose career reflects over two decades of empowering others to lead with courage, authenticity, and intention. A skillful facilitator and coach, she has guided hundreds of leaders through meaningful growth in leadership, executive presence, and inclusive culture-building. A sought-after speaker on adversity, resilience, and inclusive leadership, Monica brings a powerful blend of diplomacy, heart, and straight talk to every stage. Rooted in her Mexican and Spanish heritage and driven by a deep commitment to service, she is a champion for belonging, a mentor to rising leaders, and a living testament to the truth that healing, humility, and success are all part of a legacy built with purpose.

~ ~ ~

To my daughter, Mariah, may you walk boldly and unapologetically in the light of your God-given talents, illuminating every path you choose with grace, courage, and authenticity. May your voice echo with purpose, your heart lead with compassion, and your talents ripple outward as a blessing to the world. You are not only my greatest inspiration, but you are also the heartbeat behind every word in this chapter.

From the moment I became your mother, my life found its true direction. You gave me purpose when I felt lost, strength when I felt broken, and joy in places I never thought possible. Watching you grow into the remarkable young woman you are has been my greatest honor. Your laughter, your compassion, your resilience — they remind me daily why I chose to rise, to heal, and to build a legacy worth passing on.

This chapter is more than a story — it's a love letter to you. A reflection of the journey I've walked so that you could walk yours with fewer burdens and more light. I hope you carry this legacy forward, not just as my daughter, but as a powerful force in your own right. May you always know how deeply you are loved, how fiercely I believe in you, and how proud I am to be your mom.

.

A WHISPER TO A ROAR: HEALING THE PAST. LEADING THE FUTURE

THE JOURNEY

I spent nearly my entire life in the vibrant heart of the San Francisco Bay Area — but my story actually began in Texas, shaped by a truth that was anything but easy. My roots were tangled in a past I didn't choose.

At just 13 months old, my biological mother fled a turbulent relationship, taking my toddler brother and me to California under the cover of secrecy. She made her mother promise never to reveal our whereabouts. My biological father, away at Army training, never saw it coming. The timing was deliberate. The separation was permanent.

Growing up without extended family felt like living in a world built for someone else. My friends had two parents, cousins nearby, and grandparents at school plays. I had none of that. But I had something else — I had a love for people and a deep faith, even as a child. That spark helped me build friendships that became my chosen family, a lifeline in the absence of blood ties.

As a young girl, I recall being too patient, trusting, and naïve. But I was a happy-go-lucky kid, always smiling. It wasn't until I learned to hone my instincts that I began to see things more clearly. It took many years to learn to advocate for myself.

For the next fifteen years, we moved at least seven times. No roots. No stability. But I found strength in structure — school, sports, and the rhythm of routine. I excelled academically and threw myself into soccer and cheer, chasing moments of togetherness wherever I could find them.

Then came the moment that changed everything. I was sixteen, my brother seventeen. We walked home from school — a long trek we knew well. But this time, when we opened the door to our apartment, it was empty. Not just quiet — gone. Vanished. Our biological mother had left her kids.

What followed was a scramble for survival. Not having a home, I ended up living in a converted garage, sharing space with a peer and paying rent to her mother. This was undoubtedly the most uncomfortable situation I could have ever imagined. It was, once again, living on pins and needles.

Work became my sanctuary — a place where I could breathe, focus, and feel capable. It was my junior year of high school. After four periods, I'd climb the hill and catch the public bus to my job, quietly carrying the weight of a life few could imagine. I didn't talk about it. How could my peers understand when I was still piecing together the meaning of it all? But in that silence, I forged something powerful: resilience. Not the kind you read about in books — the kind you earn, one quiet step at a time.

Looking back, one of the most significant moments of my career came at the tender age of 16. I had a boss who looked at my work and then showed me all the ways I was doing it wrong. Each time she critiqued me, I learned how to work faster and more effectively. It was this intensity that shaped me to hustle under pressure. This took my work ethic to a whole other level.

A year later, my personal life changed again. My biological mother returned, forcing the three of us to live together again in a one-bedroom apartment. But by then, I had already stepped into adulthood. The chaos was unbearable. I should have declared myself an emancipated minor, but this was before the internet — before answers were a click away. I was navigating a maze with no map, relying only on instinct and grit.

The moment I turned 18, I moved in with roommates and began carving out a life of my own. Those next four years were a blur — equal parts freedom, uncertainty, and restlessness. I was surviving and walking through life numbly. But it wasn't until I became a mother at twenty-two that everything shifted.

In that moment, I felt something I had never truly known: grounding. Wholeness.

Motherhood didn't just give me a child — it gave me clarity. It gave me a reason to rise, to heal, and to build a life not defined by what I had lost, but by what I was determined to create. In becoming a mother, I found my anchor. My purpose. My power. This little human made me a warrior.

I remember working as a temp, pregnant and uncertain of what tomorrow might hold. Then something extraordinary happened. My boss, a kind and compassionate man, hired me during my sixth month of pregnancy. Who does that? It was an act of humanity that changed the trajectory of my life.

A few months after my daughter was born, a woman from HR approached me. She said she liked the way I spoke to people and asked if I'd consider applying for the HR Specialist role. I smiled, grateful but hesitant.

"I have a baby at home," I said. "Are you sure?"

She smiled back and said, "Yes."

That moment cracked open a door I hadn't even known existed. It was the beginning of my career in Human Resources — and the beginning of discovering my gift for helping others.

As I slowly climbed the ranks, I could provide more for my daughter and me. Money wasn't the goal — it was the tool. It gave us safety, a stable neighborhood, and the ability to say yes to softball equipment, musical instruments, and all the little things that help a child dream bigger.

Over the years, I rose to lead a team and discovered that people leadership was more than a job — it was a calling. I found joy in coaching others, in helping them grow, in navigating situations with empathy and strength.

Since then, I have coached hundreds of leaders, up to the C-suite, and have had more courageous conversations than I can count. Humor became my secret weapon — lightening heavy moments, building trust, and reminding people that even in the face of challenge, there's room for grace.

With diplomacy, fairness, and a healthy dose of humility, I've learned that almost anything is possible.

I've built training programs from scratch, facilitated sessions that sparked transformation, and grown into a coach who leads with heart. And it all started with a baby, a kind boss, and a woman who saw something in me before I saw it in myself.

These milestones weren't just about advancing my career — they were about rewriting the story I came from. Every workshop, every courageous conversation, every moment of mentorship became a way to give others what I once needed most: guidance, stability, and having their back.

I share these experiences not to place blame on my biological parents, but to tell the truth of what shaped me. They faced their own battles and did the best they could with the resources and understanding they had at the time. My story is simply that—mine. It's about how those early experiences affected me, and how I chose to transform them into something different for my daughter. Breaking the cycle isn't about judgment; it's about awareness, healing, and growth.

THE LEARNINGS

In late 2022, I was given an extraordinary opportunity: selected to lead my global company's Hispanic/Latinx Employee Resource Group.

For years, HR professionals were taught to steer clear of topics like race and culture in the workplace. So, when this role came my way, I paused. I hesitated. It would require vulnerability I hadn't yet shown at work, decisions that would impact hundreds of members and allies, and a bold step into my heritage — not as a footnote, but as a source of strength.

First serving as Co-President, then President, for the last three years, it became one of the most humbling and transformative experiences of my career. It taught me the art of balancing a demanding day job while also simultaneously leading in a mission-driven role — and the importance of showing up fully, heart, heritage, and all.

I built business plans, sat across from two of the top executives at the organization to walk through our goals and successes, and collaborated with teams across Finance, Communications, Media, Travel and Meetings, Legal, Inclusion, and Executive Sponsors. I reviewed contracts, approved keynote speakers, and made key financial decisions. It was a masterclass in cross-functional leadership and strategic influence.

But the real work — the soul work — was in harmonizing the needs of our members and allies with the company's broader inclusion strategy. It meant making tough decisions, communicating with clarity and compassion, and learning to lead a large, diverse audience with authenticity and heart. I witnessed members breathe life into our mission, bringing their gifts and passions forward to create content and experiences that uplifted, educated, and inspired.

This was a place where my speaking roles and strategic work grew, while my free time shrank. This role was not as glamorous as one might imagine. It was filled with late nights, early mornings, and weekend dedication — all driven by a purpose to expand what the ERG could be. It required navigating hundreds of opinions with limited resources and collaborating to hone an annual template for what was truly possible.

Over time, the Employee Resource Group evolved into something extraordinary — a space where voices were heard, identities celebrated, and allies welcomed not just as supporters but as co-creators of change. It became a sanctuary of support, a hub of belonging, and a catalyst for growth. My mission was simple: to leave the ERG better than I found it.

This role didn't just expand my leadership — it expanded my world. It grew my network, deepened my purpose, and ultimately led me here… to this book.

I chose to be part of this book because I believe it's time for my story to step out of the shadows and into the light. For too long, stories like mine — marked by abandonment, resilience, and transformation — have been quietly carried, rarely spoken. But I feel no shame in what I've lived through. In fact, I stand in it with pride and gratitude.

My hope is that by sharing my journey, others will see a reflection of their own strength. That they'll realize they are not alone, and that their past does not have to define their future. I want readers to feel empowered to rewrite their own narratives — to take the pain, the setbacks, the silence — and turn them into purpose.

This book, for me, is more than a chapter. It's a bridge — from survival to leadership, from silence to voice.

A book born from connection, courage, and the belief that when we lean into who we are, we unlock the power to lead, inspire, and transform.

THE INSPIRATION

Forgiveness. One of the most pivotal challenges I've faced was learning to forgive—not just others, but myself. My divorce, some years before, though necessary, cracked open a vault of memories I had long tucked away. It forced me to revisit my childhood, to tend to wounds I had ignored for far too long. While I knew leaving was the right decision, it unearthed a past that still needed healing.

Forgiveness is not a passive act; it's a radical, soul-shifting decision. When I began to release the pain caused by those who had hurt me, something extraordinary happened: I felt lighter. Happier. Free. That's when I understood what people meant by bliss. But it didn't come easily. It required deep emotional work, reflection, and a willingness to confront the shadows. Had I not invested in that process, I would never have reached the peace I now carry.

Learning to navigate life was made easier by the wonderful friendships I made, as they were like family to me. Not all friends can sit with you in grief, hold space, and listen without judgment. But those who can — they are the unsung heroes of healing. Treasure them deeply.

At my core, I'm a giver. But I had to admit — receiving? That's always been harder. I chuckle as I write this, but it's true. One poem changed everything for me in this space: *Our Deepest Fear* by Marianne Williamson.

It cracked something open. Why not lean into my gifts? Why not remember the smiling, easygoing girl I used to be? Why not become a source of light?

That shift became the foundation for how I now show up in the world. It made me a better coach, a more compassionate listener, and someone who speaks truth with love. I no longer waste time in resentment or sadness. And

I encourage others to do the same. Life is far too precious to live in emotional captivity.

The loudest lessons often come wrapped in laughter. My brother is the only person who truly grasped the silent weight abandonment can leave on a soul — and the power of humor to lift it. Where I was quiet and thoughtful, he was bold and hilarious, cracking jokes that echoed through our childhood like a soundtrack of survival.

We were opposites in many ways — my nose buried in books, his voice booming with wit — but that contrast became a classroom. He taught me not to take myself too seriously, to find strength in playfulness, and to meet life's curveballs with a clever comeback and a sly smile. I learned to spar with his quick wit, to laugh at myself, and to soften the edges of my seriousness without losing my depth.

You can't buy these kinds of lessons. You earn them through shared history — through the type of siblinghood that defies logic, so different, yet so deeply understood. He didn't just make me laugh. He helped me live lighter and more carefree.

I was also lucky to have other inspirational people around me. I worked with someone who led with unwavering kindness. One day, I asked her how she learned to lead that way, even when people were incredibly rude to her. She smiled and said, "That was my mom. She was very kind."

Through her, I witnessed the power of listening deeply, building trust, and leading with heart. She inspired me to lean into my own strengths. Her belief in me — her advocacy — helped shape me into a better leader and a better human.

When it came to my personal living situation, I was a renter for most of my life — grateful for shelter, yet quietly yearning for something more permanent, more mine. A few years ago, I took a bold step and purchased a house on my own. My brother was the first in our family to do so. Now, it was my turn. No blueprint. No inherited path. Just grit, faith, and a vision for something greater.

That home is more than four walls and a roof. It's a symbol of resilience — a testament to breaking cycles. A sacred space where healing and hope live.

It's where I find peace after long days, where laughter echoes, and where every guest is met with open arms.

My journey has been anything but conventional. But every challenge, every tear, every breakthrough has shaped me into the woman I am today — resilient, grounded, and committed to helping others rise.

I didn't just buy a house. I claimed a legacy. One that says: we strive, we build, and we welcome others into the light we've created.

THE ADVICE

You are utterly unstoppable. The only limits are the ones you set for yourself. There will be seasons of listening, observing, and grinding — years that test your patience and your faith. Keep going. Those quiet stretches are where your foundation is built.

Forgiveness isn't about letting others off the hook; it's about setting yourself free. Peace through forgiveness is one of the greatest gifts you can give yourself. When you release pain, you make space for gratitude — for the lessons, the strength, and the resilience those moments have carved into your soul.

To anyone questioning their path:

Trust your gut. It's your inner compass, and it rarely leads you astray.

Set clear boundaries — unapologetically. We teach people how to treat us, so be brave enough to advocate for yourself and never tolerate disrespect.

Lean into faith, whatever that means to you. My faith has always been my North Star — guiding me through storms and anchoring me in grace.

Get uncomfortable. Stop playing it safe. Comfort zones

Comfort zones may feel secure, but they are rarely where greatness lives. True transformation begins when you dare to step into the unknown..

may feel secure, but they are rarely where greatness lives. True transformation begins when you dare to step into the unknown.

Find a sponsor. Someone in a senior leader role who will champion you, even when you're not in the room.

Break the cycle. Be proud of building a legacy rooted in love. I am a proud mom to an extraordinary daughter whose light reminds me daily why healing matters.

Dream big — so big that future generations will follow your lead.

Invest wisely. Money is important, but it isn't everything. Be smart, start early, and invest in stocks, real estate, and, most importantly, *yourself.* Let your efforts compound over time.

As a young woman, I carried quiet confidence. As the woman I am today, that calm confidence has grown into roaring boldness.

Having fortitude is a lifelong journey — a willingness to face what's thrown at you head-on, not with fear, but with faith. Growth isn't a straight line; it's a path of courage, clarity, and conviction.

Every step you take toward healing is a step toward becoming the person you were always meant to be.

THE PATH FORWARD

If you find yourself at a crossroads, unsure of where to begin—start with what's already inside you. The answers aren't scattered somewhere out in the world; they live within you. Begin with what you're good at. Lean into the strengths others see in you, even if you haven't yet claimed them for yourself.

Ask for feedback. It's vulnerable. It's uncomfortable. But it's also one of the most courageous and transformative steps you'll ever take.

Crossroads aren't just places to pause—they're markers. What if they're not meant to confuse us, but to guide us? What if they're invitations to rise?

I remember creating a training program for a group of leaders and enlisting one of my employees to help co-create it. After the third round of edits, he asked, "When is it good enough?" I smiled and replied, "I don't want it to be good—I want it to be fantastic." He laughed, and I said, "Let's think outside the box and throw everything at it." Together, we created something exceptional. The leaders responded with enthusiasm, and the mission became clear: excellence isn't optional—it's a mindset.

My journey is proof that adversity doesn't define us—it refines us. Being taken from my family at a young age, growing up without a safety net, and navigating life without a roadmap could have broken me. Instead, it built me. It taught me resilience, grit, and the power of choosing growth over bitterness.

If you're reading this and questioning your own path, hear this: you are not alone in your struggles. Your pain can become the foundation for your purpose. You can create change. You can build a life of meaning, even when the odds are stacked against you. Your past may shape you, but it need not limit you.

> *No matter how your story begins, you have the power to rewrite the ending*

No matter how your story begins, you have the power to rewrite the ending. You can rise. You can heal. You can thrive.

This chapter is more than a story—it's a call to action. A reminder that healing is possible, that thriving is within reach, and that every one of us has the power to change the story moving forward.

This is the legacy I hope to leave—one of excellence, heart, and perseverance. A legacy that reminds others that greatness isn't reserved for the few—it's unlocked by the brave.

So if you're wondering where to begin, begin with belief. Begin with boldness. Begin with you.

ABOUT MONICA

Monica Poirier is a transformative people leader and strategic partner with over two decades of experience in leadership development, employee experience, executive presence, and talent review. She is known for her coaching prowess and facilitation abilities. With her extensive background in people matters, she brings a unique blend of diplomacy, straight talk, and light-heartedness. She has designed and delivered dozens of learning programs on leadership, career development, and courageous conversations, helping hundreds of leaders grow intentionally and authentically.

Monica currently works at a Fortune 500 global organization. She holds the Senior Professional in Human Resources (SPHR) certification and is a certified LUMA Practitioner in human-centered design. She is a sought-after speaker on topics such as leadership, adversity, resilience, and inclusion.

Monica has held the position of President of the Hispanic/Latinx Employee Resource Group, as well as Advisor. She has spent the last five years amplifying underrepresented voices, cultivating allyship, and advancing the inclusion strategy. Her leadership has spotlighted diverse talent and inspired a culture of belonging.

During her career, Monica's speaking engagements have included moderating with thought leaders such as Claudia Romo Edelman, Carolina Caro, and Dra. Carol Laine M. Garcia, PhD. Additional speaking roles include i4cp, ALPFA, and Lean In.

Monica proudly embraces her Mexican and Spanish heritage. She splits her time between Texas and the San Francisco Bay Area and is deeply passionate about supporting food-insecure communities, empowering teens, and protecting the African lion population.

Outside of work, Monica is an avid fan of her favorite NFL team, loves photography and hiking, and is a passionate traveler. She cherishes time with family and friends and lives by a powerful truth: healing, humility, and success are not mutually exclusive — they are the foundation of her legacy.

To learn more about and connect with Monica at:
www.linkedin.com/in/monica-poirier

x

PAT MARTINEZ

"We are many working as one."

\-   Pat Martinez

~ ~ ~

Pat Martinez is a visionary leadership strategist, entrepreneur, and community builder whose 30+ year career reflects bold innovation, cultural agility, and an unwavering commitment to preparing the next generation of leaders. As the founder of Leadership in the Clouds™, she has democratized the clouds by providing a front row seat to anyone wish to access to leadership development—scaling impact through executive strategy, fractional leadership, and transformative platforms like CloudChats© and Conversations in the Round©. A nationally recognized advocate and the second Latina inducted into the Women's History Hall of Fame at the Levine Museum of the New South, Pat's influence spans board service, public appointments, global consulting, and mentorship with programs like Stanford's Latino Business Action Network. Rooted in her Puerto Rican heritage and guided by a belief in mindful, purpose-driven leadership, Pat continues to expand her legacy through authorship, conferences, and retreats—building environments where innovation thrives, communities rise, and leaders grow while "building the plane as they fly it."

~ ~ ~

I dedicate this chapter to my mother, Brigida, who showed me the way of how to move forward.

LEADERSHIP IN THE CLOUDS: WHERE VISION, PEOPLE, AND POSSIBILITY ALIGN

THE JOURNEY

My leadership journey began long before I ever held a title. It started in moments of doubt, when the weight of responsibility felt heavier than my own confidence. I remember sitting alone after a difficult decision, wondering if I was truly capable of leading others. What I've learned is that leadership isn't about perfection—it's about resilience, empathy, and the courage to rise after every fall.

Every challenge I faced became a lesson, every setback a stepping stone. This chapter is my story of those moments—the victories and the vulnerabilities—and how they shaped not just my career, but my purpose: to lead with heart and to inspire others to believe in their own strength.

My journey was filled with moments of triumph and challenge—times when the path forward was clear and times when it felt like navigating in the dark. Each experience taught me that leadership is less about having all the answers and more about asking the right questions, listening deeply, and building trust.

I was raised by a single, strong, and proud Puerto Rican mom. Her work ethic was incredible. She taught herself to read and write English and provided for my sister and me without any assistance. I come from humble beginnings. Yes, we were poor, and I never lost sight of the need to strive for excellence.

One of the most pivotal challenges I faced was stepping into leadership roles where I was often the only one who looked like me or shared my background. The weight of expectations and the pressure to conform were real. But instead of shrinking, I leaned into authenticity. I realized that my unique perspective was not a liability; it was my greatest asset.

My inner strength came from a deep sense of purpose: to create opportunities for others and to challenge systems that limit potential. I relied on strategies like mindfulness and reflection to stay grounded, and I embraced a growth mindset—seeing every obstacle as a chance to learn and innovate. Scenario planning became a powerful tool, allowing me to navigate uncertainty with confidence.

I was fortunate to have mentors who believed in me. I have had mentors throughout my young professional years and, still today, I have a mentor/friend who keeps me grounded. However, there were moments when I had to stand alone and make bold decisions. Those moments taught me self-reliance and sharpened my instincts as a leader.

I've never been afraid to challenge norms. Whether advocating for diversity in leadership or introducing agile strategies in traditionally rigid environments, I've always believed that progress requires courage. Disruption isn't about chaos—it's about creating space for innovation and inclusion.

Leadership is not a title; it's a responsibility. When I first stepped into the role of CEO, I believed success was measured by growth charts and bottom lines. Over time, I learned that authentic leadership is about something more profound: empowering people, embracing change, and staying anchored in values even when the world feels uncertain.

Today, my mission is clear: to be a catalyst for growth, helping individuals and organizations unlock their full potential. Every challenge I've faced has shaped me into the leader I am today —one who leads with vision, empathy, and an unwavering commitment to excellence. This is achieved through a three-pronged approach. I analyze by assessing the individual talents, and for businesses, I seek to address the problems. Engagement to refine goals and develop strategies to ensure optimal growth. Then, to ignite with solutions and the proper tools to ensure personal and professional success that will impact and provide businesses with processes that deliver increased sustainable growth.

THE LEARNINGS

I didn't set out to become a change-maker—I set out to make a difference. Over time, I realized that real change begins when you empower others to lead, innovate, and believe in their own potential. That belief has guided every step of my journey.

One turning point came early in my career when I faced a major setback that could have derailed everything. Instead of seeing failure as the end, I embraced it as a young professional in a corporate environment. That experience taught me resilience and the importance of adaptability—two qualities that have shaped my leadership style. I quickly learned that first impressions shape your trajectory in corporate life. I learned to dress for success but never lost myself in the process. I stayed authentic, but I knew when to adapt to the situation.

The victories gave me confidence, but the challenges gave me wisdom. Every obstacle reinforced my commitment to lead with empathy and integrity. I learned that leadership isn't about being in charge; it's about creating an environment where others can thrive.

Growing up in a family that valued hard work and community service instilled in me a deep sense of responsibility. Those early lessons taught me that success is not measured by titles or accolades, but by the impact you have on people and communities.

I was raised by a single mother who taught me the value of hard work and perseverance. Coming from humble beginnings, I learned early that success isn't handed to you—it's earned through resilience, adaptability, and an unwavering belief in your potential. Those lessons became the foundation of my leadership philosophy.

Here are areas that impact me the most, and I never regret, as they have made me who I am today.

Strong Work Ethic: Humble beginnings often taught me the value of hard work and perseverance. You learn that success isn't handed to you—it's earned through effort and resilience.

Gratitude and Perspective: When you start with less, you appreciate every opportunity. This gratitude fosters a positive outlook and helps you stay grounded, even as you achieve more.

Empathy and Connection: Experiencing challenges firsthand deepens your empathy for others. It fosters compassion and the ability to connect with people from diverse backgrounds.

Resilience and Adaptability: Growing up with limited resources teaches you how to adapt and overcome obstacles. These skills become invaluable in leadership and life.

Pride Without Arrogance: Being proud of your family roots instills confidence without entitlement. It reminds you that dignity and integrity matter more than status.

Purpose-Driven Leadership: Humble beginnings often inspire a desire to give back and create opportunities for others. This sense of purpose becomes a guiding principle in your decisions.

I strive to be a catalyst for growth—helping individuals and organizations unlock their potential. Change doesn't happen overnight, but when you lead with vision, courage, and compassion, you create ripples that transform lives. I credit my mom with playing an essential role in shaping my outlook on life.

THE INSPIRATION

Inspiration for me has never been static; it has evolved as I've grown personally and professionally.

My greatest inspiration came from my mother. Her resilience and work ethic as a single parent taught me that perseverance is not optional; it's essential. Watching her navigate life with strength and grace ignited my passion for helping others unlock their potential.

My aunt, a businesswoman, embodied the ability and desire to embark on new adventures without regret or looking back. She taught me that taking chances with purpose is a way of life because, how else could you move forward?

Throughout my career, I've been fortunate to learn from leaders who modeled integrity, courage, and vision. Men and women alike, these mentors reminded me that leadership is not about titles, but about impact.

Certain books have become guiding lights during tough times, spanning science, leadership, personal growth, and resilience. These include *The Leadership Challenge* by Kouzes and Posner; *Built to Last* by Collins and Porras; *Primal Leadership* by Goleman, Boyatzis, and McKee; *The Five Temptations of a CEO* by Patrick Lencioni; and *The 360 Leader* by John Maxwell. These are among the books I have read and often reference in my personal leadership journey. These books reinforced the idea that challenges are stepping stones, not roadblocks. Keeping a clear goal of where I want to be, a roadmap for personal success, has always been my playbook in life.

> *Discomfort often signals growth.*

Moments of adversity—whether breaking through systemic barriers or leading through uncertainty—were transformative. They taught me that discomfort often signals growth. Being Puerto Rican and feeling that I was never entirely accepted by my community, and being labeled as "OTHER," forged me to be the best, no matter the naysayers. I was born in the Bronx and moved to Queens during my formative years. It was during high school that I experienced prejudice for the first time. Although I had a circle of friends, I never felt I fit in.

Over time, my inspiration shifted from external role models to an internal compass rooted in purpose. This shift taught me that leadership isn't about imitation, but about alignment. I began reading more and stopped chasing external validation. It was after college that I truly began leading from purpose—every decision carried deeper meaning. I found my voice.

That internal compass, rooted in conviction, became my anchor. It transformed my leadership from reactive to intentional, and from positional to deeply personal. It gave me clarity amid uncertainty and empowered me to define my own success—one that inspires others to do the same.

Today, I'm inspired by the possibility of creating environments where others can thrive and by the impact of empowering diverse voices.

THE ADVICE

If I could sit down with my younger self, I'd start with this: Life isn't a straight line—it's a series of pivots, lessons, and opportunities disguised as challenges.

I would also say: Embrace failure as a form of feedback. Every setback is a stepping stone, not a stop sign. Invest in relationships early. Success is rarely a solo activity built on trust and collaboration. Don't wait for permission. Create your own opportunities. The world rewards initiative.

For years, I operated from scarcity, believing resources and opportunities were limited. The shift to an abundance mindset changed everything. It taught me that growth isn't about perfection; it's about progress.

Here are a few points to consider in your life journey:
1. Define your values; they'll be your compass when the path gets foggy.
2. Surround yourself with people who challenge you, not just cheer you on.
3. Celebrating small wins builds momentum and confidence.
4. Daily reflection and journaling to clarify thoughts and track progress.
5. Continuous learning: books, podcasts, and conversations with diverse thinkers.
6. Intentional networking—building authentic relationships, not just contacts.
7. Practicing gratitude and mindfulness to keep perspective and reduce stress.
8. Find a balance that works for you; there is no cookie-cutter life/work balance; find what makes you happy.

Everyone's journey will be uniquely theirs, but here's the truth: The most significant investment you'll ever make is in yourself. Embrace growth, lead with values, and never underestimate the power of resilience.

Remember, "We are many working as one." No one succeeds alone. Be a mentor and a sponsor to another woman in need of guidance. It's truly a rewarding feeling.

THE PATH FORWARD

I want my story to remind you that where you start does not define where you finish. I was raised by a single mother with a strong work ethic and humble beginnings, and those early experiences taught me resilience, grit, and the power of possibility. Every challenge I faced became an opportunity to grow, and every lesson shaped how I lead today.

Where you start does not define where you finish.

As I look ahead, I carry a deep belief that leadership is not about position, profit, or perfection. It is about purpose. It is about serving people, staying anchored in your values, and having the courage to adapt when the world changes. Vision has the power to transform organizations, but it can also transform lives—especially when it is paired with authenticity, empathy, and integrity.

My legacy is not about titles or accomplishments. It is about unlocking potential. It is about helping individuals and organizations see beyond limitations and step into what is possible. It is about building cultures where people feel seen, valued, and empowered to lead at every level. When we put people first, embrace innovation with intention, and remain committed to continuous learning, growth follows naturally.

My call to action is simple: lead with purpose, invest in people, and never underestimate the ripple effect of your actions. Every conversation, every decision, every act of courage matters. Small choices, made with clarity and heart, can change a life—and that life can change a community, an organization, or even the world.

Remember this: we are many working as one. No one succeeds alone. Be a mentor. Be a sponsor. Be the leader who opens doors and holds space for others to rise. Ask yourself each day, *What impact will I make today?* Then move forward with vision, resilience, and the confidence that your story—just as it is—has the power to inspire the next generation of leaders.

ABOUT PAT

Pat Martinez is the visionary force behind Leadership in the Clouds™ (LITC), an organization dedicated to democratizing leadership training and empowering professionals to flourish in their careers. Now, she is leading the future with fractional executives. Pat has been a transformational strategist for over 30 years with expertise in leadership development, community relations and engagement, organizational transformation, and nonprofit management. Her extensive executive leadership experience across various sectors underscores her ability to lead, transform, and drive impactful changes, propel organizations forward, foster innovation, and strengthen community collaboration. Pat is the creator and host of CloudChats© and Conversations in the Round©. She is also the creator of the business series "Over Easy".

Her involvement has led to various appointments to serve on national and local boards, committees, and task forces. In her current home state of North Carolina, former Governor Roy Cooper has appointed her to serve on the NC Commission on Inclusion and the Andrea Harris Task Force to address the needs of the state during the COVID-19 pandemic. Her involvement in community engagement is extensive. She has received national awards and recognition for her advocacy and leadership. Among them was an award from BMW, "Paying It 4Ward," for her high impact on the community. Pride Magazine recognized her for creating "Diversity in the Clouds." Pat was one of the "25 Distinguished Women in Business" by MEA Magazine, was named "Businesswoman of the Year" by La Noticia, and received the Advocacy Award from the Diamante Organization. The Mecklenburg Times' "50 Most Influential Women" awards in 2021 recognized women leaders in the Charlotte area's legal and business communities. The awards highlight women's impact on the local economy and society through leadership, business acumen, mentoring, and community involvement. Pat Martinez of Leadership in the Clouds was among those recognized. In 2025, she was recognized in the Iconic Success Magazine as one of the Top Admired Leaders of 2025.

Pat Martinez is the second Latina inducted into the Women's History Hall of Fame at the Levine Museum of the New South. She has received leadership recognition from Toastmasters and various student organizations as she prepares the future leaders of America. She has been a recurring mentor for successful entrepreneurs participating in Stanford University's Latino Business Action Network (LBAN) scaling-up program. Latino companies are younger and, consequently, smaller than the average, but they are growing. When they reach the average size of companies in the U.S., this will add $3 trillion to the American economy. The LBAN collective goal is to accelerate this process. Since the inception of Leadership in the Clouds™ in 2013, Pat has continued to scale up her company. Pat provides strategic leadership and sustains positive business growth while embracing cultural agility within her global management consulting firm, engaging transformational leaders who ignite innovation and create environments for success across industries. The company's headquarters will remain in Charlotte, NC, and the first satellite office will be in Miami. She will continue to scale up her services and open several satellite offices across the USA and in Puerto Rico. The objective is to better serve the local business communities by providing a hybrid environment where she is leading a group of talented experts who are narrowing the learning gap and expanding the social reach. Under her leadership, she kicks off a 7-city tour in 2026 entitled "Success in Mind Women Businesswomen Empowerment Conference" in Cidra, Puerto Rico, then Orlando, Florida, in May, over to Atlanta, Georgia, and Austin, Texas, in June, then to Louisville, Kentucky, in July, and Chicago, Illinois, in August. She ends the tour in Denver, Colorado, in September.

Her dream of hosting a Destination Retreat in Costa Rica in the Fall of 2027. Her objective is to have her participants enhance well-being while experiencing transformational leadership. It is the beginning of a journey to elevate their clients' understanding of self while expanding their ability to scale their business and increase profitable growth.

Pat Martinez is also a contributing author in the Amazon-published anthology, Unveiling Legends: Women Who Rise, Inspire, and Thrive. This book is 176 pages of pure power, purpose, and transformation, released September 2025. Her leadership book, "Success in Mind," is to be released in 2026, and it will share ways to effectively manage and develop a competitive edge. It also supports belief in mindful leadership, and that each individual needs to know their purpose as well as have a strategic plan in life.

In 2027, her children's book series will be released, which is a semi-biography story, entitled "Patti Puerto Rican". It is a collection of six short stories that blends factual biography with fictional elements. It focuses on a specific period or events in the character's life and will include imagined dialogue or thoughts to enhance engagement. It aims to provide insight into the character's journey of developing self-awareness, resiliency, empathy, and the drive to excellence. It's a leadership journey.

Pat graduated with a BS in Political Science from Rutgers University. She has professional training in Paralegal Studies, Behavioral Assessments, as well as other certifications. She was born in The Bronx, New York, and her parents are from Puerto Rican. She has lived in Charlotte since 1998 with her husband, Luis, her "ROCK" and they have two adult children which she refers to them as her "BOOKENDs".

Pat believes in preparing the next generation for leadership through training, mentoring, and sponsoring activities, through her non-profit "National Council for Leadership. Together with Leadership in the Clouds™ they ignites innovation and creates environments for success in today's fast-paced world. Together, we are building the plane as we fly it!

Lear more about and connect with Pat at:

www.leadershipintheclouds.com
https://www.linkedin.com/in/pat-martinez-7a09a6232/

ROSA BELTRÉ

"Lead with purpose. Stand in truth. Leave the door wide open."

\- Rosa Beltré

~ ~ ~

Rosa Beltré (she/her/ella) is an Afro-Taina-Latiné powerhouse, author, and visionary leader whose voice has become a force for justice, healing, and liberation. As President & CEO of the Ohio Alliance to End Sexual Violence, she stands at the forefront of the movement to end sexual violence and uplift survivor-centered advocacy rooted in equity and compassion. With over two decades of national and international impact, Rosa has devoted her life to amplifying silenced voices and advancing systemic change through education, faith, and community empowerment. Her work embodies courage, empathy, and purpose—bridging worlds, inspiring collective healing, and redefining what it means to lead with heart, resilience, and unwavering conviction.

~ ~ ~

To my parents, whose courage built the foundation I now stand on;
to my children and granddaughters, the heartbeat behind every purpose I
pursue;
to my brother, his family, and all those who remind me that migration is not
loss but legacy — a testament that anything is possible when we carry faith,
love, and determination across borders.
And to every Latina walking her own road of becoming —may you always
lead with purpose, stand in truth, and leave the door wide open for those
who follow.

ROOTED IN PURPOSE: REPRESENTATION WITHOUT TRANSFORMATION IS NOT ENOUGH

THE JOURNEY

My journey began long before I ever carried a title. It started in a Dominican home where perseverance was the family language, and faith was practiced through action. As the daughter of immigrant parents, I witnessed resilience personified — a mother and father who traded familiarity for possibility, who taught me that dignity doesn't depend on circumstance, and that hard work can become a form of resistance.

Growing up Afro-Taina-Latiné in the United States meant constantly navigating multiple worlds — each with its own expectations and limitations. I learned to translate not just words, but identities. That duality taught me empathy, adaptability, and the quiet power of being both seen and unseen. It also gave me the drive to challenge the systems that too often exclude the very communities that built them.

What many don't see is how early that path actually began. Before Corporate America, before the leadership titles, before the boardrooms, there was a younger version of me—curious, determined, and already carrying the weight of responsibility with a kind of quiet courage. I studied Business Administration with a minor in finance, not because it sounded impressive, but because numbers made sense to me. They were predictable in a world that often wasn't. But even before that degree, my education started in the most formative classroom I've ever known: my parents' business in the Dominican Republic.

There, I learned what it meant to run something from the ground up— inventory, operations, customer relations, conflict management —all while witnessing the sacrifices my parents made to build generational stability. Managing their business wasn't just a task; it was an inheritance of discipline and vision.

Every summer in New York City, I worked in bookkeeping and cash flow balancing for supermarkets. While my friends were on vacation, I was counting registers, auditing numbers, and understanding systems. Without realizing it, I was training for the world I would eventually enter.

When I returned to the States as an adult, I fully stepped into the world of finance. I worked in call centers and customer service roles that often go unnoticed but are the backbone of any financial institution. And like so many of us, I had to grind. I had to work twice as hard, stay twice as late, and know twice as much just to prove I belonged. But that grit paid off.

Through work ethic, consistency, and an unwavering commitment to excellence, I climbed. Slowly at first, then suddenly. From customer service to 401(k) financial services. From entry-level to top producer. From someone following scripts on a screen to someone being trusted with strategy, equity, and impact.

Eventually, I became a Vice President of Community Relations for one of the banks—a role that allowed me to bridge my identity with my purpose. I worked closely with the Latine community, not just offering services, but opening doors. Whether I was teaching families how to build wealth, helping them diversify their portfolios, or guiding first-time homeowners through a process they had been told wasn't for them, my work became a ministry long before I ever stepped into the pulpit.

Corporate America didn't give me direction; it revealed what was already in me. Leadership. Integrity. Community. The desire to build the kind of access my parents never had. Those early experiences became the blueprint for every step that followed.

Corporate America was where ambition met reality. I entered boardrooms as one of the few — sometimes the only — woman of color. I carried the weight of tokenism and the whisper of imposter syndrome, those subtle reminders that I was expected to be grateful for being "in the room." But over time, I realized that my presence wasn't a favor; it was an opportunity — one I had earned through preparation, persistence, and purpose.

Those experiences fueled a deeper calling. I transitioned from corporate spaces into community work, where my leadership found its rhythm and purpose.

There were moments along the way that made the shift from *doing the work* to *belonging in the work* unmistakably clear.

One of those moments happened early in my advocacy career. I remember standing in a packed community room, surrounded by women who looked like my mother, my aunts, my younger self. They came seeking resources after surviving violence and injustice, and before I even began speaking, one of them whispered, *"Por fin alguien que nos entiende."*

Finally, someone who understands us.

In that moment, I felt something settle in me — a deep knowing that I wasn't just filling a role; I was stepping into a calling. I had spent years in spaces where I had to explain my presence. Here, my presence was the very thing that made the room safer.

Another moment came during an international mission in the Dominican Republic. I watched a survivor share her story publicly for the first time, her voice trembling but determined. When she finished, she hugged me and said, *"If you hadn't come, I would've never believed I deserved to speak."*

It reminded me that belonging isn't just about the room you walk into, but the rooms you help others build for themselves.

And then there was a quieter, more personal turning point — while working toward my MBA. One night, after putting my children to bed, I sat at the dining room table surrounded by notes, laptop screens, and textbooks. I was exhausted, overwhelmed, and doubting whether I could keep going. My daughter came out of her room, half-asleep, and said, "Mami, when I grow up, I want to work hard like you."

Her words became fuel. Not because they praised me, but because they reminded me that the next generation is always watching. At that table, under the warm light of a lamp and with tears in my eyes, I realized I didn't just *belong* in these spaces — I was carving a path for those who would walk after me.

And finally, there was a moment much later in my career, after becoming CEO of OAESV. I was in a legislative meeting, surrounded by policymakers and leaders I once felt intimidated by. I spoke about survivors, equity, and the consequences of silence. When I finished, the room went still. People leaned in — listening, not out of courtesy, but out of respect. That moment affirmed something I had learned over time: I didn't need to assimilate to lead. I needed to show up as myself.

These stories are not polished or perfect. They are raw, honest glimpses into the moments that shaped me. Moments where I felt, deeply and undeniably: **I belong here because purpose placed me here.**

And that is the message I want to leave with every reader — the understanding that belonging is not granted by systems; it is claimed by authenticity. It is reinforced every time we show up fully, every time we advocate boldly, and every time we refuse to let our identities be minimized for someone else's comfort.

For more than two decades, I have dedicated my life to amplifying voices that have been silenced — survivors of sexual violence, BIPOC communities, and historically marginalized populations. Today, as President & CEO of the Ohio Alliance to End Sexual Violence, I lead with both head and heart — using strategy to advance justice and compassion, and to sustain them.

My work has taken me across states and countries, advocating for survivors, training leaders, and helping communities build systems grounded in dignity and equity. Each experience, from fair housing to faith-based leadership, has deepened my conviction that justice is not theoretical — it's personal.

But behind every title is a story of endurance. As a single mother raising two children, I pursued my MBA, often studying after bedtime stories and during moments of exhaustion that only other working parents understand. Now, as I pursue my Doctorate in Strategic Leadership, I do so not as a quest for credentials, but as a testament to the fact that anything is possible. Education became my way of telling my children—and every young Latina watching— that we are not defined by barriers, but by how we move through them.

The pivotal moments in my journey were not always the public victories. They were the quiet realizations: that I no longer needed to shrink to make others comfortable; that leadership is about creating tables, not just sitting at them; and that representation without influence changes nothing.

I have learned that transformation begins when we lead as our whole selves — Afro-Taina, Latina, mother, executive, advocate — all at once. My story is not about perfection or prestige; it's about purpose. It's about redefining leadership so that those who come after us don't have to question whether they belong.

Today, I stand as an author, speaker, and advocate — but most importantly, as a bridge builder. My journey reflects a truth I want every reader to hold onto: we are not tokens; we are torchbearers. We are not merely part of change — we are the change. And no matter where you start, if you stay grounded in who you are, your story can change the world.

THE LEARNINGS

Every journey includes moments that test both courage and conviction. Mine has been shaped not only by accomplishments but by the tension between expectation and authenticity — between what the world wanted from me and who I knew I was becoming.

One of the most pivotal challenges I faced was learning to navigate spaces where my presence was tolerated, but my perspective was not always welcomed. As an Afro-Taina-Latiné woman in leadership, I often entered rooms where I was seen as a checkbox—the "diverse voice" meant to represent many, rather than a professional with expertise and strategy to contribute. That kind of tokenism can quietly erode confidence. It took time to unlearn the need for constant validation and replace it with self-trust.

There is one moment that stays with me whenever I think about tokenism and the heavy silence it carries.

Years ago, I was invited to a high-level strategy meeting at one of the banks. It was a room full of senior executives — mostly white, mostly male — discussing outreach strategies for "underserved communities." I had been excelling in my role, outperforming metrics, and building meaningful relationships with Latine families across multiple districts. I came prepared with data, lived expertise, and a plan that could transform how we engaged our customers.

Midway through the meeting, after presenting my recommendations, one of the executives leaned back in his chair, smiled politely, and said, "That's great cultural insight, Rosa, but let's wait until the *real* strategy discussion begins."

The room chuckled.

He moved on.

And just like that, I was erased — while sitting right there.

I remember the heat rising in my face, not from embarrassment, but from the familiar sting of invisibility. At that moment, I wasn't the Vice President they had promoted. I wasn't the subject-matter expert. I wasn't the strategist. I was the checkbox.

I left that meeting and sat in my car for a long time. Not crying. Not angry. Just…processing. I had a choice: shrink or sharpen. That day, I decided I would never again allow someone's limited vision to define my capacity. I would occupy spaces not because I was invited, but because I had earned them.

Another time, at a community partnership event, a colleague introduced me, saying, "Rosa is here to give us the cultural perspective." I interrupted gently but firmly: "No — I'm here to share strategies that increase market growth and community investment. My culture is a gift, not a limitation."

The room nodded, some surprised, others uncomfortable. But I learned something powerful that day: when you speak your truth with clarity, people adjust.

These moments tested me, shaped me, and ultimately strengthened me. They taught me that belonging is not the opposite of exclusion — **courage is.**

That expertise without confidence is easily dismissed.
And that representation without influence is just decoration.

Today, I walk into rooms understanding the weight and worth of my voice. I don't shrink to fit — I expand to lead. And I carry these stories not as wounds, but as reminders that authenticity is my authority.

Imposter syndrome was another shadow that lingered, especially early in my career. It showed up in moments of silence — after speaking at conferences, negotiating with funders, or leading executive meetings. I'd replay every word, questioning if I was "enough." Eventually, I realized that imposter syndrome thrives in systems that were never designed for us. The problem wasn't my belonging — it was the narrow definition of leadership around me. That realization shifted everything.

I overcame much of this by grounding myself in purpose. Every time doubt surfaced, I reminded myself of the "why" behind my work: creating safer, more equitable spaces for others. Purpose became my compass when confidence wavered. I also learned the value of reflection and community. My support system — my children, mentors, and a network of women who refused to play small — reminded me that strength multiplies when shared.

Another defining struggle was learning to lead while holding multiple truths. As a single mother, I balanced career advancement with caregiving, often moving between professional intensity and personal tenderness in the same breath. Those seasons taught me the power of boundaries, rest, and self-compassion. They also showed me that leadership isn't about perfection; it's about presence.

I reimagined leadership as an act of care — where transparency, equity, and well-being are not add-ons, but the foundation.

Over time, I became more intentional about disrupting systems that reward burnout and conformity. I began leading with a "people-first" philosophy, one that challenges outdated norms about productivity, success, and hierarchy. I reimagined leadership as an act of care — where transparency, equity, and well-being are not add-ons, but the foundation. This shift has influenced how I lead teams, mentor emerging leaders, and design organizational culture.

Through the challenges, I've learned that strength is not the absence of struggle — it's the ability to transform struggle into strategy. I no longer view adversity as opposition; it's been my greatest teacher. It taught me resilience, empathy, and the courage to speak truth to power even when my voice trembles. Our value does not depend on how others label or measure us. Too often, women — especially women of color — are invited into spaces to fill a quota, not to shift the culture. But we are more than numbers, more than representation — we are agents of transformation.

Today, I stand firmly in the belief that representation without transformation is not enough. It's not enough to be in the room; we must shape what happens inside it. We must question, disrupt, and rebuild spaces so that belonging isn't conditional — it's cultural.

My journey has taught me that the most meaningful impact begins when we stop asking for permission to exist and start leading as we are. The lesson is simple but profound: you need not fit the mold to make a difference. Sometimes, breaking it is precisely what changes everything.

THE INSPIRATION

Inspiration, for me, has never been a single moment or a person — it has been a mosaic of people, experiences, and lessons that have shaped how I see the world and the work I choose to do.

At the center of that mosaic are my parents. Watching them navigate life as Dominican immigrants in a new country, with limited resources but limitless determination, taught me what resilience truly looks like. My father modeled discipline and responsibility; my mother embodied compassion and quiet strength. They never used the word "leadership," but they lived it daily through sacrifice, perseverance, and integrity.

Becoming a mother deepened that understanding. My children have been my greatest motivation — the constant reminder that everything I build must leave the world a little more just, compassionate, and accessible for those who follow. They have witnessed the late nights, the advocacy, and the moments of doubt. And yet, through their eyes, I've seen that leadership is most powerful when it's human — when it's transparent enough to admit struggle and brave enough to rise again.

Some mentors and colleagues inspired me by challenging norms and leading with courage. I've been shaped by women who spoke truth in spaces that preferred silence, who reminded me that empathy is a strategy, not a weakness. Their examples affirmed that leadership is not about commanding attention but about earning trust.

Books and movements have played their part, too. From the writings of bell hooks on love and justice to the works of Brené Brown on

I've been shaped by women who spoke truth in spaces that preferred silence, who reminded me that empathy is a strategy, not a weakness

vulnerability and courage, I've found language for things I had long felt but couldn't name. Their ideas helped me integrate heart and strategy—to lead with intellect and humanity.

As my journey evolved, so did my inspiration. Early in my career, I was driven by the need to prove myself — to succeed against odds, to represent, to make my parents proud. But over time, that evolved into something more profound: a desire to change the systems that make representation necessary in the first place. I am inspired now by the possibility of collective transformation — by seeing others rise, by watching teams grow, and by knowing that every policy shift or organizational change can ripple outward into real lives.

Traveling internationally and working alongside communities in Latin America and the Caribbean has also fueled my perspective. Witnessing women lead with so little material power yet with immense spiritual and social strength reminds me that leadership does not depend on position — it depends on conviction.

Today, what inspires me most is impact — seeing voices once silenced begin to speak, leaders once overlooked begin to lead, and organizations once rigid begin to evolve. My inspiration is sustained by hope—not the passive kind, but the kind that builds, questions, and endures.

In every stage of my life, inspiration has been both a mirror and a catalyst — reflecting where I've come from and propelling me toward what's next. It reminds me that purpose is not found; it's lived, one courageous decision at a time.

THE ADVICE

If I could sit with my younger self — the ambitious, uncertain, determined version of me trying to balance survival and purpose — I would begin with this: you don't have to shrink to be accepted. Your voice is not too loud, your dreams are not too big, and your presence does not need permission.

When I started my journey, I spent years trying to fit into molds that were never made for me. I thought that success meant assimilation — learning to sound, dress, and lead like those who held power. But real growth began when I realized that authenticity is not a liability; it's an asset. The moment you stop negotiating your identity to make others comfortable, you start to walk in freedom.

So my first piece of advice: belong to yourself first. When you anchor your worth in external validation, you become vulnerable to every shifting opinion. But when you root your confidence in your values and purpose, no title, table, or rejection can define you.

My second piece of advice: replace perfection with progress. Leadership, motherhood, and purpose are rarely tidy. Waiting for the "right moment" or the "perfect version" of yourself only delays the impact you're meant to make. I've learned that growth doesn't always look graceful — sometimes it seems like failing forward, asking for help, and trying again. Perfection isolates; progress invites evolution.

Third, protect your peace and your boundaries. The higher you rise, the more people will demand from you — time, energy, emotional labor. But saying no is not an act of selfishness; it's an act of sustainability. You cannot lead effectively from depletion. Rest, reflection, and community are not luxuries; they are leadership strategies. Burnout doesn't prove commitment — balance does.

And finally, use your influence intentionally. Representation matters, but transformation matters more. When you find yourself in rooms where decisions are made, ask who's missing. Use your seat to open space for others, especially those whose voices are still fighting to be heard. Leadership is not about being the only one at the table — it's about making sure you're never the last.

Over time, my mindset shifted from striving to serving, from chasing success to creating impact. The habits that grounded me along the way were reflection, gratitude, and continuous learning. I journal often, revisit my "why," and surround myself with people who tell me the truth, not just what's comfortable. I've learned that humility and confidence can coexist — humility keeps you teachable, and confidence keeps you standing.

If I could summarize it all in one sentence, it would be this: Be the kind of leader your younger self needed, and your future self will be proud of. Because in the end, our purpose is not just to climb — it's to lift as we rise, to disrupt systems that no longer serve, and to leave every space a little more humane than we found it.

So to anyone walking a similar path — doubting, balancing, persevering — know this: you are not behind. You are becoming. Every lesson, every closed door, every detour is refining your strength for what's ahead. Lead with integrity, protect your light, and remember that authenticity will always be your most powerful credential.

THE PATH FORWARD

To every Latina reading these words — whether you're just beginning your journey or standing at the height of your career — I want you to know this: you are not here by accident. You are the answer to someone's unspoken hope, the continuation of someone's unfinished dream.

Our stories matter because they challenge the narratives that once erased us. We are not here to fit in; we are here to redefine what leadership looks like. The world needs our voices, our strategy, our compassion, and our courage. So the call to action is simple yet urgent: show up fully, and refuse to disappear quietly.

If there is one truth my journey has taught me, it's that change does not begin in comfort. It starts when we dare to stand in our truth — even when it shakes rooms, disrupts norms, or challenges expectations. We carry the strength of generations who fought to open doors we now walk through. Our responsibility is to keep those doors open wider.

My call to you is this: lead beyond the title. Lead in your communities, in your families, in every space where you can use your influence to amplify others. Mentor another woman. Advocate for equity in your workplace. Correct bias when you see it. Refuse to be tokenized, and when you rise, bring others with you.

To the next generation of Latinas — those watching, waiting, and wondering if they belong — remember this: your identity is your superpower. Don't dim it to survive. Use it to transform. You carry the brilliance of cultures, languages, and legacies that have endured centuries of erasure. That is power no system can contain.

What's next for me is to continue this mission — to keep creating spaces where others can lead without fear of losing themselves. Through my role at the Ohio Alliance to End Sexual Violence, I will continue to elevate voices that are often silenced and design systems where survivors, women of color, and marginalized communities are not an afterthought but the starting point.

As an author and international speaker, I plan to keep writing and teaching — not from theory, but from lived experience — reminding leaders that social change begins with human connection. And as I complete my Doctorate in Strategic Leadership, my goal is to merge scholarship with activism, building frameworks that redefine leadership through equity, compassion, and courage.

My legacy is not about titles or accolades; it's about impact. I want to leave behind organizations that are more humane, leaders who are more self-aware, and communities that are more united. I want my children — and every young Latina — to see that leadership can be bold and kind, robust and principled, visionary and vulnerable all at once.

So, to every extraordinary Latina reading this: don't wait for permission. The world is waiting for what only you can bring. Be unapologetically visible. Use your voice with intention. Walk with purpose. And remember — our collective strength doesn't just change systems; it changes history.

ABOUT ROSA

Rosa Beltré (she/her/ella), an Afro-Taina-Latiné powerhouse, is a nationally recognized author, speaker, and thought leader at the forefront of the movement to end sexual violence. As the President & CEO of the Ohio Alliance to End Sexual Violence (OAESV), she leads with an unyielding commitment to justice, equity, and survivor-centered advocacy.

With over two decades of experience, Rosa has dedicated her life's work to amplifying the voices of those most silenced — particularly survivors, BIPOC communities, and historically marginalized populations. Her leadership transcends borders, bringing a global perspective to local action as she trains, speaks, and advocates across the United States and internationally.

Rosa is known not only for her deep policy knowledge and comprehensive training expertise but for her human-centered approach to transformational change. Her work spans a wide spectrum — from fair housing and child abuse prevention to financial literacy, faith-based leadership, and community engagement — reflecting her holistic vision for a more just and compassionate world.

A dynamic communicator, Rosa is a sought-after speaker at national and international conferences, coalitions, and forums. She is also the author of several inspirational works that blend faith, resilience, and social justice.

In addition to her executive leadership, Rosa serves on several national, state, and international boards, where she continues to influence public policy, strengthen global solidarity, and advance collective healing and liberation.

More than a leader, Rosa is a bridge builder, a healer, and a catalyst for societal transformation. Her commitment to listening, learning, and leading with integrity continues to inspire movements and mobilize communities toward a future free from violence and oppression.

You can learn more and connect with Rosa at:

https://rosabeltreministries.org/
https://www.instagram.com/rbeltreministries/

ROSANNA SCARPATI

"If I want it to happen, it needs to be in my calendar!"

-   Rosanna Scarpati

~ ~ ~

Rosanna Scarpati is a dynamic Holistic Life and Executive Coach who blends two decades of high-impact banking experience with a powerful commitment to personal growth, equity, and leadership development. A global trainer with Wall Street Prep, she equips executives and analysts at top financial institutions with world-class skills in communication, executive presence, and analytical excellence. As a champion for high-achieving women and LGBTQ+ leaders, Rosanna brings strategic insight, cultural fluency, and holistic principles to her coaching—empowering clients to navigate transitions with clarity, confidence, and purpose. Her career spans major institutions like JP Morgan, Tradeweb, Credit Suisse, and Deutsche Bank, and her longstanding advocacy through INROADS and multiple nonprofit boards reflects her deep belief in representation and community. Rooted in her Colombian and Italian heritage, Rosanna leads with warmth, authenticity, and joy—helping others elevate their voice, redefine success, and live with intention and impact.

~ ~ ~

To the person who shows up for me every single day of my life like no one else possibly can. The person who willed me into existence and created me in her vision of love and valor. A mi mamá. Como siempre decías, soy tu otro yo. Y en toda esta jornada que es la vida, has sido la madre perfecta para mí. Siempre me has empoderado a sentirme segura en mis decisiones y mi camino. Te adoro y te llevo conmigo siempre.

THE WORLD SHOOK. MY SPIRIT DIDN'T. AQUÍ VOY.

THE JOURNEY

I, like most of my cousins, was raised in part by my mother, uncle, aunts, grandparents, cousins, and close family friends—aka, clan raised. I knew of my father, but as a child, I rarely saw him for more than a couple of hours every few weeks.

I grew up in Northern New Jersey and lived between my grandmother's couch and a rental in upstate NY. Both my parents were immigrants to the USA from Colombia. My roots are mostly Spanish and Italian, with a great-grandmother who was Chibcha Indian. I love looking at the one photo I have of her. It gives me peace and calm, as not many things in life can.

As a child, I always strived to get good grades in school and knew I would have to be resilient—because I saw how much my mother made possible with so few resources. "Siempre hay forma de hacer que pasen las cosas," or "There is always a way to make things happen," was her philosophy, and that belief has stayed with me ever since.

I remember crying on the first day of elementary school as my mom walked me into a classroom full of staring eyes—everyone seemed like an alien to me. They all spoke English so well! When I got my first report card, I saw a C in English and was devastated. I vowed then and there to learn to speak, read, and write English fluently by second grade. Even though Spanish had been my main language at home and with friends until then, I never wanted to see another C again.

Throughout my life, when I sensed one door closing or fully closed, I didn't dwell on the closure; I refocused on the available doors and which ones I found most interesting to knock on next. During my 20s, I made sure every move I made was toward learning the most complex products in sales and trading first. I wanted to challenge myself as much as possible, and if that meant working on the Exotics Options desk at JP Morgan, going to NYU classes at night and on the weekends, working on a non-profit start-up, all while still making time to travel, go dancing, and exercise, I was going to make it happen!

In the spring of 2001, Deutsche Bank moved us to World Trade Center 5—one of the smaller buildings in the World Trade Center complex. We merely crossed Liberty Street, but the offices seemed new and modern, with large windows overlooking the WTC plaza. It felt like I was inducted into the first-class world of finance. I spent the summer watching all the joyful performances and festivals right from my desk while I worked! On the morning of September 11th, during my commute from New Jersey, I looked up from the upper level of the ferry as the second plane struck the South Tower. We all flinched upon contact as we were docking near the World Financial Center, located directly across the street from the Twin Towers, and debris splattered down across several blocks.

In that instant, the skyline, the city, and the sense of safety we all took for granted changed forever. That day—less than a year into my full-time career on Wall Street—altered the way I viewed everything in my life and the world around me. We were ushered onto the same trains we had just stepped off of with urgency, since no one knew what was going to happen next. Were we at war? Were we being attacked? Why was my phone not working? I needed to let my mom know I was alright.

All I know is that as the train forged ahead, we all quietly stared back at the towers engulfed in smoke. A strange camaraderie with all the people I saw many a morning, but never spoke to, emerged. And I shed tears as both towers one after the other imploded within minutes of us leaving the station. It didn't feel quite real and I couldn't wrap my head around what it all would mean. Powerless and full of fear and confusion, the city skyline diminished into clouds of smoke. I sat in silence, taking in the most unexpected, jarring occurrences and incidents of my life, still to date.

We were given a couple of days to process everything before being asked to return to work, to the city that had been infiltrated. I tried to quit the following week after our office was relocated to Midtown, but my boss at the time, Shirley, took me outside. Standing beside these large Romanesque statues of human figures, she talked me through my fears and convinced me to give it one more week. She asked me what I needed, what would make me reconsider. And the very next day, she delivered the peace and solitude I needed in a cubicle across the Avenue of the Americas. To this day, I don't know how she managed to do that with so many people displaced and stuck in boardrooms elbow to elbow with colleagues. But I will forever be grateful for her determination, kindness, persistence, and belief in me.

Once I decided to stay, I embraced the challenge and pushed myself to accomplish as much as I could, as fast as I could. I went on adventurous trips, took weekend getaways to Miami with friends, read the *Financial Times* daily, and worked with more energy than ever. Most importantly, I realized how much it matters who you surround yourself with.

I signed up to take the Chartered Financial Analyst (CFA) Level 1 exam, and because I wasn't sponsored by the firm, I convinced a colleague, Yury— someone higher up with an office and more influence—to register as well so I could get access to the study materials through our company. I spent every weekend studying, sacrificing outings with friends and shopping trips, but I kept my eye on the prize: becoming an Emerging Markets (EM) salesperson one day. That was my goal, and nothing was going to stop me.

Fast forward 7 years to 2008, and I was on the Fixed Income Emerging Markets Institutional Sales desk at JPMorgan and graduating from NYU with my MBA. Yay! My dream had come true. I was also the Finance Director and Founding Board Member of a nonprofit that my college roommate started to help girls and orphans in Liberia. We were in our third year, had hit all our budget goals, and had set up a house to support girls in becoming leaders.

Guess what else was happening? 2008 — the year the financial world turned upside down. Lehman Brothers collapsed, Bear Stearns was absorbed by JPMorgan, and the mortgage crisis sent global markets into freefall. On our trading floor, people were being laid off daily, entire desks disappearing overnight. I had to re-evaluate what I was doing with my life once again. As colleagues packed up their boxes, I wondered who would be next and whether the cuts would ever stop.

Given the volatility and uncertainty of the financial system, I began to seriously consider a new challenge outside Institutional Sales and Trading —

somewhere that might offer a bit more stability. That's when I applied to join the Private Bank as a sales trader on the Private Equity Sponsors Desk. While an unconventional move, I just went with my instinct and accepted the position.

There is always another door ready for you when you are, and even though that opportunity didn't turn out as expected, it taught me invaluable lessons about what I wanted — and what I didn't — in both my career and my life. So at 32, a decade into Institutional Banking, I realized it was time to take a different path.

I hadn't planned it, but the moment I saw my bonus numbers and realized my compensation had gone down after moving to the Private Bank, I knew I was done. I quit on the spot — something nearly unheard of for someone living in the city without a plan for what came next.

I decided to focus solely on my mental and physical health for the entire next year — something not often heard of from a Gen Xer. Looking back, I realize I had truly burned out. The year before, I had gone through a divorce while also dealing with a series of health issues: migraines, joint pain, and aches that spread through my back, feet, and neck until my whole body hurt. Eczema had broken out across my face and lips so badly that I could barely smile without worrying about the skin cracking and bleeding. I even developed an eye twitch that came and went unpredictably — all while working in a high-pressure environment where symptoms like mine were often seen as an inability to "handle" the job. And, to some extent, maybe that was true.

My whole life had been about striving — always chasing the next goal, the next step up, both financially and experientially. What I didn't realize at the time was that much of what drove me came from a deep need to prove to my father that I was enough — that I was worthy of love, worthy of being his daughter.

We had reconnected a few months after September 11th. A cousin had told him I worked in one of the World Trade Center buildings, and by February 2002, he left me a voicemail. It took me a few months to call him back, but when I did, we agreed to meet. We hadn't spoken or even said goodbye to each other since before my senior year of high school — almost seven years. When we finally sat down together, I cried and poured out my heart. That

meeting became the beginning of a decade-long process of rebuilding —
learning to form a somewhat healthy relationship with the father I also had
to learn how to love.

The need for a father figure and a nurturer led me to marry my first husband,
my college sweetheart and best friend in the whole world. Without him, I
would have had a completely different college experience. He was a senior,
and from the moment we met in November of my freshman year, he helped
set me on the right path. I had already made several mistakes by then, and I
don't know where I would be without his love and support in those first two
years of college. For me, I only have beautiful memories of my first real
boyfriend, first everything really. Looking back, he deserved someone who
would love him unconditionally. The love I had for him was meant to fill a
void left by not having a father who showed me paternal love as a child.

My father passed away unexpectedly just a few weeks after my daughter was
born in early 2022. He had slipped in the bathroom and hit his head. It was
not the time or the kind of passing I had imagined for him. Though I believed
I had long since healed the wounds of our past, his sudden death — and the
resurfacing of his words in his will he had written back in 2000 — haunted
me for the rest of that year. He had named me in his will, only to say I was
to get nothing of his. I found myself reverting to old feelings of unworthiness,
of being unlovable, unimportant, and unwanted. Fortunately or by design, I
didn't need even a penny from him, but the gesture hurt nonetheless.

And yet, with the birth of my long-awaited and miracle daughter — my
purpose — came something else: the quiet death of my need for admiration
and love from the man who brought me into this world. Healing that final
part of my story took time, but by the end of my daughter's first year on this
earth, I had finally made peace with it.

In 2023, a two decades-long chapter of my career in Fixed Income came to
a close with the official end of LIBOR—the London Interbank Offered Rate.
For over 40 years, LIBOR had been the global benchmark for short-term
interest rates, shaping trillions of dollars in loans, derivatives, and financial
contracts worldwide. Its discontinuation marked the end of an era in modern
finance — and, coincidentally, the end of one in my own life as well.

That transition had been on the horizon even before I accepted the role of Global Product Head, where I was tasked with revamping the LIBOR Reset Risk market and launching an electronic trading platform in under four months from my start date. I knew that once LIBOR was gone, my time in that sector would be too.

When the change finally came, it felt as if the universe were giving me permission to begin again. I realized I needed distance — not just from the markets, but from the pace, the pressure, and the version of myself that had lived in that world for so long. The choice was easy: Florida. More specifically, Southeast Florida.

That year became one of profound rebirth. Coming off the life-changing experience of giving birth to my miracle baby, 2023 brought its share of trials and turbulence. I knew it would take a year — maybe two — to fully feel like myself again.

THE LEARNINGS

I've had many challenges over my lifetime that really fueled my resilience and forced me to find alternate routes that exceeded my expectations, usually.

Most recently, I would say it was the miracle of conceiving naturally at 43 without actually trying. After two miscarriages, one worse than the other, and 5 years of trying, along came COVID, and my husband and I just put that thought on the back burner. I was simply content to be safe, able to work remotely and spend more time with my son, while looking after my mom.

In 2021, one year into the pandemic, I spent a month in Miami Beach while my husband and son spent time with my mother-in-law in Toronto. That month opened my eyes to what the rest of my life could look like. I worked for Tradeweb during the day, and did a Wharton Fintech Revolution Certificate class at night. The main difference of being there during the pandemic was being able to work outside on the patio, under the shade of palm trees, with the sun lighting everything around me and the warm breeze that only a winter in South Florida could bring.

At night, I would go out to eat or make something in my little kitchen (extended beachfront hotel stay) and then go for a walk or stargaze on the beach. One night, I remember when I sat up, the moon was as big as the earth, it seemed, and was right in front of me at the end of the ocean, smiling back at me. It was then that I realized I couldn't wait until I retired to live here. I realized I deserved heaven on earth — my version of it, anyway, even if most people can't get past the hurricanes and humidity.

In fact, I'd been coming to Miami since I was little, spending summers with my aunt and cousins. Crazy enough, I was here the month Hurricane Andrew hit—August 23, 1992—the same day my twin cousins were born. You'd think that experience would've scared me away from ever wanting to live here again. My aunt's sunken living room turned into a swampy mess, water poured in through the front door and kitchen windows, and tiles flew off the roof while I hid under her king-sized bed, praying the whole ceiling wouldn't lift off. And the mango tree I loved so much? Gone—probably a little consolation gift from Andrew to one of her neighbors.

But, I digress. When I left Florida after a little over a month during that pandemic break for me, I knew I would be back very soon. My husband and I reunited back in New Jersey, only to reveal that the marriage, like his job, might not survive the pandemic. Something in me had shifted, and I saw that I wasn't living all of my core values with him by my side. As we navigated the talks, he began to show signs of improvement, with help from a professional and a lot of his own research. I believed our union might flourish if there was a big enough shake-up for him, for us, and so I pitched the Florida idea as a possible way forward.

It landed, and he was in. That was all I needed. I set my intention, and within a month, I found and put an offer on the perfect house. It had everything I had dreamed of at the price I expected. All via FaceTime and in a town I had never visited before in my life, over an hour north of Miami.

My daughter was conceived on the precise day my son and I landed in Florida, as my husband had driven down in one of our cars and met us that night at a hotel. Good thing for getting upgraded to a suite, as she would not be here if not every single thing was just right that day. It still blows my mind when I look at her to think about how perfect the timing was.

The challenges began the week after she was due. Because I was so scared of miscarrying, I did the bare minimum in movement during my pregnancy. I worked hours at my desk, would walk up and down the stairs at home a couple of times a day, and then sleep in my bed. That was the extent of my 'exercise' so my health and recovery paid the price.

She finally entered the world healthy and strong, and beautiful at the end of week 42, a week after they had been trying to induce me with every pain-inducing device possible. Unlike my firstborn, this time I was at level 13 in Pitocin when they broke my water, and even though I tried the laughing gas for a good half hour, I quickly realized I could barely breathe between contractions. Getting an epidural was my only option to not pass out or end up with a C-section.

A month after she was born, I was still a mess. Pain everywhere, my feet, my back, everything felt like it was falling apart on me. I opted for a tubal ligation as I didn't think my body could handle another pregnancy. Then, six months after she was born, I ended up with Shingles - the pain of which reminds you what contractions feel like when there is nothing at the end of the tunnel! It was horrible, painful, and took days to diagnose properly, as one doctor thought I had IBS.

After that, I focused entirely on becoming pain-free. I had never experienced so many aches and issues throughout my body all at once—or for such a long period of time. It felt like my 2010 burnout all over again, only amplified. I was still working full-time from home, praying my tenure would end soon so I could finally devote myself fully to recovery. I felt sorry for myself at times, my hormones were completely out of balance, and I started to wonder if I'd ever get back to my pre–baby number two self.

Knowing I needed to be there for my children motivated me to forge ahead with the power to find answers, try various methodologies, and figure out exactly what needed fixing. I was granted freedom from my corporate career at the beginning of 2023 and immediately kicked my post-baby health recovery regimen and self-development journey into high gear.

I did everything from meditation, acupuncture, cupping, chiropractic, infrared sauna, red light therapy, massages, muscle stimulation, vibration plates, pilates, weight training, HIIT, HRT, bike riding, walking, supplements galore, removed sulfates, added this and that – you name it, I tried it. And, between a combination of all of those things or maybe just time, the pain began to subside, and I came back stronger mentally and physically than ever before.

My daughter was walking around like a little boss babe and discovering all the amazing things nature and her discovery of life have to offer. Getting to go for a walk, a bike ride with her, to the park, playing with chalk, or swimming in the backyard all gave us both so much joy. Getting to make plans with her each day still feels surreal at times.

She and my son have given me the ability to love unconditionally and without abandon. To not expect anything in return, nor to judge myself for not being the perfect parent every second of the day. She teaches me not to be so hard on myself and to remember my purpose in life is to be of service to others, to those who need me most, and those who look up to me for guidance and direction. And it's okay if they learn on their own, too. I am not attached to the outcomes either way.

By the end of 2023, my vision for the next chapter of my life was clear. I was deeply engaged in the Executive Coaching program I'd chosen and exploring new business tools that reignited my creativity. I had returned to one of my greatest joys—Latin dancing—and even made two wonderful new friends. I was once again living with intention, both with my family and with myself. Life felt full, vibrant, and finally aligned—all thanks to that unshakable resilience that has carried me through every season of change.

THE INSPIRATION

There were two books, beyond my formal schooling requirements, that shaped how I view my life and the world. One was given to me by my mother when I was a teenager, called the *Silva Method Mind Control Method*.

At the time, the author held in-person workshops, and my mom convinced me to go with her to an introductory seminar. We walked into a plain room filled with rows of closely packed chairs. It was nighttime, and I remember there not being much to look at except bodies in seats. Everyone there was an adult—most of them even older than my mom. It was the first time I was introduced to meditation, and I was horrible at it! I kept opening my eyes and looking around at all these people who seemed to be in a trance or something. I left that experience wondering what it was really all about and a bit skeptical.

Reluctantly, I gave the book a chance, and once I began, I couldn't stop. I even experimented with remembering and writing down my dreams for several weeks, and surprised myself by the outcome. First, it was one, and then by the end of the week, I was remembering 3 and 4 dreams and writing them all down. That was just the beginning. I envisioned getting into every college I applied to and being offered every internship I interviewed for. It all began to actually happen. I was admitted to all ten schools I applied to and was offered internships at all three companies. It actually scared me, but what it 100% gave me was confidence in my ability and power to make great things happen in my life.

The other book I read was because of a boy I really liked (he was a 22-year-old DJ at Tribecas), about 5 years older than me suggested, *The Celestine Prophecy,* written in 1993. This book, though fictional, profoundly shaped how I viewed people and the world at large. The premise was that we are all energy, and that life is full of synchronicities. This was the first time I didn't feel so alone in the world.

The book spoke of a collective spiritual awakening the world was undergoing, one that would bring us all to a higher consciousness. I remember it made me realize that if we raise our vibration to live in harmony, we can more confidently trust the path our intuition guides us on. No boy had ever given me a book to read before, let alone a boy that I adored. I valued it beyond measure and let the positive messages stay with me long after the crush on him had dissipated.

Many books and people have inspired me throughout my life, but without those two books before I turned 18, I don't think I would be the woman I am today. Small changes made at that pivotal time in my life ensured that I would walk a special path of resilience, intention, and fortitude in the face of adversity.

THE ADVICE

Looking back, I realize how much I've learned about perspective, courage, and self-worth. I would tell my younger self, *We see things as we are, not as they are.* So when life feels unfair or overwhelming, take a deep breath and remember that how you see the world depends on the lens you're looking through. Change your lens, and you change your life.

> *Every time you choose healing over hurt, growth over comfort, truth over silence—you're rewriting the story for those who will come after you.*

I would also whisper: *Be brave enough to disrupt generational cycles.* Your legacy depends on the courage you show now. Every time you choose healing over hurt, growth over comfort, truth over silence—you're rewriting the story for those who will come after you.

Another truth I've come to know deeply is this: *Own your worth so you can change your worth.* I spent too many years thinking I had to prove my value through hard work, titles, or recognition. What I know now is that worth is internal—it begins when you decide you are enough.

And above all, I would remind myself: *You are enough. You are worthy. You deserve to give and feel great love.*

Self-care became the anchor that continues to keep me balanced through every difficult season of life. I've learned that when my cup is at least 85% full by the start or end of every week, I show up as my most present, patient, and compassionate self—for my children, my work, and my community. Friends and colleagues often tell me they admire how I make time to travel, even alone, or to go dancing, or to attend a sound bath meditation at an ashram. Those aren't indulgences—they're necessities. They are how I stay grounded in joy, peace, and purpose.

Life will always test your resilience, but when you nurture yourself first, you meet those tests with grace instead of exhaustion. Fill your cup. Protect your energy. And never forget—you are already everything you need to become who you're meant to be.

> *Life will always test your resilience, but when you nurture yourself first, you meet those tests with grace instead of exhaustion.*

THE PATH FORWARD

So many women hit their 40s and feel as if they've lost their spark—their sense of direction, their confidence, their "mojo." Whether it's after having kids, facing divorce, being passed over for a promotion, getting laid off, or navigating perimenopause, it can feel as if life has quietly shifted beneath your feet. I want every woman reading this to know: you are not alone, and this is not the end of your story.

This is the moment to pause, breathe, and ask yourself what truly brings you joy and fulfillment. It's your time to realign—to make choices rooted in your values, not in fear or obligation. Reinvention is not a failure; it's a form of wisdom. Transformation is how we return home to ourselves, stronger and more certain than before.

Keep moving forward—with intention, with clarity, and with faith in your ability to rebuild at any stage. Learning never stops. Growth never stops. And even when change feels uncomfortable or uncertain, trust that you are being guided toward a life more aligned with who you truly are.

Above all, remember that you are worthy—of love, success, peace, and joy— simply because you exist. Stay resilient. Keep showing up. And as you rise, extend your hand to lift another woman beside you.

That, to me, is legacy. It's not about titles or accolades—it's about the quiet courage to evolve, to keep becoming, and to remind others they can too. Our stories matter because they light the way forward for someone else's becoming.

El Amor que Quedo'

No fuiste mío en ningún momento,
pero sí la persona que siempre quise impresionar,
con mi inteligencia, mis logros, mi intento constante
de ser independiente, de brillar.

Me di cuenta, cuando murió mi papá,
que un dolor todavía existía:
ese dolor de nunca sentirme querida,
cuidada, o siquiera pensada,
por alguien que uno cree debe amarte
incondicionalmente.

¿Por qué no?
Sí, pudiste amar...
¿pero nunca a mí?
Nunca de verdad.

Te gustaba que fuera fuerte,
que nunca me dejara vencer,
que luchara con toda mi energía
cada vez que había un tropiezo o un amanecer.

Siempre tenía planes,
una lista de cosas por hacer,
ver, comprar, sentir, lograr,
y casi siempre lo conseguía.
No te lo decía — era para mí,
para probarme que valía,
que sí merecía llamarme tu hija,
que sí tenía peso mi vida,
mi presencia en este mundo.

Te empecé a querer
como al padre que nunca tuve,
te empecé a admirar
como al hombre que en ti descubrí:
trabajador, genio, cómico,
y de familia, al fin.

Tu atención, tu preocupación,
tu pasión por mi bienestar,
me conmovían,

me hacían creer en segundas oportunidades,
en sanar.

Tres años sin ti,
y ya respiro en calma plena.
Aprendí que, al aceptarme completa,
te abrazo más profundo,
más tierno, más alegre,
y más nuevo.

Sin ti, yo no sería yo.
Y tengo tanto amor hacia mí…
tanto, que sé que sí me quisiste,
porque esa verdad me da paz,
y te agradezco la jornada
que llamo mi vida.

Hoy entiendo que mi valor
nunca dependió de tu mirada,
sino del amor que floreció en mí
cuando tuve el valor
de mirarme sin cuentos.

No sé si te lo dije lo suficiente,
pero siempre te admiré, te aprecié,
y te extrañaré.

Y en cada paso que doy con amor y certeza,
sé que, de alguna forma,
te llevo conmigo.

ABOUT ROSANNA

Rosanna Scarpati is a Certified Holistic Life and Executive Coach who blends over two decades of high-impact banking experience with a deep passion for personal growth and leadership development. As a Professional Skills and Banking Consultant with Wall Street Prep, she trains executives and analysts at the most prestigious financial institutions across the globe—delivering world-class instruction in communication, executive presence, and analytical excellence.

Rosanna's coaching practice focuses on elevating high-achieving women and LGBTQ+ leaders, helping them navigate transitions, unlock their full potential, and lead with clarity, confidence, and purpose. Her unique approach combines strategic insight with holistic principles, empowering clients to set bold goals, embody resilience, and achieve sustainable success in both career and life.

With a background spanning sales, risk, and product management at JP Morgan, Credit Suisse, Deutsche Bank, Top Broker Dealers and Tradeweb, Rosanna has led large-scale business transformations and driven team success. Now, she brings this corporate expertise to her coaching work—guiding professionals in leadership roles to break through internal and external barriers and thrive at every stage of their careers.

A long-time advocate for equity and empowerment, Rosanna has mentored underserved youth through the INROADS program for over 20 years and has served as a founding director and board member for multiple nonprofit organizations. Her work is driven by a steadfast belief in the power of community, representation, and purpose-driven leadership.

Rosanna holds an M.B.A. from New York University and embraces a holistic lifestyle rooted in wellness, creativity, and connection. Of Colombian and Italian heritage and bilingual in Spanish, she brings cultural fluency and warmth to everything she does. Whether dancing, traveling, or simply enjoying time with loved ones, Rosanna leads by example—helping others find their voice, redefine success, and lead lives of meaning and joy.

To learn more about and connect with Rosanna at:

Website: www.empowerevolutioncoaching.com
LinkedIn: https://www.linkedin.com/in/rosanna-scarpati/
Instagram: https://www.instagram.com/coach_rosanna_s/

Burnout Quiz!

SIERRA DOMB

"In a world that often promotes conformity, insecurity, self-serving systems, and appearances over substance, choosing to be yourself and focusing on what you contribute and how you treat others are important acts of rebellion. We cannot choose the health or appearance we are born with, nor how others will treat us, but how we respond shapes our character. Do not fear being different. Suffering is inevitable, but leaving it meaningless is optional. Amidst injustice or hardship, let your actions foster resilience, kindness, and the change you hope to create for yourself and others, knowing that as long as you try your best, that is enough."

\- Sierra Domb

~ ~ ~

Sierra Domb is a globally recognized medical advocate, health communicator, and research collaborator who has helped advance care for under-recognized neurological and chronic conditions, including Visual Snow Syndrome, Erythromelalgia, and autoimmune disorders, while also highlighting critical yet often overlooked topics such as women's health, homeostasis, and the role of neurotransmitters in overall health. She has forged research collaborations, globally accessible educational resources, and patient-centered initiatives that promote health literacy, physician-patient communication, resilience in the face of adversity, and healthcare reform. Drawing on her personal experience living with complex medical conditions, Sierra has transformed challenges into actionable initiatives that educate, inspire, and drive impactful change worldwide.

~ ~ ~

To all who suffer, feel different, unheard, or unseen, and to those who remain kind, offer support, take action, or try their best despite life's hardships.

TRANSFORMING PAIN INTO PROGRESS: A LIFE SHAPED BY ILLNESS, RESILIENCE, INQUIRY, AND ACTION

THE JOURNEY

From the moment I was born, I had no choice but to stand out. Even when I longed to fit in, I often felt judged for my health, my appearance, and my personality, which did not match society's expectations. From an early age, I understood that society often assigns value and treats people unkindly based on superficial traits or circumstances beyond their control, particularly women, and especially those living with medical challenges. Not fitting in taught me to think independently, to question societal norms, many of which are rooted in long histories of injustice and prejudice, and to reject narratives that prioritize appearance, conformity, and idle chatter over substance and constructive action. I hope readers take away that embracing difference, forging their own path, practicing self-care, and cultivating kindness are essential acts of resistance and liberation.

For anyone who has faced challenges not of their choosing, I hope they feel empowered to reclaim control by shifting their perspective and transforming the pain of those challenges into purpose, whether that purpose leads to positive change for others in similar situations or to learning to accept, love, and honor themselves for surviving. Do not fear being different. The path may be lonely at times, but it also has the power to attract a life shaped by authenticity, courage, knowledge, and, with intention and effort, to make a positive difference in your own life and in the lives of others.

My life has been shaped by medical struggles, loss, and profound physical and emotional challenges, experiences that provoked reflection, cultivated resilience, questioned conformity, and guided me to approach the world with open-mindedness, compassion, and a drive to make a positive impact. These formative years were defined by what my body demanded and what my mind had to navigate. My path to founding a global nonprofit, working in health communication, and collaborating in medical research began long before I understood the challenges ahead.

Since childhood, I struggled with Autoimmune Dysregulation, a chronic immune condition, and Erythromelalgia, a neurovascular disorder. I juggled school, activities, and social life while navigating chronic pain, frequent medical appointments, and periods of being immunocompromised. I maintained a composed exterior to meet societal expectations while silently enduring pain. The visible effects of my conditions made hiding impossible, and daily bullying became routine. I built walls around myself, always on the defensive, longing to be healthy and "normal".

By young adulthood, both conditions were managed mainly through medication and lifestyle adjustments. University marked a turning point: life felt full of possibility, and my goals seemed attainable. I embraced opportunities in writing, photography, studying communication, and hosting a campus radio show. These experiences led to commercial and animation voiceover work, prompting me to pause my studies and move to Los Angeles.

While in Los Angeles, I learned that someone close to me was terminally ill. I returned to Miami to care for them until their passing. During that time, they encouraged me to resume my studies. After their death, I returned to the University of Miami, weighed down by loss, mortality, and the helplessness of witnessing suffering I could not stop.

In 2015, at age 21, I developed Visual Snow Syndrome (VSS). My symptoms began subtly, then later that day, my vision went black while driving. When it returned, I faced relentless visual and sensory disturbances, including flashing lights, double images, distortions, tinnitus, paresthesia, derealization, brain fog, and migraines. Fear consumed me as I tried to understand what was happening.

Doctors were unfamiliar with VSS, misdiagnosing me and warning of possible blindness or death. I struggled to explain a disorder I barely understood, and some questioned my sanity. Every medical test showed nothing abnormal. Unable to work, drive, attend classes, or recognize familiar places or loved ones as I once knew them, I left school again, consumed by fear of losing my sight or life. I soon learned I was one of millions worldwide with VSS, who were disbelieved and misdiagnosed.

A crucial discovery was an academic paper that described VSS exactly as I experienced it. I contacted the author, neuroscientist Dr. Peter Goadsby, who confirmed my diagnosis and explained that medical professionals still dismiss VSS patients. Globally, resources and awareness were virtually nonexistent, leaving patients disbelieved, misdiagnosed, or falsely institutionalized. Only a handful of researchers studied VSS, and none had funding.

Seeking answers online, I also found others with VSS; some offered empathy, others hostility. A few urged me to end my life, conveying the condition and the medical community's dismissal made hope impossible, and some responses turned disturbing after learning I was a woman. It was clear that countless people with VSS were suffering. The combination of severe symptoms and neglect by the medical community had devastating effects on both physical and mental health.

All my life, I resented my medical conditions for the pain they caused. Before VSS, I quietly adapted to challenges, striving for normalcy. VSS changed everything, arriving with debilitating symptoms yet without awareness, support, or solutions. Affecting 2-3% of the global population, it was a widespread neurological condition that medicine had ignored. Faced with a grim outlook and millions affected worldwide, I felt compelled to act. I realized I could no longer hide my differences or fear judgment. As a coping mechanism and way to help others, I decided to turn my health challenges into a catalyst for positive impact.

In 2018, at age 23, I moved back to Los Angeles, organized the first Visual Snow Conference at UCSF to unite researchers and individuals with VSS worldwide, and founded the nonprofit Visual Snow Initiative (VSI) to advance awareness, education, recognition, and research. I established a Global Research Team, sparking collaborations across seven countries and securing funding from institutions including King's College London and UCLA. Since then, VSS research has quadrupled, producing advances in biomarkers, pathophysiology, symptomatology, and treatment options. We created the first official diagnostic criteria, the first Global Physicians Directory, the first pediatric resources via VSI 4 Kids, a multilingual website, numerous educational materials, and online awareness content. I collaborated with the AnCan Foundation to launch the first VSS video chat support group. I partnered with the Oxford Mindfulness Foundation to create a globally accessible app integrating evidence-based therapies for VSS's neurological and perceptual features.

After being told it was impossible, I secured the first ICD-11 recognition of VSS and its hallmark symptom, visual snow, from the World Health Organization, a historic milestone in global clinical and scientific acknowledgment. I facilitated multidisciplinary research collaborations with institutions including MIT, UC Denver, the University of Perugia, Monash University, the University of Bern, Johns Hopkins, the Mayo Clinic, and more.

I also served on the International Advisory Board for the Columbia-WHO Center for Global Mental Health, addressing stigma, improving access in underserved regions, and highlighting marginalized medical topics in neuroscience and women's health. I have spoken for the Erythromelalgia Association, delivered a TEDx Talk on VSS and VSI's founding, and was recognized in the University of Miami's 30 Under 30 list for global impact after completing my degree.

Integrating health and intercultural communication, neuroscience, behavioral sciences, qualitative analysis, and lived experience, my work translates research into accessible educational resources and actionable initiatives for diverse audiences, connecting professionals across disciplines to advance equitable knowledge sharing and address complex medical and systemic challenges. The models I have developed extend to other underserved conditions and global issues, laying the groundwork for progress guided by compassion, science, and collaboration.

THE LEARNINGS

I have come to accept that while I can control my actions, so much remains beyond my control: my health, how others respond to me, and the shifts unfolding around us all. I often wondered why life led me down specific paths, but I have learned that some things simply happen. All I can do is move forward, applying my skills where possible, stepping into new chapters, or adjusting my role as needed. Life often unfolds while we are busy making other plans, and all I can do is try my best.

Studying neuroscience, psychology, and human behavior revealed how much of what drives us happens beneath the surface. Our actions and beliefs are often shaped by layers of societal conditioning, personal experiences, insecurities, and projections we may not even recognize. While each of us is unique, much of who we are is influenced by unseen forces beyond our immediate awareness. People often believe their perspective is the one true reality. Understanding this helps us recognize that opinion is not fact and that it is essential to consider the source of information. When someone says something is impossible, it may reflect their limited view rather than the objective truth.

Many people told me what I set out to do was impossible. They questioned not only my goals but my very presence, suggesting that a woman with strong opinions who values intellect over appearances, along with sensitivity and kindness, would never find her place. My health challenges seemed only to strengthen their doubts. Yet the real challenge is not that I do not fit the mold, but that society expects everyone to fit into a single, narrow mold. So long as no harm is caused to oneself or others, differences should not only be accepted but celebrated. Yet many want others to conform to their views, often overlooking the richness of diverse perspectives and experiences.

Despite these doubts, I persisted. I forged my own path, refusing to let others define the limits of my potential. By showing up, taking risks, and remaining true to myself, we made progress that might not have happened otherwise. This taught me a lesson I carry into all endeavors: innovation and change rarely come to those who wait for permission or certainty. Real impact arises when you embrace your whole self, continue despite skepticism, and act to help others and challenge systemic injustice, even when it feels impossible.

Persistence despite doubt separates those who spark change from those who accept the status quo.

Whenever you introduce something new, whether a creative work or an effort to improve a system, resistance is inevitable. It arises not because the change is wrong but because it challenges norms and comfort. Change can sometimes provoke skepticism or opposition. Embracing resistance allows you to refine ideas, strengthen resolve, and build understanding. Real progress happens step by step, and persistence despite doubt separates those who spark change from those who accept the status quo.

Letting yourself be seen honestly, flaws and all, is not weakness but a quiet strength. For a long time, I masked myself to make others comfortable. But even then, you cannot be everyone's cup of tea. Genuine connections and experiences matter more than appearances or conformity. Life is constantly changing, from health to perspective, and while we do not have to welcome every change, we must live with them. I strive to grow, improve, and build what I can while treating myself with kindness, even if I am still becoming who I hope to be. Personal victories, however small, are worth celebrating.

THE INSPIRATION

My health challenges, particularly VSS, have shaped my work, and by learning about the suffering of millions affected by overlooked conditions. Beyond this, I have always carried a deep sensitivity to injustice and empathy for those who struggle. Though often celebrated, these traits can feel heavy in a world where fairness and understanding do not always prevail. For years, I viewed my sensitivity as a burden, feeling others' pain without the ability to change it. Over time, I realized it was not a weakness but a compass, guiding my advocacy and humanitarian work.

Holding space for both seriousness and joy, logic and creativity, keeps us grounded and human.

I am drawn to resilience, critical thinking, and the courage to challenge convention. Reducing a person to a single trait erases their depth. Society often forces people into narrow definitions, forgetting that humans are layered and multifaceted. Adversity, intellect, empathy, and strength can coexist and even strengthen one another. Life is rarely linear; struggle and progress, fear and courage, fragility and determination coexist. My identity is a mosaic of abilities, passions, and contradictions. Negative experiences can give rise to positive change, and exhaustion can coexist with perseverance. One can work in medicine or science and still love the arts. One can strive to solve complex problems while needing lighthearted moments. Holding space for both seriousness and joy, logic and creativity, keeps us grounded and human.

My family laid the groundwork for these beliefs. Growing up in a multicultural household taught me that unity rests on respect and openness, not uniformity. Diversity enriches innovation and broadens understanding. My parents and grandparents taught that courage and empathy are intertwined, that strength lies in patience, integrity, and kindness, and that doing your best without expecting perfection is enough. They taught me to speak up even when others tell me not to.

My significant other and best friend has been my steady anchor through every high and low, showing that true love blends attraction and compatibility with support, growth, dedication, desire, the celebration of differences, and the treasuring of each other's authenticity. Together, our love makes anything feel possible.

My sister figure and best friend, who passed too soon, showed me the power of artistic expression and of embracing difference. What once made me feel isolated became a source of direction, teaching me to face hardship with creativity and empathy.

I am grateful to everyone who has supported me and believed in my causes, especially my teammates, whose intelligence, care, and tenacity made VSI a reality. Hearing from people affected by VSS and other health issues in 93 countries, I am honored to have a positive impact on even one person's life.

I have learned the value of reflection, adaptability, and intention. Inspiration evolves through people, experiences, and challenges. It grows through every encounter, struggle, and shared moment of humanity. This blend of insight, persistence, and compassion drives me to create change, guided by the belief that within hardship lies the seed of progress and within pain, the possibility of purpose.

What defines my work is a willingness to explore unconventional solutions when traditional ones fall short. I do not accept impossibility simply because it has not been done. I rely on analysis, creativity, and independent thought. When I believe in something, I take an uncharted path. The only way to know what is possible is to try, and I commit fully, even when the outcome is uncertain.

I am passionate about bringing humanity back into medicine and science. These fields need not feel distant or sterile; clarity and empathy benefit both professionals and patients. I connect individuals across disciplines, identify shared goals, and merge complementary strengths to create real solutions. Collaboration between patients, clinicians, and researchers is essential, as lived experience provides insights that data alone cannot capture. Beyond validation, people need practical resources and accessible education to navigate their realities. I hope to continue building bridges through culturally relevant resources, global collaborations, and honest conversations that break health stigmas, ensuring individuals are acknowledged and their perspectives recognized.

THE ADVICE

Not fitting in taught me to think independently, to question societal norms, many of which are rooted in long histories of injustice and prejudice, and to reject narratives that prioritize appearance, conformity, and idle chatter over substance and constructive action.

It is unrealistic to feel happy every moment of every day. Society promotes the illusion of constant contentment, but reality is far more complex. There is much suffering in the world, and many have endured far worse than I have. These realities are not a reason for pity but an invitation to awareness, empathy, and positive action. I do not believe every hardship has a grand design, but I do believe we can choose to make meaning from our experiences. Often, the most difficult moments open doors we would not have otherwise found, shape us into stronger people, or bring irreplaceable individuals into our lives. I look for any good that might emerge from the bad, whether it is wisdom, resilience, empathy, or clarity about what truly matters. At the same time, I accept that some pain is simply pain, and survival alone can be enough.

Success is a subjective term, and so is failure. For me, it is not simply a matter of pass or fail; it is about giving your best effort and doing everything you can, while recognizing that some obstacles will always be beyond your control. Accepting this makes it easier to focus on what you can change and keep moving forward. What matters most is continuing to move forward and giving your best, because without that, nothing changes, and the outcome remains fixed. No matter how challenging or unpredictable life may be, I act with intention, balance perseverance with self-compassion, and embrace both perceived setbacks and successes as part of the journey.

Ultimately, what you contribute to the world is your responsibility. Whether you lift someone up or dismiss them, your choice reflects your character. We never fully understand what others face, and some may lack empathy. Sometimes what matters most is not the setback itself, but how you respond. Did you show up despite the challenges? Did you try to improve something for yourself or someone else? Did you continue moving forward when stopping would have been easier?

I have learned to stand in uncertainty with resilience and adaptability. I show up even when outcomes are unclear, value reflection and growth, and measure progress by effort as much as result. Personal growth and helping others, whether through daily acts of kindness, listening, sharing insights, creating resources, or contributing on a larger scale, hold significance even when they require facing challenges and discomfort.

An essential component of my work is that it goes beyond research alone. It is about bringing multidisciplinary collaboration and humanity back into medicine, bridging the gap between science, patients, and everyday understanding. I believe in accessible, practical, evidence-based communication that connects people across different fields, levels of health literacy, and cultural backgrounds. By blending various perspectives and ideas, we can create comprehensive, well-informed solutions to challenges that once felt insurmountable. Striving to achieve something unprecedented requires embracing the unknown and exploring paths others have not yet imagined.

Different cultures, influences, and interests do not cancel each other out; they bring complexity, perspective, and variety to life. After all, we all bleed red. As long as no one is causing emotional or physical harm to themselves or others, differences can coexist, be appreciated, and even expand our horizons. Through respectful dialogue and global teamwork, these differences can help us build a better world together.

At every funeral I have attended, no one mentions looks, business success, perfect health, or academic records. What endures is how a person treats others and the feelings they inspire. Kindness, compassion, and genuine connections outlast any external measure of success. I am grateful for the support of loved ones and advocates, and for the lessons forged through anguish: resilience, self-care, persistence, critical thinking, nonconformity, innovation, curiosity, and a multifaceted identity blending science, creativity, and humanity.

THE PATH FORWARD

I have come to accept that while I can control my actions, much remains beyond my control: aspects of my health, how others respond when I am true to myself, the harsh realities of the world around us, and obstacles embedded in systems. I often wondered why life led me down this path, but I have learned that some things simply happen, and all I can do is move forward. Whether that means stepping into a new chapter, applying my skills in different ways, staying hands-on, or taking a step back, I give my full effort. Our "best" looks different for everyone, and it can change from day to day. All I can do is strive to give my personal best each day, knowing that life has its own course, often unfolding while we are focused on our plans.

Society often responds critically to those who do not conform to typical norms or ideals, as if existing outside the standard challenges others, even when being different was never your choice. Yet it is precisely our diversity and varying perspectives that make life abundant, beautiful, and interesting, while also driving innovation and progress.

The world is filled with inequality, discrimination, and systemic barriers in medicine and society. Despite these obstacles, it is through our response to adversity, both our own and that of others, and by embracing what makes us unique, including our differences, that we can discover the power to create transformative change.

Life is not fair, and suffering is universal. Some endure more than others, and the pain they carry may never fully fade. Life's hardships can leave lasting marks, but they can also awaken a calling within us. Within that pain lies the potential to cultivate resilience, illuminate what truly matters, deepen empathy, foster compassion and understanding, and transform suffering into purpose. Whether that purpose lies in changing the world, helping others, or accepting and advocating for yourself, imperfections included, while nurturing self-care and personal growth, it can guide us toward transformative action. Even the smallest step forward, taken with courage, opens the door to transformation more than a lifetime spent wondering "what if?".

True impact is not determined by wealth, status, or appearances. It is defined by the content of your character, the courage to remain kind despite how much you have been hurt, the choice to act ethically, challenge injustice, and help those in need along the way. Recognize that you have survived days you never thought you would, and know that you do not have to love yourself every day. Practicing self-acceptance and self-care allows you to be the best version of yourself for both yourself and others, no matter what life throws your way. In a world that often encourages conformity, fosters insecurity, thrives on chatter, and fixates on appearances while overlooking substance, choosing to be yourself and prioritizing your contributions and the way you treat others over superficial impressions is an important act of rebellion.

For anyone who has faced challenges not of their choosing, feel empowered to reclaim control by shifting their perspective and transforming pain into purpose, whether that purpose leads to positive change for others in similar situations or simply learning to accept and love themselves and find peace within. Do not fear being different. The path may be lonely at times, but it also has the power to attract a life shaped by authenticity, courage, and knowledge and, with intention and effort, to bring positive change to your own life and to the lives of others.

ABOUT SIERRA

Sierra Domb is a global health innovator, research collaborator, and consultant in intercultural and scientific communication. She has advanced initiatives for under-recognized medical conditions by fostering interdisciplinary collaboration, building research infrastructure, and creating accessible, multimodal medical resources. Her work has promoted recognition, research, and problem-solving for overlooked issues, supporting more equitable knowledge dissemination. She founded the Visual Snow Initiative and has served on the International Advisory Board for the Columbia-WHO Center for Global Mental Health. Sierra has delivered a TEDx Talk and been recognized as a 2024 University of Miami "30 Under 30" Award recipient and a 2025 Extraordinary Latinas Award nominee in the "Amplifying Voices" category for her advocacy on underrepresented health topics, including women's health, homeostasis, and chronic illness.

Sierra's diverse professional background includes experience as a voice actor in Los Angeles, a writer and photographer published in The Miami Herald, and a DJ and radio show host. This combination of creative and communication roles informs her ability to engage diverse audiences and bridge the gap between scientific research and accessibility. She has also contributed as an author and collaborator to organizations such as Oxford Mindfulness and the Erythromelalgia Association, where she has served as a member and guest speaker.

Sierra coordinated the effort that secured the first-ever ICD recognition of Visual Snow Syndrome (VSS) and its hallmark symptom, visual snow, from the World Health Organization, marking a historic milestone in global clinical and scientific acknowledgment of this complex neurological condition. She simultaneously facilitated multidisciplinary research collaborations with institutions worldwide, including King's College London, UCLA, MIT, UC Denver, University of Perugia, Monash University, University Hospital of Bern, Johns Hopkins, and the Mayo Clinic, focusing on biomarkers, pathophysiology, symptomatology, advanced technologies, and treatment development.

These initiatives contributed to establishing foundational diagnostic criteria, creating a global physician directory, producing comprehensive multimodal educational resources for healthcare professionals and patients, and organizing an international conference uniting researchers and affected individuals.

Drawing on expertise in health and intercultural communication, neuroscience research, behavioral sciences, qualitative analysis, humanitarian initiatives, organizational management, and lived experience with medical conditions, Sierra has developed integrated methodologies to identify complex patterns, foster cross-cultural understanding, and inform global initiatives. While much of her experience centers on medical conditions, the frameworks she developed are broadly applicable to fields seeking ethical, accessible, and compassionate solutions for underserved populations and systemic challenges.

By translating scientific research into strategic initiatives and integrating it with creative and multimedia expertise, Sierra has connected professionals across disciplines to facilitate collaboration, foster nuanced problem-solving, and develop accessible, outcome-driven resources that advance equitable knowledge dissemination and inform ongoing efforts addressing complex medical, social, cultural, and systemic challenges.

To learn more about Sierra and connect with her:

Website: https://sierradomb.com/
LinkedIn: https://www.linkedin.com/in/sierradomb/

Surround yourself with Extraordinary Latinas who encourage you to thrive.

ABOUT UNITED LATINAS

Elevating the Voices, Leadership and Impact of Extraordinary Latina Leaders.

UNITED LATINAS is a collaborative leadership community devoted to empowering, amplifying, and connecting Latinas and those who champion Latina leadership. We exist to elevate leadership impact and presence through upskilling workshops, public speaking programs, mentoring, leadership development opportunities, visibility platforms, strategic networking, and intentional community-building experiences.

We believe that finding community and building meaningful professional alliances can be transformative. That's why we cultivate spaces where Latinas from across industries, generations, and geographies can gather in shared ambition, cultural pride, and collective growth. We also welcome allies and partners who are committed to expanding opportunity and advancing Latina leadership in every space.

At UNITED LATINAS, we believe Latinas deserve to be seen, heard, valued, and represented at every level of influence. We work to amplify voices, expand visibility, and strengthen leadership presence across corporate, entrepreneurial, nonprofit, academic, and creative sectors. Whether you are a seasoned executive, an entrepreneur, an emerging leader, or someone just beginning to explore your voice, there is space for you here.

This is a community rooted in courage, connection, and collective advancement.
If you are ready to grow, lead boldly, and build alongside other extraordinary women — we invite you to join us.

www.unitedlatinas.com
https://unitedlatinas.mn.com
hello@unitedlatinas.com

ABOUT THE PUBLISHING AUTHORS

ILHIANA ROJAS SALDANA

Ilhiana Rojas Saldaña is a Human Potential & Culture Expert, international keynote speaker, award-winning executive and leadership coach, seasoned multicultural business strategist, and bestselling publishing author. Her mission is to help leaders find their voice, align it with their evolving aspirations, and translate it into meaningful impact.

With more than 20 years of global executive experience across Fortune 500 companies in Mexico and U.S. headquarters, Ilhiana has led large-scale business transformations, coached high-performing teams, and guided professionals through pivotal leadership transitions. As Founder and CEO of BeLIVE Coaching & Consulting, she partners with organizations and leaders to build resilient, collaborative, and high-performing cultures grounded in clarity, confidence, and human-centered leadership. To date, she has designed and delivered coaching and leadership development programs impacting more than 4,500 professionals across industries worldwide.

Driven by her belief in the power of community and representation, Ilhiana co-founded UNITED LATINAS Group Corp, where she serves as Co-Founder and President. UNITED LATINAS is a global leadership and empowerment platform dedicated to amplifying women's voices through upskilling programs, mentoring, visibility opportunities, and high-impact community experiences. She has spearheaded the launch of multiple international leadership initiatives across Europe, Latin America, and the United States and is the publishing author of six bestselling anthology books featuring the stories of nearly 100 women leaders.

Before launching her companies, Ilhiana built a distinguished corporate career as a global business leader and strategist at organizations including Procter & Gamble, Hanesbrands, and Hasbro. She drove double-digit growth across multiple businesses, led successful turnaround initiatives restoring profitability after years of losses, and earned recognition for her strategic insight, innovation, and ability to cultivate engaged, high-performing teams across diverse markets.

Her honors include recognition as a 2025 Top 100 Latina by Latino Leaders Magazine, a 2024 Most Influential Woman Powerlist by COLOR, recipient of the 2023 P&G Alumni Leadership Award, the 2023 Top Coaches Award by WomELLE, and the 2022 Women in Business Stevie Gold Award, among others.

Beyond her coaching and speaking, Ilhiana continues to contribute to leadership advancement initiatives across corporate and nonprofit sectors. She currently serves as a Power Council Member for Poderistas, Champion Member of the Women Business Collaborative, and Founding Board Member of Thousand Faces. She has previously served as Chief Development Officer for ALPFA Boston, Vice President of the Board of Directors for the National Wellness Institute, Vice Chair of the Rhode Island Hispanic Chamber of Commerce, and in additional advisory roles. She is also an Executive MBA Career Advisor for Hult International Business School.

Ilhiana holds a Chemical Engineering degree with honors from Mexico City and resides in Rhode Island with her family.

Learn more and connect with Ilhiana at:

www.belivecoach.com
www.ilhianarojas.com
https://www.linkedin.com/in/ilhiana-rojas7
ilhiana@unitedlatinas.com

SANDRA NOEMI TORRES

Sandra Noemi Torres is a dynamic Public Speaker and seasoned Marketing and Business Strategist with over 20 years of consulting and scaling small and medium sized business owners and entrepreneurs.

Sandra has managed multi seven figure ad marketing budgets and is an expert in strategies that connect, convert and build customer loyalty. With a focus on high-impact and results-driven solutions, she has earned a reputation as a trusted advisor and key decision maker in mission-critical brand messaging campaigns.

Sandra is the Founder and CEO for UNITED LATINAS, a thriving women's personal development organization that empowers Latina women, She spearheaded the creation of Latina Speakers Club, a leading Latina Speakers Directory where Hispanic women are showcased and highlighted and promoted as the thought leaders they are.

Sandra is also the Founder and CEO of Sandra Noemi & Co, dba/ Plan Your Company, a full service digital marketing agency with coaching and consulting services, Sandra brings her years of expertise in marketing, sales, business development strategies to every project and every conversation she takes on.

Sandra is a two-time published author with her book The Life Agreement and a collaborative project & #1 Amazon Best Seller through United Latinas, Extraordinary Latinas Vol II - Breaking The Narrative & Redefining Our Power. And the creator of the MindCreatesMatter Series of Books that will be released in 2024, that helps Individuals, Entrepreneurs and Marketing professionals help reach their goals

Learn more and connect with Sandra at:

https://www.linkedin.com/in/sandratorres/
https://planyourcompany.com/

www.ingramcontent.com/pod-product-compliance
Lightning Source LLC
Chambersburg PA
CBHW051503150726
47997CB00001B/101